A
HUNDRED
YEAR HISTORY
OF THE

P. & O.

PENINSULAR AND ORIENTAL
STEAM NAVIGATION COMPANY

BY BOYD CABLE

QUIS NOS SEPARABIT

1837—1937

IVOR NICHOLSON AND WATSON
LIMITED   LONDON

Contents

v

CONTENTS

Illustrations

For convenience the plates of P. & O. vessels are placed throughout the book in chronological order and do not necessarily appear opposite the relevant text.

vii

Acknowledgments

For the invaluable help given me in my writing of this History I am anxious to offer my grateful thanks to :

The many known and unknown friends who went to such trouble to lend and send me private and family letters, books, papers, diaries and other documents, many of which provided otherwise unobtainable facts and knowledge of relatives and friends connected with the P. & O. ;

To the Press here and abroad, and to the editors through whose courtesy I was enabled to get in touch with many of those correspondents ; and to the Company's foreign and Overseas Agents and offices for their help in this and in collecting out-of-the-way items of historical interest in their respective localities ;

To such official bodies as the G.P.O. Records Committee and the Record Office of the India Office, and others, unofficial and voluntary, like the Postal History Society and the Flag Circle, for providing and checking up information and data ;

To Mr. Frank C. Bowen for his contribution of the article, " The Development of the P. & O. Fleet," with its wealth of technical detail, which I am sure will be appreciated as it deserves ;

To the compilers of the other article on " P. & O. Capital," with which I was incompetent to deal but without which such a History as this would have been incomplete ;

And—finally, because I feel they would wish it to come last even if I know it should come first—to the Management and Staff, collectively and individually, of the P. & O., without whose cordial co-operation and guidance to the old books, records and documents of the Company this History could not have been attempted or made in any sense authoritative ; and also to the associated companies for the material facts of their respective histories.

I have received such generous help and encouragement in all these directions that it has made a pleasure of what would otherwise have been a heavy task, and I can only say to my many helpers and well-wishers—Thank you !

Boyd Cable

ADDENDUM

Since the printing of this book was commenced, the Hon. Alexander Shaw has succeeded to the title of Lord Craigmyle.

CHAPTER ONE

" A Hundred Years Ago "

THERE is an old sea chantey which begins :

> (*Solo*) " A hundred years is a very long time.
> (*Chorus*)   (Oh, yes, oh !)"

and has a last chorus line to innumerable verses—

> " A hundred years ago ! "

The chantey is now a memory and a museum piece, like the tall ships that were worked to the swing of it, and like the dwindling handful of shellback survivors who knew and served those ships.

There are no chanteys sung at sea to-day—except perhaps when some kind performer takes the platform at a liner's concert party, and the audience is invited or induced to join in the chorus lines of a well and wisely expurgated version of the old full-blooded words.

Yet it is a curious fact that in nautical history it is only now, and when applied to steamers, that there is truth in the line, " A hundred years is a very long time " ; and that in the thousands of years of Sail history, a century, as a measure of evolution and progress, was a mere passing breath, a light puff of air in the Doldrums, a lift-and-let-fall of the idle canvas that hardly shifted the ship a measurable length.

How vastly and strikingly different is the story of " steam navigation," of steamer design, building, and propulsion can be indicated clearly and simply by an illustration from the history of the P. & O. and another from the previous history of Sail.

I can find no century of known Sail history that marked any important or revolutionary advance in the whole matter of ship designing

B   I

and handling. The Romans found the advantage of a balancing sail on a mast projecting forward from the bows ; but in this knew no more than the Chinese had applied in their junks centuries before. The Norse vikings used a single big square-sail that the Egyptians had used a thousand years earlier.

If you look at a picture or model of the ships of Vasco da Gama or Christopher Columbus at the end of the 1400's, and then at one of the Pilgrim Fathers, " Mayflower " of 1620, you'd have to be an expert to find any major difference.

Even in the " revolutionary " clipper ships, there was no more than a lengthening and narrowing of the hull, an increase in the height and spread of spars, and a piling on of " fancy " sails, all of which had been used in the lumbering East Indiamen a hundred years before.

If Columbus and his men could miraculously have been brought back to life a hundred years later and had the " Mayflower " handed over to them, they would have had the anchor hoisting and their sails spreading after no more than a hasty look round and a trial pull or two on braces, halyards, and lifts.

So if the " Mayflower " crew had been put aboard Cook's " Endeavour " they would have been able to reef, hand, and steer as well as her own crew did in the later century. Equally could captain and crew of an East Indiaman of, say, 1750 have run an Atlantic packet ship or a racing clipper of 1850 ; and the clipper crews of that latter date would find little or nothing to puzzle them in the handling of one of the big grain ships of to-day.

We can take a more gigantic stride back through the centuries and find proof of how little that " hundred years " meant in Sail. If you show an intelligent boy from the " Conway " or " Worcester " training ships a picture of one of the carvings of ships in the Red Sea on Egyptian monuments of two thousand to three thousand years ago, the boy will point out, name, and describe the use of every rope and spar in the prehistoric vessel.

Now let us take from the history of the P. & O. a comparison of the progress made in the evolution of the steamship and of Steam Navigation. Imagine again that a captain and crew from the first

2

P. &. O. liners of 1837 returned to life or wakened from a long Rip van Winkle sleep and were handed over, say, the " Strathmore " or " Stratheden " and left to take her to sea.

Neither the deck officers nor the engineers of 1837 would be able in 1937 to make the wildest guess at where to begin on their job. If you told them they had a steamship or steamboat to handle, they would first look in vain for the spars and sails which were so important an asset in propulsion in their day and for many years after. They would also be stumped by the lack of any paddles, because the screw was only in its first experimental stage in 1837, and this P. & O. centenary year also marks the centenary of the screw's first practical application.

Imagine that 1837 Commander led up the covered gangway and in through a door in the middle of the towering cliff of the 1937 liner's side, and by a labyrinth of passages and alleys and companionways up to his bridge, and left there to get on with the job. He would find himself surrounded by an array of " gadgets "—devices of depth echo-sounding, smoke-detection indicators of fire anywhere in the ship, levers and wheels for closing bulk-heads, for signalling the engine-room to go Ahead or Astern, Fast or Slow, innumerable switches and telephones for use of the electricity of which he had never heard save as a fantastic dream.

Imagine again the 1837 Chief Engineer dumped down in the engine-room of the 1937 P. & O. liner. Under, over, and around him he would find a nightmare tangle of polished steel and gleaming metal, the accumulated mass of intricate machinery for propulsion and for subsidiary electric lights, refrigeration and cargo, lifeboat winches, power, and the rest, packed into a space incredibly small to us, but more incredibly large to him as a mere section in any ship's hull. He would also find a jungle of indicator dials, switches, and instruments even more numerous and hopelessly bewildering than the unfortunate Commander found confronting him up on the bridge.

Such an illustration of the difference to the mind and knowledge of the man is the best I can find or offer to indicate the progress made in the science of marine propulsion and ocean navigation since " A hundred years ago."

3

All the story of that progress is nowhere better, or even so well, carried step by step than in the *Hundred-Year History of the P. & O.* The P. & O. story is the more strange and fascinating, because it is tied up with a side that comes into no other steamship company's history, the problems and difficulties of land communication and " navigation " by the Overland Route across Egypt—a fantastic mixture of ship management and the carriage by canal, river, and waterless sand desert of passengers and mail, goods, and even coal for the ships' bunkers on the other side of Suez.

To all this is added another unusual interest of political complications, fierce battles fought in Press and Parliament between commercial and party and vested interests, national and international politics and policies, wars and world events—to say nothing of unforeseen and unforeseeable progress and developments like the opening of the Suez railway and canal, compound engines and screw propulsion, the then new policy of foreign Governments heavily subsidising their own steamship lines in opposition to ours.

Some of these events threatened little short of ruin and extinction to the P. & O. A whole fleet of liners was at one time thrown on the scrapheap and required staggering sums for replacement ; or profits were wiped out by the leaping price of coal and expense of keeping depots supplied half the world away, while mail contracts held the company rigidly to the maintenance of service and time schedules ; or the whim of an Eastern potentate or opposition of English statesmen equally endangered the life of the Company.

There is the stuff of Romance as well as of History in all this record and tale of the Company which began life " A hundred years ago." Perhaps the most striking period of the whole story is in the rise of the first founders from the chartering of a few little paddle-steamers running to Spain to the management of a network of mail liners covering the Eastern hemisphere, touching the major ports of the Mediterranean, India, The Straits, China, Mauritius, and Australia, totalling in tonnage, horse-power, and gun-power the equal of many or most maritime Powers of their day.

Through all the century there has been one item which has not changed in the Company's ships—and it is about the solitary one which the ghosts or spirits of those 1837 seamen would recognise if they came alongside a P. & O. liner to-day.

When the founder partners began their little business in the Peninsular trade, and were enabled through it to render certain services to the Royal House of Portugal and then of Spain, they adopted as the Company or House Flag a diagonally quartered flag, the upper or first two quarters' colours of white and blue being the Royal colours of Portugal, and the lower or third and fourth quarters' red and yellow the colours of Spain.

The flag, according to some early paintings of the first little paddle-steamers, was of pennant or triangular shape to begin with, but this quickly gave place to the square-ended or oblong shape which has continued to fly to this day. The crest of the Rising Sun and Motto of " *Quis Separabit* " were adopted in 1840, when the Peninsular Steam Navigation Company extended to the Peninsular & Oriental, but the flag colours and device go back to the first days and first steamers of the original Company.

CHAPTER TWO

Founders of the P. & O.

ON the 22nd August, 1837, a contract was signed between the Admiralty (which then conducted all " Packet Ship " business for the Post Office) and the Peninsular Steam Navigation Company for the conveyance of Her Majesty's Mails between England and ports of the Spanish or Iberian Peninsula.

In September of that year the Company advertised its first monthly sailing list, so that September 1937 marks the completion of the Hundred-Year History of the Company's official founding and regular sailings as carriers of the Royal Mail—a service which has continued unbrokenly from then until now.

But before we come to that story of the Peninsular and the P. & O. Company, there is much to be told of the founding of the Company and of its founders, of the slow but steady building up of the business and the fleet, of the battle with the Government to secure the mail contract.

The originators of the Company were two partners, Brodie McGhie Willcox and Arthur Anderson, the former being the founder of the business which later became that of Willcox & Anderson. It was in 1815, after the battle of Waterloo and close of the Napoleonic Wars, that Willcox opened a little office in London as a shipbroker and commission agent ; and in the same year he took Anderson into his employment as a clerk.

Of the early history of Willcox little is known to-day. W. S. Lindsay, the famous historian, in his *History of Merchant Shipping*, says :

"In the year 1815, Mr. Brodie McGhie Willcox, then a young man with no influence and but limited pecuniary means, opened an office in Lime Street, London, and commenced business on his own account as a shipbroker and commission agent."

A footnote to this says: "Mr. Willcox was born at Ostend, but of English and Scottish parentage, his second Christian name, McGhie, being that of his maternal grandfather. He, however, spent his boyhood at Newcastle-on-Tyne, where he received the chief portion of his education."

Beyond this the records are dumb, except for the regular appearance of Willcox's name in the printed Annual Reports of the Company as one of the Managing Directors and as Chairman, with an occasional—very occasional—report of a letter or a speech to the Proprietors from him, or some activities in the House after he became a Member of Parliament.

With Anderson there is a very different story, perhaps because he led the more colourful, active, and romantic career both before and after he joined Willcox, or perhaps because he left behind him voluminous records both in his reports to the Company and its shareholders—or rather "Proprietors" as they were and are described—and to the "Court of Directors" (a much more imposing title than the name of "Board," which was substituted in 1873); and finally we have Anderson's speeches in the House as a Member of Parliament, his evidence on Committees and Commissions, and before then his own writings in the *Shetland Journal*, a newspaper which he established, edited, largely wrote, and entirely paid for out of his own pocket, having it printed in London and shipped to the Shetlands at more or less monthly intervals.[1]

It may seem that the early life and antecedents of Arthur Anderson hardly come within the proper scope of this P. & O. History; but I have the more reason at least to outline them, because I believe his early days and struggles had a marked effect on his activities as a partner

[1] All this material has been very fully collected and published in a book, *Arthur Anderson*, by John Nicolson, to whom I am greatly indebted for full permission to extract what I want to fit into this History of the P. & O. Those who would read the full story of a remarkable man and life may still obtain this book from the publishers, T. & J. Manson, Lerwick.

of Willcox & Anderson, the founding of the Company, and, in particular, on his continuous effort to establish and extend ocean mail services and the rapid, regular, and cheap carriage of letters.

It was inevitable that his parentage, his upbringing in a seafaring community, and his later service in the Navy should have bent his thoughts afterwards to the sea and shipping ; and indeed there was no other life or business of which he had the slightest knowledge.

His early days too must have made clear to him that there was no such prospect of advancement in life for a seafarer as there might be in business ; and, finally, his service in the Navy gave him an insight into the running of a ship and dealing with ship stores, victualling, and supplies—even if that learning was of the system, wasteful alike of men and material, in a warship.

Because I think that those first years of Arthur Anderson's life came to have a marked effect on his later career as one of the founders of the Peninsular and P. & O., because the tale of them gives an indication of the character and personality of the man, and finally, because his life is so interesting in itself I shall outline it briefly in the hope that others will find it so.

CHAPTER THREE

Arthur Anderson

Arthur Anderson was born with no silver spoon in his mouth, and indeed in his young days he was much less concerned with what spoon he had than in whether he would have porridge or potatoes enough to sup with it.

He was one of a family of eight, and was born on the edge of the cold, grey, storm-lashed waters of the Shetland Isles, near Lerwick, on 19th February, 1792.

Mark the date. It, or the world events which we now connect with it, mattered nothing to the infant but much to his parents, to all their friends and acquaintances, and to every soul, even in the far-away and shut-off Shetland and Orkney Isles of those days.

That year saw the declaration of the Republic of France, and the beginning of the incessant Napoleonic Wars which over-ran all Europe except Great Britain, and even here upset the whole normal life of the nation and took its heavy quota of life through our continental armies and our Navy.

It was the sea service and war which had a direct bearing on the inhabitants of the Shetlands. To a man and boy they were literally born to the trade of the sea, and practically everyone of them made a scant and hard-won living as fisherman or seaman. Every British warship that came within hail of the Shetlands went out of her way to land press-gang parties, who swept up every man and boy they could find. On the news flashing round the island of a warship in the offing, every able-bodied man and boy over 10 or 11 fled from their homes to lie hid in the hills until the press-gangs had departed and the next

9

morning's daylight showed the sea and horizon clear of any suspicious sail.

Apart from these dreaded raids of the press-gangs, life in the Shetlands ran its normal course of struggle to win a livelihood from the fish of the sea, their curing and exporting by tiny little sailing vessels to the mainland of Scotland, or to some ports of England and the Continent.

The women took their full share of the battle for existence in the curing of the fish, in the stripping of the tiny sheep, and in spinning, knitting, or weaving the wool into the garments that clothed their men and families.

From earliest childhood Arthur Anderson shared that bitterly hard life. His parents were poor—so poor that his father could not afford to join with any of the slightly better-off neighbours in subscribing to bring over a tutor from the mainland for the education of their children. There was no other schooling in all the Shetlands then, because there were no schools of any kind.

Arthur's first education was from his parents—and from his own testimony it was at least a foundation of the best and soundest. The father must have found Arthur a good and promising learner, because, somehow, he managed to send him for a brief spell of tuition to the local church minister.

But no thirst for knowledge could compete with the cruder demands of food for the body, and Arthur was put to earning his keep at about the age of 11. The work was as a " beach-boy," and it would be hard to imagine a more rigorous mental and physical killer of that knowledge-thirst. A chief export was dried salt fish, and Arthur's job was to assist in the curing, scrubbing, and washing of the fish, spreading them out on the rocks to dry, gathering them in heaps, and covering them at night or when rain fell.

But even at that he gave every spare minute to his self-education, and when his employer noticed this, he afforded the boy a chance by giving him a certain amount of work in the little office. Low as it was, it was at least a first rung of the ladder in business training.

While still a child, Arthur narrowly escaped being carried off by the press-gang, being saved only by the vigorous protests of his employer, who was the agent of Lord Dundas, the local " laird " and property owner. A stern warning was offered that Arthur, as an employee of the agent of Lord Dundas, was equally a servant of his Lordship, and that the press-gang officer would certainly be called to strict account for this interference with his Lordship's service and business.

I hardly suppose the noble lord would have given a second thought to an unknown beach-boy impressed into the Navy ; but the bluff worked, and Arthur was reluctantly released. Possibly his father thought it might not work again, and that " better a volunteer than a pressed man," so in 1808 he entered Arthur as a volunteer in the Navy at the age of 16. This was the year when a British army was sent to Spain, when it fought the battles of Vimiera and Corunna, and so opened the first of those fierce years of the Peninsular War—a war which made " Peninsular " a household word in England and led to an extensive trade (and mail or dispatch carrying) between England and the Peninsular ports. It was that trade and shipping business into which some years later Willcox and Anderson entered and out of which came their " Peninsular " Steam Navigation Company.

Anderson's career in the Navy little is known, and he seems to have said or written little or nothing about it himself. He served in the Baltic and off the coast of Spain and France. At some time in this period, he was appointed Midshipman, but was fortunate (or clever) enough to get (or, as we'd say nowadays, to " wangle ") a transfer to the post of Captain's clerk, in which he would have had some opportunity of improving his knowledge on the " business " side of a ship's management.

After Napoleon's abdication and retirement to Elba, Anderson, with his ship's company, was paid off at Portsmouth. He tramped to London, arriving practically penniless, without introductions, connections, or any means or method of earning a living except in his writing a " fair round hand " and his determination to fight a way into business.

He lived, or rather existed, precariously for a year on such scanty work as he could find as a copying clerk. His normal food was twopenn'orth of bread and penn'orth of cheese a day, with a pint of porter every other day. His courage and perseverance were sustained through all his hardships by correspondence with his home, a correspondence only carried on by real sacrifices at both ends.

A letter then cost 1s. 6d., and if he paid half and his parents the other half, it meant he had to go on short rations to make up the postage. The 9d. was an equally serious sum for his parents to spare. Arthur was to tell often in later years how much his home letters had meant to him, and it may well be that his personal experience of slow and costly letters first turned his thoughts to the speeding up and cheapening of the posts, and so to the securing of the mail contracts on which were based the early fortunes of the P. & O.

At the end of his year in London, the news came of Napoleon's escape from Elba and the beginning of the Hundred Days' War. Anderson footed it back to Portsmouth, which he reached in the last stages of exhaustion and starvation. He made for the docks, and was fortunate enough to secure a post again as Captain's clerk in a warship. Throughout the Hundred Days' War he served, apparently uneventfully so far as war went, but no doubt usefully in picking up further knowledge of ship running and management, until the Battle of Waterloo ended the war and the need for a full-strength Navy.

Again his ship paid off at Portsmouth, and Anderson, seeing no prospect of advancement in a peace Navy without private means or influence, took his discharge and returned to London.

This time he was more fortunate than last. He found an uncle there, called on him, and was given an introduction to a Mr. Christopher Hill, a Scarborough shipowner, and to his daughter Miss Mary Ann Hill.

Here wafts in a whiff of Romance, on which I wish I could elaborate. But all we know now is that he met Miss Hill in 1815, and that he married her in 1822; and that Mr. Hill was so favourably impressed at that first meeting with young Anderson's life-story and personality that he introduced him to a Mr. Willcox, who was then just opening a little office as a shipbroker and commission agent.

What impression was made on Mr. Hill by young Anderson, or what impression was made on Miss Hill and passed or pressed on her father, can only be left to the imagination of the reader . . . or perhaps of some film producer who one day may make a better story of it than I can hope to do in a history.

What is more important in this History, however, is that the introduction to Mr. Willcox resulted in his engagement of Anderson as a clerk. Again we have a gap in the details both of business and courtship, and I can only record that in 1822 Anderson was taken into partnership, that the firm became Willcox & Anderson, and that in the same year Anderson married Miss Hill.

Dates make rather boring reading, I know. But in this pre-history of the P. & O. they are of consequence, so I may be forgiven for quoting them.

Willcox opened business and engaged Anderson in 1815, when the Napoleonic Wars ended. By 1822, Willcox and Anderson had established a small but promising business in the running of little sailing vessels to ports of the Spanish or Iberian Peninsula. Through 1824–5–6, the accumulating troubles of the Royal dynasty of Portugal and the insurrection against her Queen brought the humble firm of Willcox & Anderson into the turmoil of world events, and threatened their business with disruption and disaster.

Their regular trading, the delivery of cargo in Portuguese ports, and securing of a homeward cargo, became more and more difficult and hazardous. They either had to cut out their Portuguese trade and find another, or definitely take sides. They decided for the Queen, and threw all their resources into helping her, Anderson especially taking a vigorous and active part in the support given.

They bought a schooner which had stranded near Dover, salved her, fitted her out more or less as a warship, and set her on gun-running to Portugal. Anderson sailed in her on her first run. Later he went to Portugal as " Mr. Smith," brought back two of the Queen's representatives disguised as his servants, lodged them in his home at Norwood while they tried to raise a loan in London for the Queen's cause. Willcox and Anderson also gave useful introductions to financiers, and any other assistance they could.

Largely as the result of that loan raised in London by the representatives Anderson brought over, an expedition was landed in Portugal in 1832, the Queen's naval squadron being under command of Sir Charles Napier. This marked the turn of the tide in favour of the Queen, and on her triumphal entry into Lisbon in 1833, the insurrection collapsed.

No sooner was the Portuguese trouble ended than war flared up again, this time in the Carlist rising in Spain. Willcox and Anderson, faced with the same upset of their trading, again supported the Queen of Spain against the pretender Don Carlos, chartering and running ships to her, taking their risks of losing all if she lost.

The " Royal Tar " landed the first troops of the British Legion recruited in England for service in the cause of the Queen of Spain in the Carlist War. James Grant, the famous war historian, wrote :

" On the 10th of July, 1835, the ' Royal Tar ' steamer, having on board the first portion of soldiers for the Legion, anchored in the Bay of San Sebastian. As the anchor plunged into the water, the booming of artillery from the castle and the universal clanging of church bells in the city saluted the arrival of the 1st Regiment in Spain."

The Queen of Spain finally won her war and the firm of Willcox & Anderson began to reap their reward from both the Royal houses of Spain and Portugal, in trading facilities, and in Royal and official favours.

When the Spanish Minister in London sought to establish steam communication with the Peninsula, the benefits of steam having been demonstrated in the few little steamers employed in the wars, the Dublin and London Steam Packet Company provided the chartered steamers, and Willcox & Anderson were given the management of the line.

Whatever Royal or Government influence or favour may have helped in the selection of the partners as managers, there was probably no firm in London more entitled to the position on the firm basis of business ability and knowledge. Willcox and Anderson had proved their business aptitude by building up from nothing, and with a minimum of finance or influence, a good, solid, paying shipping concern. They had been trading with the Peninsular ports for over a dozen years, and Anderson had travelled often to and fro, had visited the main ports and cities repeatedly, had established friendly connections, correspondents, and agents, had learned the ways of buyers and sellers, traders and shippers ; and finally he had learned to speak and write Spanish—no small asset then when few Spanish houses knew any English.

The partners had been in close contact for some years with Messrs. Bourne, of the City of Dublin Steam Packet Company, and that successful Company must have been well impressed with the energy and ability of the two to have agreed to their management of steamers chartered from the Dublin Company.

They further confirmed their good opinion of the partners later, when their influence and capital did much to set the Peninsular Steam Navigation Company afloat. This appointment of Willcox & Anderson as managers of the line to Spain was a definite step to the founding of the Peninsular and the P. & O. Company.

CHAPTER FOUR

Early Steamers to the Peninsula

In the list of " Past and Present Fleet " published in the *P. & O. Pocket Book* in 1888, under the Chairmanship of Sir Thomas Sutherland and largely contributed to by him, the names of two little paddle-steamers hold pride of position at the head of the roll.

First is the " William Fawcett," given as : " Built 1829 ; Gross Tonnage 206 ; Horse-power 60 " ; and, second, the " Royal Tar " : " Built 1832 ; Tonnage 308 ; Horse-power 260."

These two appear to have been included in that list of the past fleet, because both were owned by the Peninsular Steam Navigation Company after its formation. They were evidently chartered from the Dublin and London Steam Packet Company in the service of the Queen of Spain (and perhaps the Queen of Portugal prior to then), as other steamers were from the same Company and from the General Steam Navigation Company.

These two companies were at that time amongst the few which owned steamers running on open sea services, so that it was natural charterers should turn to them for vessels suitable for the Peninsular trade. The Dublin Company's steamers went from London to Plymouth, Falmouth, Dublin, and Belfast, so had to make their passages in waters by no means sheltered. The General Steam was founded in 1824, and within a year or two had steamers trading to various continental ports and down to Lisbon and Gibraltar.

Admiral Napier, who went out to take command of the Queen of Portugal's fleet in 1833, was taken there in the Dublin Company's " City of Waterford," and with him went one of those Portuguese

S.S. "WILLIAM FAWCETT," 206 tons. Built 1829

From a painting by Norman Wilkinson, P.R.I.

16]

Ministers Anderson had brought to England and helped to finance a loan. This vessel, therefore, may have been one of the first run under charter and managed by Willcox & Anderson, but she would not be included in that " Past and Present Fleet," because she was not owned later by the Peninsular Company, as the " William Fawcett" and " Royal Tar " were.

The " Fawcett " was built by Caleb Smith, and engined by Fawcett & Preston of Liverpool. Fawcett later engined a number of P. & O. vessels, and the " William Fawcett " apparently bore his name. She ran for a time as a ferry-boat on the Mersey, later went on that Belfast–Dublin–London service with odd charterings to Willcox & Anderson, and in the end was bought by their Peninsular Company, enlarged, and re-engined.

The " Royal Tar " was similarly employed in turn on the Dublin–London service, chartered for the Peninsular service, returned to the Dublin Company's run, was rebuilt and re-engined, and bought by the Peninsular Company. She did sterling service for many years, being only sold out of the fleet in 1847.

It may well be that the figures given in the *Pocket Book* of the " Tar's," 308 tons and 260 h.p., are a confusion of her original tonnage and her final engine power.

This supposition is based, not only on the improbability of a 300-ton steamer having 260 h.p. (no steamers then or for many years after having much more than a fifth or a fourth of the measurement of h.p. to that of tons), but also on a note in a Prospectus for increase of capital of the P. & O. dated 1841. This gives a list of the fleet then owned, and includes the " Tar " as of " 681 tons, 260 h.p. (built 1832. Had new engines and extensive alterations at a cost of £16,000, in 1838)."

The practice of lengthening a ship, rebuilding her upper structure, and greatly increasing her tonnage and engine power was a common-place in those early days and for some considerable time after, and we come across records of this being done with many of the P. & O. liners. We hear nowadays a good deal of such " surgical " operations on ships as something rather wonderful in our own day ; but our shipbuilders are doing no more now than those of a hundred years ago.

It may be outside the story of the P. & O., but yet have some relation to it, and certainly deserves a place in these notes on the early steamers to the Spanish Peninsula, that the first steamer owned by Spain (and previously chartered to Portugal) was the British-built, -engined, and -owned " Royal William."   She was built at Quebec in 1831 for service on the Canadian coast, was sent to London for sale in 1833, and holds her niche in steamer history as the first to cross the Atlantic under steam all the way.

The " Royal William " was owned by a group of Quebec and Halifax merchants, who included the three brothers Cunard, founders of the Cunard Line.   On arrival in London she was chartered to the Portuguese Government, then was sold to the Spanish, and successfully used as a warship.

True that we may only now hazard a guess on how much or little influence that tiny 300-ton paddler " Royal William " (or " Ysabel Segunda " as she was renamed) had on the decision of the Spanish Government to induce the Dublin and London Steam Packet Company to run steamers between England and Spain.   But at least her story to some extent ties up with that of the first charters of steamers to Spain under the management of Willcox and Anderson, founders of the P. & O.

The earliest records I can find, however, of regular steamers to Spain and Portugal are in the sailing lists of the General Steam Navigation Company.   These advertise, in a list of about 1826, sailings from London (calling at Brighton and Portsmouth) for Lisbon, Oporto or Vigo, and Gibraltar, of the " George the Fourth " and the " Duke of York."   How closely Willcox & Anderson were connected with the General Steam so far back I do not know ; but that the two firms were associated before the Peninsular Company was formed we do have recorded in the chartering of a General steamship to Willcox & Anderson.

It is therefore the more fitting that nearly a hundred years later that old connection was firmly renewed, and that the General Steam Navigation Company is now included in the world-wide ramifications of associated companies included in what is known as " the P. & O. group."

CHAPTER FIVE

Willcox & Anderson in 1836–7

By 1835 the firm of Willcox & Anderson was well and firmly established, both in their own private business and as managers of the steamers to the Spanish Peninsula. That the two partners were men of substance is clearly indicated in the case of Anderson, who was in 1835–6 spending a good deal of effort and cash in an endeavour to improve the conditions of life in the Shetlands.

He founded in 1836 the *Shetland Journal*, paying out of his own pocket the cost of its publication in London and shipment to Shetland ; and—fortunately for the sake of this history—he published in his *Journal* names and details of the steamers put on the Peninsular service before and after the Peninsular Steam Navigation Company was formed.

Anderson also initiated a scheme for migration of Shetlanders to Brazil, where of course he had considerable influence owing to the firm's support of Dom Pedro, the Emperor, and his daughter, the Queen of Portugal, in the insurrection against her.

Further activities to improve the condition of his fellow-Shetlanders had a direct and speedy link-up with the Peninsular Steam Navigation Company. In 1835 and 1836 he was fighting for a postal service between the mainland of Scotland and the Shetlands, with steamers providing cheaper and more regular communications. In 1837 he was offering the Postmaster-General a steam packet service to replace the slow, irregular, and expensive sail packets to Shetland, undertaking to pay the cost and an additional £500 a year to the Post Office, taking in return what postage the service might bring in—

the return from postage then being about as many shillings as he offered pounds.

The Post Office declined this offer (although next year they made a mail contract with the Aberdeen, Leith & Clyde Shipping Company for a steamer service to the Shetlands); but how determined Anderson was on the establishment of the Shetland steam service, and how this was upset by the needs of the Peninsular service, is shown in an item of the " Local Intelligence " in the *Shetland Journal* dated Aberdeen, 29th May, 1836. It reads :

" The Steam packet ' Peninsula,' built here by John Duffus & Co. for Messrs. Willcox & Anderson of London, and in which Mr. Anderson and a party of friends were expected to have visited Shetland, has been ordered to proceed to London with all dispatch, her services being required immediately on the coast of Portugal. . . . The ' Peninsula ' is a very fine steamer of great speed, and just the description of vessel which would answer to run between this and Shetland."

The next we hear of this steamer is in an advertisement of November 1836, where at the foot of a list of steamers managed by Willcox & Anderson and running to Spain appears :

" ' Peninsula.' Branch Steamer."

Her particular service is further explained in another advertisement of 1st February, 1837, where again she appears at the foot of the list of steamers from London and Falmouth :

" Steam conveyance from LONDON AND FALMOUTH to OPORTO, LISBON, GIBRALTAR, and MALAGA, and vice versa, by the following new powerful, large and splendidly fitted up Steam Ships, carrying mail from His Majesty's Post Office.

STEAM SHIPS

DON JUAN	.	.	.	.	935 tons,	300 Horse-power		
TAGUS	.	.	.	.	900 ,,	300 ,,	,,	
BRAGANZA	.	.	.	.	650 ,,	250 ,,	,,	
IBERIA	.	.	.	.	600 ,,	200 ,,	,,	
LIVERPOOL	.	.	.	.	500 ,,	160 ,,	,,	
MANCHESTER	.	.	.	.	600 ,,	220 ,,	,,	(Chartered Ship)

PENINSULA (Branch Steamer on the Cadiz and Seville Station)."

There are two items in this advertisement worthy of note. The first is that, although the Company then had no contract for the carriage of mails, the Post Office was evidently using the steamers as supplementary to their Sail Packet Services from Falmouth ; and the second is, that this mention of " His " Majesty's mails reminds us that 1837 was the year of the Accession of Her Majesty Queen Victoria. The Queen's Jubilee in 1887 was also the P. & O. Jubilee, fittingly celebrated by the Company in the building of their famous four " Jubilee Ships."

For one or two years before the Peninsular Company made its first mail contract with the Admiralty and Post Office, the Company was running its services to the Peninsula with a fleet of six " large and powerful " steamers, two of which, the " Don Juan " and " Tagus," it was able to boast as " the largest and most powerful that have yet been put afloat."

I find it a little curious that this particular fact of the P. & O owning the largest and most powerful steamers of their day was noted one hundred years ago, and was repeated at intervals with several notable vessels, but that little attention has been paid to this leadership and progress of the P. & O. in the story of " Steam Navigation " as recorded by nautical historians, and that it is now so often overlooked by the Press and public, which in their day acclaimed loudly and enthusiastically this evidence of our British maritime supremacy.

In the published advertisements of Willcox & Anderson through the years 1835–6, there is evidence of a shrewd knowledge or even anticipation of the wants and needs of travellers ; and, indeed, they were then using methods of attracting passengers to their line which are in common use to-day.

For example, in order that enquirers might be spared the troublesome task of visiting one of the steamers to inspect the cabins and accommodation, it was advertised that :

" The Managers have adopted the plan of having at the Chief Office complete models of the whole of the Cabins, by which a Passenger may see at once the size and situation of any cabin or bed-place as well as if he were on board the ship—a facility which they have found engraved plans cannot give."

One might comment on this last fact, that there are still many people to whom an " engraved " map or plan conveys little or nothing, and that many more can take in and understand a model, whether of a landscape or a house or a ship's accommodation, much better than they can any drawing of it. Some passenger lines to-day follow that old plan of displaying models of the cabins.

Another item. In each steamer was placed a book with a notice printed in it in English, Spanish, Portuguese, and French, inviting passengers—or rather " any gentleman " of them, without regard to complaints of ladies, or perhaps supposing no lady would be so unlady-like as to complain or write to a personally unknown gentleman manager —to lodge a complaint if they should " experience any want of civility or attention on the part of the cabin attendants, or any want of cleanli-ness in the cabins or bed or table linen or scarcity in the provision department." Such a " Complaint Book " is a commonplace of catering to-day.

As early as November 1836, the advertisements of vessels sailing to the Peninsula ports added to these that :

" One or two of the vessels will also proceed in the Spring and Fall of the year to Madeira for the accommodation of Invalids and others visiting that Island."

Here again the partners were anticipating by a hundred years the present-day offers of passage to Madeira as a " health resort " for those who wish to avoid a British winter by going abroad in " the Fall of the year," as the autumn is described now only in the American.

Up to the beginning of 1837, the six " large and powerful " steamers were announced as sailing every fortnight, but early in 1837 a note was added that in the spring they would commence running every week.

This is very early proof of a policy which was followed through succeeding years of the P. & O. under the Willcox and Anderson management to go well beyond the needs of the existing trade and to build up a non-existent or trifling traffic by placing steamers on a route and waiting until the facilities offered to shippers created or increased the trade.

They gambled more than once on this belief that trade would come to the ships and the route if the ships were there to receive it, but that the trade would not begin to flow freely until and after the ships were there to carry it.

But of all the gambles the partners took, there were none so serious, or even desperate, as this first placing on the Peninsula trade of a fleet of steamers which apparently were more than ample to carry it, or which could not make it pay to carry.

On the first one to two years of the steamers which were run under changing titles of the " Peninsular Steam Navigation Company," the " Peninsular and Mediterranean Steam Packets," or simply as " Willcox & Anderson," the Company ran at a loss. Within a year or so of its launching, the Line was faced with a crisis and the imminent danger of being " Sunk without trace " beyond an obscure paragraph in history which was to be the fate of so many other steam companies of that and much later date.

Possibly Willcox and Anderson had started their venture on the hope or expectation that they would be so well able to prove the advantages of mail carriage by steam that they banked everything on doing so and securing a contract ; or it may be that, faced with their crisis, they woke to the possibility that they might obtain a mail contract which would be the saving of the Line. Whichever it may have been —and I incline to the belief that it was a first and far-seeing plan to fight for and force on the Post Office the obtaining of a mail contract— it is certain that it was the first mail contract which saved the Company from failure and possible extinction.

The belief that it was a predetermined part of the plan to start running the steamers on a trade which did not and could not pay on a purely trading basis is supported by the early and clearly indicated efforts of the partners to bring pressure on the Post Office to adopt the system of contracting to a private company instead of continuing the centuries-old, inefficient, and extravagant system of Government-owned, more-or-less-controlled Post Office Packet Ships.

To understand now why the merchants here were ready and willing, or even eager, to support a fight against the Admiralty's Post Office

Packets, we must take a cast back and look at the system under which the sailing packets had been run, and the reasons why the system, the Admiralty, the Post Office, and the packet ships were distrusted and disliked by the business community.

It is a story of the famous " Falmouth Packets," which for many years played a part in ocean mail transport, distinguished by a fine record of gallant and desperate actions and fights with enemy ships against impossible odds with the highest credit to the Packetmen ; but is also a tale marred by a long-tolerated creeping in of many evils, ranging from minor dodgings of regulations to the most flagrant jobbery, chicanery, and corruption.

CHAPTER SIX

The Packet Ship Service

T HE services of the Post Office on land in carrying by "post" stages on horseback of mail "pacquets" were first extended to sea in the time of Queen Elizabeth, although it was not until 1633 that there are records of a postal or "Ship Pacquets" service under the Post-master for Foreign Affairs. The first service was by boats rowed or sailed across the English Channel.

In 1688 the first use of Falmouth as a mail packet port began, and the use of this port was so firmly established when Willcox & Anderson began their steam service to the Peninsula that in 1835, and for some years after, they continued to use the port, although the reason for doing so had practically gone with the coming of steam.

The first selection of Falmouth for the packets is explained by a glance at the map and the knowledge that then, as now, sailing ships in the ports higher up the Channel might be held storm-bound for days or weeks by westerly gales which prevented them from beating out to the west or round the corner to the south for Spain and Portugal.

So firmly was the Falmouth packet port and service established when the Peninsular Steam Navigation Company was formed that it remained the arrival and departure point, although the steamers sailed from London one day and were advertised to sail from Falmouth two days later, demonstrating thereby that steamers could get out of the Channel against the prevailing westerlies, and were not under the restriction of the old sail packets of requiring a port which allowed them to push out to sea and safely clear the land no matter what the direction of the wind.

25

The first Falmouth packets ran to Corunna and Lisbon, and later were put on the run to the West Indies and North America. By 1800, two packets a week were sailing for Spain and Portugal, and from two thousand to three thousand passengers passed through the port in a year. The town, a tiny village of a few houses when the Post Office started the Falmouth packets in 1688, had grown by 1800 to a busy and prosperous centre, with private carriages, mail stage-coaches, and wagons clattering and rumbling in and out all hours of the day and night, the inns crammed with arriving and departing passengers, a fleet of ships and boats filling the harbour, and one or two packets sailing or arriving each week, the ship repair yards, rope-walks and sail-lofts, victualling and refitting stores giving wide employment.

But in the same year of 1800 and up to the end of the Spanish, French, and American Wars, the mercantile community had been thoroughly disgusted by the abuses which had crept in to the Falmouth packet service, and it was a card which Willcox and Anderson did not fail to play in 1837 that the deep-rooted hold of the system of the official Post Office-owned and controlled packet service was something that might and ought to be broken.

Up to the end of the Napoleonic Wars, the packet ships were hired by the Post Office, nominally from the commanders, but actually through them from private syndicates or owners. When a packet was captured or sunk by the enemy, the owner lodged a sworn " protest," and was paid by the Post Office the value of the ship. The crew were employed and paid by the Post Office. In the packet ports a Post Office agent was supposed to guard the Postmaster-General's interests, see that full crews were employed, that no goods for sale in foreign ports were carried, and that the ship was properly and well found.

The whole system became rotten with corruption and jobbery— and worse. The captain or commander, if he could satisfy the Post Office agent he had good reasons of health or anything else for staying ashore, could send his ship to sea without a single competent navigator. The agent, too, often held shares in the ship, or had a " private venture " of goods aboard, or had friendly or family relations with the com- mander. How readily he would accept the captain's reasons for staying ashore and recommend these as good is instanced in a Minute by the Postmaster-General in 1793 that " There are now twelve packets at sea ; and no less than ten captains of them ashore." Again in 1798, the Postmaster-General in reply to an application by a captain to stay ashore, wrote that this captain had " been absent from duty during many years, assigning no other cause than the death of his mother in 1792."

The major complaint of the shippers and merchants on this point was that captains were allowed to send their ships to and fro with their mails with no other in command than a seaman, who had not even the rudiments of navigation, and for lack of such knowledge might lose their ships and the merchants' mails.

But the worst malpractices grew out of permitting the packets to carry goods for sale in foreign or home ports. This was, from the first institution of the packet service, prohibited, but was officially winked at or even condoned by the Postmaster-General in official Minutes requiring agents to see that cargo was not so heavy or so stowed as to interfere with the trim, sailing, or handling of the ship.

The natural result was that every packet sailed with every ounce of cargo she could collect, the goods being owned by captain, officers, crew, and private shore venturers and merchants. Large profits resulted, and " a good time was had by all " concerned. Worse followed from this illegal trade.

The merchants, whose first and vital concern was in the safe carriage of their letters, began to notice that ship after ship was captured by privateers (especially American) on the homeward passage, while very few were taken outward bound. Investigation following their protests and agitation, proved to the hilt that these captures handsomely paid the ships' crews—through the insurance companies.

The simple method was for all aboard to ship some private goods for sale abroad, to sell these, to send home the proceeds in bank drafts or letters of credit ; and then, if the ship was captured homeward bound, to claim on the insurance company for the value of the goods bought abroad from the proceeds of sale of the outward cargo.

The clamour of the merchants, whose mails were always, according

27

to regulation, weighted and sunk before the ship struck and surrendered, led to a close investigation. The result was startling.

The crew of one packet attacked by a privateer refused to work the ship, and went below when the captain would have fought his ship with every hope of success and escape. Another packet, chased by an enemy for some daylight hours, struck her flag at dusk, although the enemy was a mile off, and had not even fired a gun demanding surrender. Then, lest the enemy had not seen the flag hauled down, the ship was hove to and the captain sent off a boat to inform the privateer of the surrender.

It was proved that eight of those seamen who had refused to work ship, and so allowed her to be captured, had previously received value for insured goods in other ships in which they had been " captured." In the case of the other packet which had hove to and surrendered at dusk, the surgeon, who had urged the captain to surrender, had been captured three times before, and had been heavily insured against loss of private goods he carried. The ship's steward claimed that he had taken out goods, failed to sell them, had lost them by capture on the homeward passage, and had been paid £250. Three fo'c'sle hands had been captured on this passage for the fourth time, and one of them received £200 insurance on the last " loss "—previous amounts not discovered.

In 1810 and 1814 the packetmen went on strike for more pay. This was the last straw on the patience of Post Office and public. The first strike was met by transferring the station from Falmouth to Portsmouth for some months, and the second by manning the packet ships from other ports.

The strikes shocked the merchants to an understanding of how completely their business, the whole of their communications with Spain, the Mediterranean, the West Indies, and North America were at the mercy of a comparative handful of Falmouth packetmen. It was a lesson not forgotten for many years by the whole business community.

All this is now very ancient and forgotten history; but we must remember that when the proposals of Willcox and Anderson were put forward for the carriage of ocean mails by private contract, the mercantile community was still rankling under the losses and sufferings to their trade which they had suffered so long and so recently.   They were the more ready and eager to back the proposals of Willcox and Anderson, because they could see that a privately owned steamship company would be free from the shackles of officialdom, of the slackness and incompetence and extravagance of Post Office and Admiralty management and running of the packets.

Willcox and Anderson played well and wisely on that string, and on the comparison which they could (and thoroughly did) prove was all in favour of their steam service to the Peninsula against the Post Office sail packets.

CHAPTER SEVEN

The First Contract—1837

In 1836 Willcox & Anderson were advertising a fortnightly service from London and Falmouth, but that this would soon be improved to a weekly sailing to and from the Peninsula. In November of that year they advertised the following steamships :

DON JUAN	.	.	.	.	.	.	800 tons, 300 Horse-power.	
BRITANNIA	.	.	.	.	.	.	800 ,, 300	,, ,,
BRAGANZA	.	.	.	.	.	.	650 ,, 240	,, ,,
IBERIA	.	.	.	.	.	.	600 ,, 200	,, ,,
MANCHESTER	.	.	.	.	.	.	600 ,, 220	,, ,,
LIVERPOOL	.	.	.	.	.	.	500 ,, 160	,, ,,

and again were announcing that the fortnightly service was soon to be made a weekly one.

It is probable that the weekly sailings were not justified by the volume of trade, but that they were necessary to the partners' plans, which they were then urging, for a steamer mail contract to compete with the service of the Admiralty sailing ships.

The service was by then in the hands of the Admiralty and not of the Post Office, the strange fact being that, through the many years of wars, the packets were run by a civil or peace Department on what was as fully a war as a peace service, because the packets were armed and gunned to protect themselves against warship and privateer attack, and did so in innumerable brilliant actions ; but some three years after the war ceased with the Battle of Waterloo, the service, which had become a purely peace one, passed under the control of a War Department— the Admiralty.

The grounds on which the Admiralty claimed and gained control of the packets against the most vigorous opposition of the Post Office was that the Navy needed them for the training of seamen and the employment of half-pay officers. These were arguments little likely to appeal to the merchants whose first and most urgent concern was that their mails should be carried with regularity and certainty. They could not see that this need would be furthered by ships manned by training-ship seamen and elderly officers who had to be found jobs, no matter what their competence or efficiency.

The Admiralty packet service to the Mediterranean and the East was run in stages. The sail packets left once a week for Lisbon, and the Gibraltar mails were carried on to there once a month. Up to 1830, mails for Malta and Egypt went by sail packets, but in that year the Admiralty sent out the first of their steam packets, the " Meteor," and followed her with another eight for the Mediterranean.

But even with the help of these steam packets, the service was slow and irregular. The sailing brigs from Falmouth ran once a week, " wind and weather permitting," and took anything up to three weeks to reach Lisbon. Mails for Egypt went to Malta, and were transhipped for forwarding once a month ; and the steamers also had to serve Greece and other Mediterranean ports.

But in those days Lisbon was by far the most important port of this service, being the centre of the Peninsular trade and financial interests which had been built up there for so many years. It was therefore on the Peninsula part that Willcox and Anderson concentrated in their effort to obtain a mail contract.

They prepared a plan and proposals for such a service and placed these before the Admiralty, pointing out that they could guarantee greater regularity and speedier delivery, guaranteeing, in fact, to take no more and usually much less than five days between Falmouth and Lisbon ; and at the same time producing figures to show that their steam service would cost very much less than the country was paying for the Admiralty packets.

The Government turned the proposals down flat, but Willcox and Anderson continued to agitate and to bring to the commercial and banking interests the superiority of their steamers over the Government sail packets. They circulated reports of the comparative times taken by various steamers and by sail packets, and on the 1st June, 1837, obtained Press publications of a report on a striking performance of outward-and-homeward steamers. The paragraph ran :

MARCH OF STEAM

" The ' Iberia ' steamship, belonging to the Peninsular Company, sailed from Falmouth on the 22nd May and arrived off Oporto on the 25th, IN 66 HOURS. The ' Braganza,' belonging to the same Company, left Oporto on the 25th and arrived at Falmouth on the 28th in 70 HOURS, bringing letters from the ' Iberia's ' passengers. So that in 136 hours, or something SHORT OF 6 DAYS, from their leaving England, advices of their safe arrival in Portugal were back in England."

By this time the pressure of public opinion and business circles could no longer be resisted, and the Government called on Willcox & Anderson to submit plans for a steam-packet service. These were promptly supplied, whereupon the Government called for public tenders on the plans submitted.

Two tenders were submitted, one by a firm called the British & Foreign Company, and the other by Willcox & Anderson. For some reason not known, but suspected to have been official dislike of the forcing tactics of the latter tenderers, the British & Foreign Company were given a marked preference, and their tender was on the point of being accepted when it was made widely public that the Company had not the ships or means to carry out their undertakings.

The Government obligingly postponed a decision for a month to allow the British & Foreign to provide suitable guarantees, but these not being forthcoming, the tender of Willcox & Anderson was at last accepted, and a contract with the Peninsular Steam Navigation Company was formally signed on 22nd August, 1837.

Even before the new mail service began, a Post Office notice indicated a benefit resulting to the public in cheaper postage—an attainment always dear to the heart of Arthur Anderson especially. The

S.S. "PRECURSOR," 1,817 tons. Built 1841

Notice gives a useful indication both of the postal rates of a hundred years ago and of the packet service in the Mediterranean covered by the Admiralty :

NOTICE

GENERAL POST OFFICE.
18th August, 1837.

" A great reduction is made in the postage upon Letters conveyed by Her Majesty's Packets in the Mediterranean. Letters for MALTA, GREECE, the IONIAN ISLANDS, EGYPT and the EAST INDIES, if forwarded by way of FALMOUTH and by Her Majesty's packets in the Mediterranean will, in future, be subject to an uniform rate of only 2*s.* 6*d.* Single—5*s.* Double—7*s.* 6*d.* Treble—10*s.* per Ounce weight, and so on in proportion, from whatever part of the United Kingdom they may be despatched, instead of the former rates, which varied according to the distance the Letters were conveyed to FALMOUTH.

" Single Letters for the above destinations in the Mediterranean, if specially directed ' via Marseilles,' will be liable to an uniform British rate, wherever they may be posted, of 10*d.* and the French rate of 1*s.* 10½*d.* in all 2*s.* 8½*d.*, and Letters for the East Indies, by the same route, will be liable, in addition to those rates the further charge of 1*s.* Single, and so on in proportion.

" By Command,

" W. L. MABERLY, *Secretary.*"

With that note about " Letters for the East Indies " I shall deal later in the story of the Overland Route, so that it is sufficient for the moment to say that across and beyond Egypt mail transport was haphazard and slow in the extreme.

An advertised Sailing List, dated 1st September, includes a reference to a Liverpool Line or branch service with the " Manchester " and " City of Londonderry " sailing fortnightly. This Liverpool branch had run for months before, although now, even in Liverpool, it is little remembered that the Company once had regular sailings from there. Previous advertisements give the " Manchester " as of 600 tons and 220 h.p. and the " City of Londonderry " as of 513 tons and 200 h.p.

Both vessels had belonged to the Dublin and London Steam Packet Company, and its proprietors, Messrs. Bourne, had from first to last played a leading part in the support of Willcox and Anderson and the formation of the Peninsular Steam Navigation Company. Captain Richard Bourne, R.N., had a seat on the Board of the Company and of the P. & O. Company ; and Mr. James Allan, a clerk from the Dublin Office who was sent to London to assist the management, gave a life-time's service to the P. & O. He was first appointed as Secretary and Transfer Clerk at a salary of £300 a year, but in ten years had risen to a seat on the Board (or rather Court) of Directors and was a Managing Director with Willcox and Anderson, and he held those positions until his death in 1874.

The announcement giving official notice to the birth of the Peninsular Steam Navigation Company and the first month's sailings which began on 1st September is of historic importance enough to justify quotation in full :

HER MAJESTY'S PENINSULAR AND MEDITERRANEAN MAIL PACKETS

STEAM conveyance from LONDON and FALMOUTH to VIGO, OPORTO, LISBON, CADIZ, GIBRALTAR, MALTA, GREECE, the IONIAN ISLANDS, EGYPT and INDIA.

One of the following vessels of the Peninsular Steam Navigation Company, viz. :

DON JUAN	.	.	.	.	.	.	933 Tons, 320 Horse-power.
TAGUS .	.	.	.	.	.	.	900 ,, 300 ,, ,,
BRAGANZA	.	.	.	.	.	.	650 ,, 264 ,, ,,
IBERIA .	.	.	.	.	.	.	600 ,, 200 ,, ,,
LIVERPOOL	.	.	.	.	.	.	500 ,, 160 ,, ,,

Will on and from This Day (the 1st of September) start from London every Friday, and from Falmouth every Monday, with her Majesty's Mails for Vigo, Oporto, Lisbon, Cadiz, and Gibraltar, returning Weekly by the same route.

In connection with the Company's vessels, Her Majesty's Steam Ships run every alternate Week from Gibraltar to Malta, and from Malta to Corfu. Also, once a month from Malta to Alexandria, in connection with the line of Steam communication through the Red Sea to India. Passengers for Malta, Corfu, and Greece, should proceed by the Company's vessels, which leave London on the 1st, 15th and 29th September. Those for Egypt and India by the vessels of the 1st and 29th of that month.

THE FIRST TWO VESSELS ARE THE LARGEST AND MOST POWERFUL THAT HAVE BEEN YET PUT AFLOAT. The whole of them have been fitted up so as to combine the first style of elegance with comfort to the passengers. Separate cabins for Parties and Families can be engaged.

A liberal Table, with Wines, &c., is provided, and included in the Fares ; and numerous unsolicited Testimonials from parties of the first rank and character, confirm the superiority of the management on board.

The average time in which the Vessels make the passage is—from Falmouth to Vigo, 54 hours ; to Lisbon 84 hours ; to Gibraltar, including 24 hours stay at Lisbon and 6 hours at Cadiz, 7 days. The passage from Gibraltar to Malta is about 5 days ; from Malta to Corfu 2 days ; from Malta to Alexandria about 4 days.

LIVERPOOL LINE

Fares the same as from London.

The large and powerful steam vessels MANCHESTER and CITY OF LONDONDERRY, run from Liverpool to Oporto, Lisbon, Cadiz, Gibraltar, and Malaga, once a fortnight.

RATES OF FARE

	Chief Cabin	Second Cabin
London to or from Vigo, Oporto or Lisbon .	£15 0 0	£9 10 0
London to or from Cadiz or Gibraltar . .	18 0 0	12 0 0
Falmouth to or from Vigo, Oporto, or Lisbon .	13 0 0	7 10 0
Falmouth to or from Cadiz or Gibraltar . .	16 0 0	10 0 0

It may have been noticed that no mention is made in these sailing lists of the " William Fawcett." This was because she was employed on the Madeira run, and an advertisement in *The Times* of 4th October, 1838, has an " N.B." saying the " William Fawcett " will make a second trip to Madeira from Lisbon about the 20th October.

It may also have been noticed that in the advertisements I have quoted on the Peninsular Company's sailings, there are variations in the tonnage and horse-power of some of the steamers. This apparently was due to alterations to ships or to their engines, which increased their gross tonnage and the horse-power.

The contract rate was for £29,600 a year for at least one passage a month between Falmouth and Peninsular ports round to Gibraltar. The amount no doubt made all the difference of turning previous losses into a profit, and the Company was launched on the first short stage of the Far Eastern routes which the P. & O. were to cover so completely well within a score of years from this first sailing for the Peninsula in September 1837.

CHAPTER EIGHT

Fateful Years—1837–40

THE first years of the Peninsular's mail contract were of vital importance, not only to the fate of the Company itself, but also to the whole system of mail carrying by private contract instead of by Admiralty-controlled packets.

It was, in fact, only after the Peninsular had proved the success of the system that consideration was given to its extension to the Atlantic services. Neither the Cunard nor Royal Mail service was then in existence, and if the Peninsular Company's contract had not proved to the hilt the superiority of the private company contracts in speed, regularity, and economy over the Government sail and steam packets, it would certainly have set back for years the Post Office plans which led to the advertising of a call for tenders for an Atlantic steamer mail contract, which in turn led Samuel Cunard and his brothers to seek the capital and ships which won them the first cross-Atlantic mail contract, and set the first Cunarders and their Company successfully afloat.

I have mentioned that for a year or two before Willcox & Anderson secured their contract for the Peninsular Company in 1837, their Line had been running at a loss, and that it was only the cash earned by the contract that turned this into a profit. There was a desperately narrow margin between the signing of that contract and a loss which might have sunk the Company if it had not had the financial backing of the Post Office contract behind it.

As already quoted, the fleet which began the Peninsular service included two steamers then advertised as " the largest and most powerful yet put afloat," and the first of these was the " Don Juan," of 933 tons and 320 h.p.

The contract was signed on 22nd August, 1837, the first liner sailed under it on 1st September ; and on the 15th of that month the " Don Juan," homeward bound from Gibraltar, ran aground off Tarifa, 20 miles from Gibraltar, and became a total loss. She was carrying the mails, specie to the value of 21,000 dollars, and some passengers, including Arthur Anderson and his wife.

The ship had been built at a cost of some £40,000, and the loss to the Company was the more severe in cash, because she was only partially insured, and in prestige because she was wrecked so very quickly after the inauguration of the mail contract and when it was hoped the crack liner would set up a record on the homeward passage.

The saving factor in the casualty was that Arthur Anderson was aboard the ship, and that his individual efforts and initiative saved the loss of the cash consigned in her. The whole story was told by him soon after in that *Shetland Journal* which he had founded and edited, and in which he told the story in detail both as an explanation of why that issue had been delayed in publication, and perhaps because it was also an excellent piece of press " copy."

Within half an hour of sailing from Gibraltar, a thin mist had thickened to a solid fog, and Anderson, on the quarterdeck with the Captain, gave up a hopeless peering into " the thick " and went below to his cabin. Before he reached it, he heard loudly shouted orders to stop and go astern, and before he could rush up on deck again, felt the grate and grind of the bows striking.

The mist thinned, revealing a long ridge of rocks close to and the shine of the Tarifa lighthouse some way off. The sea was smooth, but the ship's bows were firmly aground, and no efforts of engine or man power could get her afloat again.

A little Spanish fishing boat approached, and Anderson hailed her, brought her alongside, and entered into an urgent but lengthy bargaining for the boat to carry the mails and news of the disaster to Gibraltar. It was his (and the Company's) good fortune that his fluency in Spanish

ARTHUR ANDERSON, ESQ.
One of the Founders of the P. & O.
Managing Director 1837–1868
Chairman 1862–1868
From a painting by T. F. Dicksee

enabled him to conclude the bargain and to embark the mails, with himself in charge and his wife for company.

Arrived at Gibraltar, a British warship and Government packet readily offered their aid. The warship took the mails, put a squad of Royal Marines on board the packet as a safeguard against possible looting, and ordered her off in haste. Anderson went with her, and on arrival at the " Don Juan " found her listing badly and with part of the decks awash. The Captain had decided that the ship was done for, and had turned the crew on to salving what they could.

They had got a good deal ashore, including the boxes containing the specie. The locals from Tarifa and around had swarmed down and had given plenty of indication that they were ripe for plunder. Anderson and the captain of the packet hurried ashore with a party of sailors and the armed marines, intent on recovering the boxes of cash and getting them safely aboard.

Tarifa town is connected by a causeway with a little island, on which there was a lighthouse and fortified wall or fortress. Anderson and his party landed, found the gate through the walls open, and no interference with their proceeding to where the boxes of cash had been placed. They gathered these up and were marching them back to their boat, but this time they found the gate closed with an officer and two sentries posted outside.

Anderson's polite request to be allowed to pass was refused point-blank, the officer answering all remonstrances with a stolid but stubborn reply that he was acting on direct orders from the Governor. We may imagine how anxious Anderson was to retrieve the cash which, if lost, would have to be accounted for by his Company on top of what was by then the certain loss of their best and biggest ship.

He told the officer that he insisted on seeing the Governor (who was on the other side of that locked gate), that he must take with him the Captain of the armed packet who commanded a British Government vessel, that the Captain would naturally resent what was virtually an attempt to make him and his uniformed troops prisoners, and, if refused access to the Governor and an explanation of his orders, would at once signal his ship to open fire and continue it until the walls were battered into ruins.

In brief asides to the Captain (in English) Anderson warned him to pass the word quietly to his men to stand by ready, to make no sign of a move until the gates were well open, and then to grab up their boxes and make a rush for it.

In those days the British Navy carried matters with a high hand abroad, and no doubt the Spanish officer was well convinced that the threat of bombardment would be carried out if he did not give way—as indeed it probably would have been, with the later approval and support of the British Government. He ordered the gates to be opened, and bowed Anderson and the Captain through.

They marched gravely past him, and, close on their heels, followed a rush of sailors and marines carrying the treasure boxes, jostling and hustling aside the indignant officer and sentries and returning only rude laughter and ruder gestures to their violent language and gesticulations. The sailors jogged down to the beach and their boat with the boxes, and the Spanish officer could hardly dare offer physical interference to them and the steady covering party of armed marines.

With the boxes safely aboard the packet, Anderson took the Captain back with him to interview the Governor, and without waiting to hear more than the beginning of a fierce tirade about the insult to Spain of landing an armed force, pointed out that the insulting boot was on the other leg, that the Governor had failed to prevent the local people interfering with salvage parties and trying to plunder a stranded British ship; and finally, that he had apparently ordered his troops to keep British sailors and marines in uniform in restraint and as prisoners. The Governor, said Anderson, would assuredly hear more of this from the British Government when the Captain made his official report.

The Governor, no doubt with some visions of himself being made the scapegoat and his own job in jeopardy, cooled down rapidly, and in the end did what he could to make amends with useful help and protecting the salvage work.

As a sidelight to this episode, consider the physical endurance Anderson displayed. He embarked at Gibraltar, no doubt after a full and busy day on the work of embarkation of passengers, cargo, and those cash boxes ; he was on deck with the Captain until the ship struck in the darkness, was very active in the efforts to get the ship off, embarked with the mails in an open fishing boat and sailed back in her 20 miles to Gibraltar, had all the urgent business to put through of arranging for the mails to be taken on, and an armed party sent back to the " Don Juan " in the packet.

He may have had an hour or two of sleep or rest on that run back, or he may (and probably did) not, since he would know (and the Captain would not) just where the " Don Juan " was stranded. Then there was all that affair of going ashore, getting the treasure through, going back to interview the Governor, and so keeping his diplomatic equanimity that he turned hot hostility into at least moderate and useful friendliness and help. I should imagine that Anderson must have kept his feet, and kept his mind and body on the stretch, for anything from two to four days and nights without a break.

All his efforts failed to save the ship. She became a total loss, and the Company had to face this and find another ship to carry on the contract of the mail carriage. The Sailing List of the next year (1838) tells how this was done with the full lot of steamers required, including, with the TAGUS, ROYAL TAR, BRAGANZA and IBERIA, the LIVERPOOL, and CITY OF LONDONDERRY, both the last being chartered from the Dublin Steam Packet Company.

The next year (1839) saw a new development in mail carriage to the East which, if successful, might well have put a stopper on the further extension of the Peninsular Steam Navigation Company to Malta and Egypt and into its " Oriental " services and have stifled the P. & O. at, or before, birth.

That year (1839) an agreement was made with the French Government for the carriage of mails from England across France to Marseilles. There the mails were shipped by Government steam packet for Malta, and thence carried on by another Government steam packet to Egypt for the East. Then (as now) land transport was swifter than sea, and the short cut across France could not fail to be quicker than the long sea passage round Spain up to Marseilles.

But our Government were not altogether satisfied with this method of sending mails across France, a major factor against it being that they distrusted or disliked the possibility of official dispatches to and from the East being tampered with while in transit through France. Also it was found that the mail connections at Marseilles were irregular and unsatisfactory and too liable to long delay because wind and weather often prevented the Admiralty steamers being there to meet the land-transported mails.

The Company had so well established its reputation for regularity of sailings and for carrying out its undertakings that when Lord William Bentinck, the Governor of India, was preparing a case to press on the Government for a steamer service to India and to express the increasing demands for this in India, he went to the Peninsular Company and urged them to make an offer to undertake the service.

The Company, however, was then too fully occupied with its Peninsular service and in getting that firmly on its feet, and so declined to consider the further Indian service. But they went exhaustively into the possibilities of the India–Egypt steam mail, and supplied Lord Bentinck with all the data gathered from their experience and with the application of this to an Indian sea mail. Lord Bentinck made the fullest use of all this in evidence he gave before a Commission of Enquiry on Steam Communication with India, and gave all credit to those in the Company who had supplied him with invaluable facts and knowledge.

The upshot of it all was that the Government asked the Company for any plans they could offer to extend the service to Egypt and to India, and the plans were promptly produced in full and itemised detail, together with an offer to undertake the through service with a suitable fleet of the class of steamers they recommended.

The Government having carefully considered the plans and proposal and found them good, repeated the rather shabby trick they had played on Willcox and Anderson over the first Peninsular contract. This was that, having " sucked the brains " of the only men who could supply the facts, information, and estimates, they adopted these root and branch, in whole and in part, and proceeded to advertise them and call for public tenders for the contract to carry the mails between England and Egypt.

Four tenders were put in, one by Willcox & Anderson for £34,200, and theirs being not only the lowest but the only one backed by experience and the substantial offer of suitable vessels at their command, their tender was accepted.

Out of that contract came the Incorporation by Royal Charter in December 1840 of the Peninsular and Oriental Steam Navigation Company, and an extension which in two years reached out to India, included a development unheard of in steamship companies of a difficult and complicated overland route as part of their system, and within five years had branched out into lines to Italy, Greece, and the Black Sea, and regular running to Ceylon, Madras, Calcutta, and China.

But those giant strides were not made without a hard struggle, complicated negotiations, and efforts to reconcile well-founded rival interests and competitors. On top of all were the heavy responsibilities and the onerous conditions attached to the granting of the Royal Charter of Incorporation of the P. & O. Looking back now on all these obstacles, one can only wonder that a Company then well and profitably established in its own specialised trade should have been willing to undertake the make-or-break, win-or-lose-all conditions which the Company risked.

The terms of the Charter included an undertaking that, within two years, the P. & O. would establish a mail service with suitable steamers between India and Egypt ; and this undertaking was given without any contract or offer of payment for the service except that the East India Company promised an annual payment of £20,000 if they made four voyages in the first year, six in the second year, and one a month in the next three years. In view of one fact, that the steamers required on the service would cost several times this amount, and of another, that the East India Company had been trying for years to run steamers between Bombay and Suez with no better success than to make one round voyage a year, the offer was by no means generous.

By 1838–9 the Company had successfully turned the corner, and were showing a profit, where up to 1837 Willcox and Anderson had lost upwards of £30,000 on their Peninsular service. It may well be wondered why, with the prospect of steadily increasing profits from the Peninsular trade, they were so ready to venture all and risk the wrecking of their whole soundly established enterprise by the extension into the Indian service.

They appear to have staked everything on certain fundamental beliefs held by both of them as Managing Directors and as men experienced in steam navigation.

First, they were convinced of that principle that trade follows facilities for it, that although liners when first put on a route might not pay, the traffic attracted to regular and speedier communication would quickly make up early losses and turn them into a profit. Anderson especially in later years often propounded in speech and writing that theory or belief, and offered plenty of proof of past experience that he was right.

The second belief was that traffic to and from India would benefit their Peninsular trade, and that, having contracted for a mail service between England and Egypt, there was the more need to encourage an increased traffic of passengers and mail between India and Egypt, since, obviously, that increase would swell the flow between Egypt and England.

A final factor which cannot be ignored is that Anderson, as ever, was keen on that speeding up and cheapening the carriage of letters between scattered communities and families, which had resulted from his own early youthful experiences of the hardships of being cut off from his own parents by the cost of letter postage.

It must be remembered that the project for an establishment of " Steam Communication with India " was by no means new, that the need for faster mails had been urged vehemently by soldiers and statesmen from the Duke of Wellington down for years before, and that for nearly twenty years before Willcox and Anderson negotiated the Charter for the P. & O. to put the project into being, one attempt after another had been tried to collect the cash and to use it profitably to run steamers on the India–Egypt—or, as it was then called, the " Oriental "—end of the route.

The history of the P. & O. is essentially the history of steam navigation to the East, and although the P. & O., as such, had nothing to do with the first attempts (and failures) to establish that through communication, the Company and its Managers certainly were closely concerned with those early efforts, and the lessons to be learned from their failures, as well as in financial difficulties met in rival plans and companies which were still very much alive just before and after the Royal Charter of the P. & O. was granted.

In the next chapter, then, I must 'bout ship and go back to the story of first steam enterprises in the East, and how the success of the P. & O. was built on their intentions, efforts, and failures.

CHAPTER NINE

Steam to India—Early Failures

IT is rather astonishing to find, from an examination of the contemporary newspapers and journals, Reports of Commissions, Committees formed and meetings held, and discussions in both Houses of Parliament, how intense was the interest in the subject of steam navigation to India in the 1820's and 1830's, and how violent the war between rival supporters of various schemes.

It was in 1819 that the American steamship " Savannah " made the first crossing of the Atlantic from America and back, and although it is a matter of dispute to this day whether it can be fairly claimed that she was the first to cross " under steam," because for a good part of her passage the patent paddles were hoisted in and stowed on deck while she proceeded under sail only, her performance fired the ambitions and imagination of men in the direction of ocean steam navigation.

It was natural, or indeed inevitable, that the route to India should draw first attention, because of the richness of the trade that had been carrying to and fro for over three hundred years, because of the enormous wealth and power it had brought the East India Company, and because the desperate slowness of the old East Indiamen round the Cape called urgently for improvement.

Four, five, and even six months was no abnormal time for dispatches to take between England and India, which meant anything up to a year for a reply to be received. This was an intolerable state of affairs, not only for the important circle of merchants here and in the East, but also for the large public whose relatives were serving in India both in commerce and the " civil service " of John Company, and in the large army there, and all these fastened eagerly on the calculations of enthusiasts who figured that with the aid of steam a ship could make the passage in 70 or 80 days.

From letters and articles in the Press, the matter moved to Parliament, where a Report was laid before the House in August 1822; and from the realm of speculative surmise moved again to that of practical and business possibility when, in that year, a public meeting was held in London for the purpose of forming a steamship company for the Indian trade.

There appears to have been no consideration given then to the possibility of a route by the Red Sea, and the route on which it was decided to pursue investigations was the old one round the Cape by which the riches of East and West had been exchanging since the days of Vasco da Gama. We cannot but admire the boldness of the promoters of the proposed enterprise, when we remember that the only steamers then regularly trading were little vessels on river, estuary, coastal, and cross-Channel services, and making journeys of no more than a few hours or at most a day or so in adverse weather.

At the London meeting of 1822 a certain amount of financial support was promised, but both because this was not sufficient for the undertaking and because the promoters wished to ascertain the views in India on what support might be counted on in cash and trade, a Lieutenant (later Captain) Johnston was sent out to India to enquire into both items.

This, of course, was years before Willcox and Anderson had given a thought to India or even taken any step into the new world of steam navigation; and yet the journey of Lieutenant Johnston was to have results on their future business, and by 1840, when the P. & O. was formed, led directly into an association with Mr. Waghorn, the man whose name has always stood out as that of the pioneer and progenitor of the Overland Route across Egypt.

That route was even then quite well known, although the difficulties of it had tempted to travel by it only those of hardy and adventurous spirit, or those to whom the possibility of saving weeks or even days on the journey made it worth trying.

Johnston went out by that route, and although his employers had commissioned him to advocate the Cape route, he himself was so converted to the greater advantages of the journey by Egypt that he gave his personal adherence and preference to it. This was to prove later of momentous importance both to Mr. Waghorn and the P. & O.

Johnston held several meetings in India, and at one in Calcutta, in December 1823, Lord Amherst, the Governor of India, gave his warm approval to the proposals, and promised to recommend to his Council that they should make a gift of 20,000 rupees to any British company or individuals who, by the end of 1826, should have established a permanent service of steamers which would make two out-and-back voyages each year ; taking not more than 70 days to each passage each way.

This, with the rupee valued at about 2s., meant, say, £2,000, so that the Governor was not promising anything very extravagant for a 70-day passage to replace the existing normal one of 4 to 6 months. But at least his promise had a moral value, and it is important that he made his promise for a service either by the Cape or Red Sea route. Johnston must already have begun to sow the seed of the Red Sea route, and on good ground.

Johnston raised 80,000 rupees in India in addition to this conditional promise of 20,000, and when the news of this reached England, the promoters held another meeting, at which sufficient further capital was secured to order an experimental steamer, the " Enterprize," to be built for the voyage out round the Cape.

She was built at Deptford, was a wooden paddler of 479 tons and 120 horse-power, and was built at a cost of £43,000, of which £7,000 went in the notable feature of her copper boiler, made in one piece and weighing 32 tons. It was believed that the copper would stand up to continuous service without the repair or replacement which was then impossible in the East better than an iron boiler would do.

Johnston returned from India by an Indiaman round the Cape, and on completion of the " Enterprize," was given command of her. She sailed with 17 passengers from London on 16th August, 1825, and arrived 113 days out at Calcutta on 7th December.

This passage of 113 days was a severe blow to the hopes of the pro-moters, and offered little or no prospect of the regular 70-day passages required to earn that promised 20,000 rupees. The ship was sold to the Indian Government for £40,000, and was put into service carrying dispatches between Calcutta and Burma during the Burmese War.

She lost her owners £3,000 on her building cost, plus an unknown but heavy amount of her expenses on the outward passage. Her failure was, as we shall see, a severe setback to the whole enterprise of steam navigation to India for years to come.

Her passage, however, had one accidental but very important side-line result. When she arrived off the mouth of the Hoogly, the pilot who took her up the river to Calcutta and who heard from Captain Johnston all about his passage and also about that former journey out by the Red Sea route was Mr. (later Lieutenant, R.N.) Waghorn, who from that day became a devoted and ardent disciple and spreader of the gospel of steam navigation to India, and of the " Overland Route."

His, however, is a story that needs its own telling, and meantime I'll carry on with that other story of the failures that pointed a way to success.

In the following years every effort was made to force the Govern-ment, the Admiralty, and the East India Company to establish steam communication, and the East India Company in particular came in for the most bitter attacks and accusations of hindering rather than helping the establishment of a steam service.

It was said frequently, freely, and very loudly that a quick and regu-lar mail service was not wanted by the East India Company, because this would bring them into too close touch with the home authorities, curb their independence and authority, and lead to searching reforms. Even when the East India Company were at last moved to make an effort to run steamers to Egypt from Bombay, the failures of those steamers were held up as merely another attempt to prove that steam communication was impracticable. Certainly their first venture on this service did a good deal to bear out these views.

The first steamer to attempt this Red Sea service was the East India Company armed vessel " Hugh Lindsay," built at Bombay, of 411 tons and with two 80-h.p. engines sent out from England. It can only be said that if John Company had any serious intention of proving the Suez voyage possible, they or their ship designers were singularly short-sighted, not to say stupid.

The " long leg " of the passage was between Bombay and Aden, a distance of 1,710 miles, which, at the estimated best speed of the steamer, she could hope to cover in 10 days, with a lake-smooth sea all the way. Yet for this 10 to 11 days' steam, she was given a full bunker capacity for about 5½ days.

She sailed from Bombay on 20th March, 1829, and in the hope that she might be able to steam to Aden, she was crammed to the last available corner with coal. Even the passenger saloon and cabins were filled with coal, so that only one passenger was carried. Instead of drawing her proper depth of 11½ feet, she drew nearly 14, and was so deep that her decks were almost awash, her transom was under water, and her paddles could only with difficulty turn round. Those who watched her start rather neatly nick-named her " the Water-Lily " or " Pond-Lily."

She made all possible use of her sails in favouring winds, and dragged into Aden on the last sweepings of her coal bunkers about noon on 31st March. She took six days to get coal aboard, went on to Mocha, and anchored there on the 7th April. More coal taken in, she made Jeddah on the 12th, and, after another four days lost in coaling, reached Suez on the 22nd.

On the whole, fair weather was met ; but on one day, when the wind was ahead, the best that could be made was a speed of about 3 knots. It was quite evident that the vessel was hopelessly under-powered to make all-the-year voyages against the strength of the monsoon winds and seas which are adverse from June to September.

An examination of the Log Book for that voyage reveals how unsuitable the " Hugh Lindsay " was in other respects than that lack of bunker space. One of the first entries is two hours after sailing— " 4 inches in the well," and next day there is another entry—" The two engine pumps kept going to keep down the water, which came in very fast, apparently through the paddle-shaft blocks." One might have

S.S. "HINDOSTAN," 2,017 tons. Built 1842

Leaving Southampton, 1842, to open Indian Mail Service

supposed this water came in because the paddle-shaft apertures were sunk too deep ; but against this is the fact that right up to the arrival at Aden the entries continue of " the two bilge pumps kept going."

The Log also shows a continual succession of notes of the engines being stopped to repair this or that damage, loosening or breaking of bolts and working loose of paddle boards. The Log sets down exactly the time lost from the stopping of engines until they " set on steam again." The whole passage to Suez took 32 days 16 hours, of which the ship was at sea 21 days 6 hours ; and of the 10 days 19 hours to Aden, just on 10 hours were lost in engine stoppages for repairs.

It was only the time lost in bunkering that might be cut down with better organisation on a regular service. At Aden, for example, as soon as the anchor was down a boat was sent in with a request that the " Sooltan," as the Log has him, should order the coal there to be sent off. The officer who went in brought back a message that the Sultan was up-country at his residence there, that the Sheik in Aden did not dare ship the coal without orders, so had sent off a message asking for instructions. Next day a polite message was received from the Sultan that he wished to invite the Captain to come and pay him a visit. The harassed Captain rushed off an answer begging to be excused because of urgency of re-bunkering and getting away ; and at last, after another day had gone, the order came—although the coal only began to do so next day, at the rate of only two boat-loads a day.

Whatever else went badly, the keeping of the Log Book was all that an historian could desire in its meticulous detail, not only of speed, paddle revolutions, inches of water in the well, but down to such items as " Killed two sheep weighing 55 lbs.," " Carried away the tiller ropes ; rove new ones," and even " Missed a silver tea-spoon belonging to the gov' mess."

But, unsatisfactory as the voyage was, it did at least show that it could be made in the favourable months of the monsoons, although not against their adverse winds and seas. This was so plainly proved that the " Hugh Lindsay " made only the one voyage a year from then until 1836, while over all those years the storm of criticism and complaint beat stronger and stronger about the ears of the East India Company.

But although in that year the East India Company began to put on more powerful steamers, these by no means gave the regular monthly service which was promised.

I quote an extract from *Parbury's Oriental Herald* of 1838, which is a fair or even a mild sample of some of the expressions of opinion of that period. Said Parbury :

" It is quite true that steam vessels have been sent out with the ostensible view of carrying on Steam Communication, and the East India Company have done no more. But who now, conversant with facts, will believe that such was the real intention ? It could not have been, because these vessels are notoriously inefficient in size and power ; and the experience of the past few months has clearly shown this because during the months of June, July, August, and September the communication between Bombay and Suez was completely suspended."

Such attacks on the East India Company and on our own Admiralty and packet service were strengthened both by the regularity with which the Peninsular Steam Navigation Company had by then (1838) been running to the Spanish ports against all the gales of the notorious Bay of Biscay ; and also by comparisons made between the official mail times and those made by Mr. Waghorn, who from 1829 had been devoting himself to developing and speeding up communication by the Overland Route.

Waghorn's career deserves a place in this history, all the more because his efforts did so much to increase the demands for the service to be put in the hands of a private company by contract and the subsequent incorporation of the P. & O. by Royal Charter for that purpose ; and because Waghorn was for a time offered or was in the direct employment of the P. & O. to act as their sub-agent.

CHAPTER TEN

Lieutenant Waghorn, R.N.

Y OU may at times have heard or read of Waghorn as " Mr." and at other times as " Lieutenant," so to begin with I may explain that this was because he resigned from H.M. Navy and Bombay Marine as Midshipman or " Mr." about 1829, and was only granted the rank of Lieutenant many years later, in 1842.

Thomas Fletcher Waghorn, born at Chatham in 1800, joined the Navy aged 12, and served in it for 4½ years.

I have only in recent weeks been fortunate enough to receive from Australia a letter from Mr. Carr-Comyns, a grand-nephew of Waghorn's, who has given me some facts about his grand-uncle which I have never previously heard and which I find well worth including here.

Mr. Carr-Comyns tells me, for example, that after this spell in the Navy, Waghorn, " at the age of 17, passed in Navigation for Lieutenant, and joined as third officer of a free trader to Calcutta in 1819. He joined the Bengal Marine (Pilot) Service and was with the above Company until 1824, when he volunteered for the (Burmese) Arracan War and received command of the East India Company's ' Matchless ' and a division of gunboats. Waghorn saw much service, was in five engagements, and was badly wounded."

Much, or most, of this detail is new to me and may be to others, so is therefore the more gladly quoted.

Waghorn returned to the Pilot service, and, as already mentioned, piloted the " Enterprize " up the Hoogly when she arrived there in 1825, and heard from her Captain Johnston the story of the passage out and also of Johnston's earlier journey out across Egypt.

We have Waghorn's own word for it that it was this chance encounter that first turned his attention to steam. In the evidence he gave before a Select Committee on Steam Navigation to India in 1834, he said, " I have been on board the ' Enterprize,' and it was on board of her that I first gave my attention to the subject of steam navigation, and afterwards joined His Majesty's Navy on board the steamers and remained there until I passed for Lieutenant."

It was later a minor but insistent grievance that, although he passed, he was not promoted then, and he spent long efforts, letters, and petitions pleading for this official recognition of his service in the Royal Navy.

From that same evidence before the Committee, it appears that Waghorn's first thoughts were of the route by the Cape. He began his warm advocacy of steam communication, and in this had made himself so prominent, that in 1827 he was selected by the Indian Government to proceed to England for the purpose of endeavouring to establish steam transport.

He himself summed up the results of his efforts with a flavour of bitterness : " I went to London, Liverpool, and Manchester. I stated my plan in various parts of England, and all the success I could achieve after three years' toil was the loan of two 50-horse-power engines from the East India Company."

He went back to India to report progress (or rather the lack of it), and found there that a Steam Committee which had been formed had collected over £4,000 towards the enterprise. He was offered this money to return to England and try again whether with this backing he could raise further capital. It was about this time (1829) that he resigned from the East India Company service, because a continuance in it must hinder his work for Indian steam transport, on the establishment of which he had by then come to be deeply impressed, or one might even say obsessed.

Back in England again with his £4,000-and-odd and offer of two 50-h.p. engines, he failed again to raise enough enthusiasm, or cash, to provide a steamer.

It is always easy to " be wise after the event," and it is now generally regarded as a disgrace to our Government and commercial community that they were so stupidly short-sighted in refusing to accept Waghorn's proposals and provide him with the moderate amount which would have given the proposed plan a fair trial. But there were circumstances existing then which at least show some very good reasons why Government, merchants, and investors or speculators alike might hesitate to embark on the venture.

It was in 1827 that Waghorn first came to England to raise support for the project of a steamer service round the Cape and across Egypt. It was only in December 1825 that the " Enterprize " had arrived at Calcutta, that her passage had proved impossibly slow and costly, and in 1827 it would still have stuck in the memory that a year before she was sold at a dead loss to her owning Company. There was little then, or for the next year or two, to encourage investors to put up cash for a similar venture.

The prospects of an Overland Route across Egypt were even more doubtful at that time. Little was known of it so far as the journey across Egypt went. The only people who had made it were hardy and adventurous travellers, who told and wrote of the trials and difficulties they had endured ; and those harrowing tales, while redounding no doubt to the heroic courage and physical endurance of the travellers, were hardly good publicity for the route.

The first voyage of the " Hugh Lindsay " again had brought forward all the difficulties of the Red Sea passage against the monsoons, and the probability that only one voyage a year could reasonably be accomplished between Bombay and Egypt. That particular difficulty had already been rubbed in by those few hardy travellers who had crossed from India by sail and had told repeatedly how the irresistible monsoon winds blew for months on end down the Red Sea and so many other months up it and across the Indian Ocean.

The service from England to Egypt was also then in a state of irregularity and slowness, such as to offer little encouragement to promoters of a service to connect with one across Egypt and beyond to India. Let me recall that then and up to 1830, the Admiralty's Falmouth packets went by sail to the Peninsula, monthly on to Gibraltar, and then by one ship to Malta and another on to Egypt each month, with frequent irregularities and disconnections.

Even after 1830, when the Admiralty put steam packets on the Gibraltar–Malta or Marseilles–Malta and Malta–Egypt services, there was little if any improvement in the Mediterranean service. This continued right up to 1836 and 1837, when Willcox and Anderson were regularising the mail carriage to Gibraltar—and this was years after that period of Waghorn's first disappointing efforts to enlist support had failed. It was not until 1840 that the P. & O. inaugurated a regular, reliable, and consistent service betwen England and Egypt.

There was another nasty snag in the path of the traveller across Egypt, especially from the East, before those P. & O. days. Egypt was so subject, or believed to be subject, to regular annual periods of plague, that at Malta or any Italian and French port the traveller almost certainly had to undergo a period of quarantine. This meant weeks' shut-up imprisonment within the walls of a lazaretto house with a good deal of discomfort and cost in cash and time.

The reports of those who ventured the journey in those days were certainly discouraging, to say the least of it—and, however exaggerated we now believe those "travellers' tales" to have been, they were the only tales our public heard.

I can quote one example of these reports out of many published at the time. It was that the better-class dweller in Egypt took infinitely less risk of plague than the traveller. As soon as the plague period began, the fixed-inhabitant Egyptian simply shut himself up in his house and did not stir out for weeks or months until the plague was declared over, or dying out.

The traveller, on the other hand, ate food, slept in beds, travelled in boats all plague-tainted, jostled elbows with the plague-ridden poor, and even picked up the plague on his boots in walking through the streets. Whether this was the truth, or whether (as we should suppose now) the plague was conveyed by way of the flea-infested rats or the mosquitoes, bugs, and lice which were always a prominent feature of the tales told by travellers, matters little. What did matter to the preaching of those pressing for the support of the Overland Route was that THE PLAGUE dogged the footsteps of the traveller, and that a slow four- or five-month clean and healthy voyage round the Cape was more attractive than the possibility of a week or two's quicker journey with the added prospect of a dirty death or illness in the middle of all the plagues of Egypt.

Add to all this that the reports were that Mehemet Ali, the Pasha of Egypt, was by no means friendly to Europeans, and was much more likely to fight rather than favour any plan which would bring through his country a regular stream of busybody travellers and officious officials poking their inquisitive noses into affairs which he much preferred should not be known outside Egypt.

At that time, for example, we had a very strong body of public opinion here hot against the system of slavery; and in the middle of Cairo (through which every traveller by the Overland Route must pass) there was a female slave market where the slaves were exposed for sale in pens or dens ranged round an open space in the centre of the public square and described in the *Hand Book for Egypt and India* of as late as 1842 as "more fitted for wild beasts than human beings." Actually that exhibition and market of slaves, almost nude negro girls with ugly faces but beautiful forms, white Circassian or Georgian beauties bought by Constantinople merchants for sale to the harems of Egypt, were an advertised "attraction" to travellers, and for many years P. & O. passengers visited the "show" and wrote at length in our journals about it.

There was another and very serious discouragement to those who might have been tempted to invest in promoting steam transport by the Red Sea. Just at the time Waghorn was pressing his views, there were very strong claims afoot for a mail service by the Euphrates route. These proposals were for a route which went by road from a port on the Mediterranean to the highest navigable waters of the River Euphrates, by steamer down (or up) the river, and by way of the Persian Gulf to India.

Later surveys and investigation proved this route to be less practicable than that by the Red Sea; but in the 1820's and 1830's the alternative was a very live subject indeed. As late as 1834 a Select Committee of the Government was still giving the most serious consideration to the Euphrates route and recommending the most exhaustive enquiries and surveys being carried out officially into its possibilities. The one outstanding fact that the Government had voted an expenditure of £30,000 to a survey and experimental trial of the route was in itself enough to put off those investors who might otherwise have put their cash into Waghorn's plans for the Egyptian route.

A final blow to Waghorn and his plans was in the announcement that the East India Company in 1829 was starting to run a steamer service between Bombay and Suez, beginning it with a trial voyage of the " Enterprize." Even the most reckless speculator might well have hesitated to put his money into establishing a service in competition with the all-powerful East India Company of those days.

Here, out of the many points that deserve it, I touch my hat to Waghorn, to his courage and enterprise, and his swiftness to snatch from impending collapse of all his plans the possibility of turning failure to success, of using a turn of the tide against him to float him on to later progress. He had cut himself adrift from the East India Company to further his pet project ; and it could have been no less than shattering to him to learn that the East India Company were to set afloat, without any help from him, the stage of the route for which he had been pleading and begging outside support.

Waghorn hurried to the London office of the East India Company, and obtained a special permit to act as courier to carry dispatches from Lord Ellenborough to India by the Overland Route, and an order to the captain of the " Enterprize " to embark him at Suez and carry him to Bombay. Waghorn's intention was to demonstrate beyond question the speed with which mails could be carried on his plan.

He left London on 28th October, 1829, having been advised that the " Enterprize " was due at Suez on the 8th December. He travelled across Switzerland and down to Trieste, went on to Alexandria by a Spanish ship, up the Nile to Cairo and post-haste across the desert to Suez, arriving there on the day the " Enterprize " was due.

He waited two days at Suez, consumed with impatience, and there still being no sign of the steamer, he hired an open native boat and embarked himself and his dispatches on rather a needle-in-a-haystack search of the Red Sea for the steamer.

Outside the offices of the Suez Canal Company at Suez to-day, there is a bronze bust of Waghorn, and on the base of it a relief depicting this incident of his embarkation in an open boat on his determined and desperate effort to make the record-breaking mail trip on which his heart and hopes were set.

He made first for the port of Cossier, some 250 miles down the Red Sea, thinking that the steamer might have called there for coal, and arrived there 4 days after leaving Suez, only to be disappointed again in finding no sign or word of the steamer. He left a letter there for her captain in case he missed her, and pushed on in his open boat down and across the Red Sea to Juddah or Jeddah, the Arabian port used by the pilgrims bound for Mecca.

This was another normal coaling port for the " Enterprize," but she had not arrived, and Waghorn was informed that she was no longer expected, because a report had been received that her engine had broken down and she was laid up for repair. The stout-hearted courier was still determined to push on, but he had to waste a month at Jeddah before he could engage a passage for India in a native sailing dhow ; and a few hours after his sailing, there arrived the East India Company sailing brig-of-war " Thetis," which had been in to Cossier, where her Captain, having received the letter left by Waghorn for the "Enterprize," set out to find him.

The " Thetis " picked him up off Jeddah and carried him to Bombay, where he arrived on 20th March, having taken 4 months and 21 days from England, including all detentions. But out of this grim discouragement, Waghorn took fresh courage, being in particular convinced that the Overland Route across Europe and then across Egypt offered every certainty of greatly speeding up the carriage of mails. He estimated that, if a steamer had been waiting him at Suez as arranged, he should have been in Bombay in 55 days from London. He found that only the day before he arrived at Bombay in the " Thetis " the East India Company new steamer " Hugh Lindsay " had been sent off from there to meet him.

This was the first voyage of the " Hugh Lindsay " already des-cribed, and it would seem from the time she took that the estimate of a total of 55 days from London was a very optimistic one. Waghorn took about 40 days from London by Trieste to Suez, which would have left him 15 days to reach Bombay by steamer. Actually the "Hugh Lindsay " took 33 days on that first return passage Suez to Bombay, and in subsequent years never took less than 32 days.

Waghorn returned to England and set about the task of building up on his own a system of transport for passengers and mail across Egypt and across Europe. On his journey out to connect with the " Enter-prize " he had met with a good and friendly reception from the Pasha of Egypt and his officials, and he was now able to confirm this friendliness and obtain the support of the Pasha in his undertaking.

I quote again from that letter from Waghorn's grand-nephew, Mr. Carr-Comyns in Australia, who says that Waghorn wrote :

" Once in the enjoyment of the Pascha's friendship I was enabled to establish mails to India and to keep the service in my own hands for four years. On one occasion I succeeded in getting letters from Bombay to England in 46 days by means of a fast French brig hired by me from Alexandria, lying in ballast and ready to start at a moment's notice to Marseilles."

Those four years apparently began with an experimental trip made in 1835 by Waghorn himself carrying a parcel of mails with him to India. He issued a circular, dated 8th January, 1835, addressing it to merchants having business with India and saying that he was leaving Falmouth for Alexandria on 5th February on a journey to India. " On this occasion," said the circular, " I shall take charge of any letters given me, at Five Shillings each. . . . I shall return to England in November, and in all probability I shall travel this route early in February, so that once a year you can count on rapid communication with India."

In the later years, however, he improved on this service by making his route " overland " across Europe as well as Egypt, as exampled in that instance of fast delivery by brig to Marseilles.

In this year (1835) Waghorn actively continued his endeavours to secure the formal appointment to the rank of Lieutenant, on which he had set his heart. In September he wrote to the Editor of the *Naval and Military Gazette* in London alluding to " the Memo I left with you referring to my claims for promotion to the rank of Lieut. in the Navy." In another letter to the Editor from Alexandria in November 1836 he sends a copy of a letter to the Earl of Minto and saying, " The fact is I would sooner be Lieut. in the Royal Navy than receive anything else."

In his letter to the Earl of Minto of 25th November, 1836, from Alexandria, he draws attention to his efforts to speed up the mails, saying that he " did in July last, unaided, accomplish the transit of H.M. Mails between Falmouth and Bombay in 63 days, personally taking it himself from Cairo to Mocha (without solicitation or recompense) on its way."

His letter continues, " The writer craves promotion to the rank of Lieut. in the Navy—nothing on earth would gratify him compared to it " ; and he proceeds to give reasons why his wish should be granted : " Sir Thos. Hardy can attest, if applied to, that he persuaded the writer in 1831 to return to H.M. Navy in order to be eligible for that rank, and the writer feels his is the only instance on record where a man who had once commanded a Vessel of War of the E.I. Compy. in the Burmese War and had been mentioned for his services there oft-times to the Bengal Govt. and to the Court of Directors of the E.I. Compy, consented to return to fill the station of *Midshipman* at the age of 31 in order to complete 16 months of time to be eligible for promotion."

It is at least some satisfaction to record that, whatever other disappointments he met in life—and there were many which embittered him—this dearest wish was at last gratified years later, when on 23rd March, 1842, he was appointed to the rank of Lieutenant, R.N.

I quote again from that letter of Mr. Carr-Comyns in which he says that Waghorn wrote of keeping the mail service in his own hands for four years, and to which Waghorn continued, " and immediately after, the Government and the East India Company, at the pressing solicitations of the London East India and China Association, started mails of their own and taking from me the conveyance of letters without a sixpence compensation from that time to this. Had this deprivation of my income been adjudicated upon by any commercial tribune in the world, £20,000 is the lowest sum that could have been in fairness awarded me."

It must not be supposed—as it might be—from the above that at the end of the four years (which would make the date about 1839 or 1840) Waghorn ceased to run his own private service or agency for passengers and mail. He certainly continued it actively, advertised and improved it, for some years in co-operation, and later in competition, with or even opposition to the P. & O. When the latter took over the Egyptian transit, spending a great deal of effort and money on it, Waghorn had his agents across Europe and Egypt and in India and was offering his services either to expedite travellers or mails by his faster route. One of his first London agents was Smith, Elder & Co., and another was a firm of Wheatley, which still continues as a shipping agency.

Those who collect postal packets and wrappers of the past are familiar with the covers stamped " Care of Mr. Waghorn—Marseilles," or Alexandria or elsewhere. The procedure in sending a letter was to take it to Mr. Waghorn's agent fully addressed, and (having paid the due charge on it) have it stamped " Care of Mr. Waghorn," and leave it to be forwarded by the speedier route.

This apparent ability of Mr. Waghorn to be anywhere at any time to receive letters to his care created for him almost a legendary fame. Thackeray, the novelist, saw him once in Cairo and wrote of him : " Lieut. Waghorn is bouncing in and out of the courtyard full of business. He only left Bombay yesterday morning, was seen in the Red Sea on Tuesday, is engaged to dinner this afternoon in Regent's Park, and (as it is about two minutes since I saw him in the courtyard) I make no doubt he is by this time at Alexandria, or at Malta say, or perhaps both."

In 1840, the story of Waghorn begins to merge with that of the P. & O., so I shall leave that part of it to deal with in a chapter on " The Overland Route," and here will conclude briefly his personal history.

Waghorn's efforts to establish his travel-agency business could not have paid, because the Australian grand-nephew has written that

S.S. "RIPON," 1,908 tons

Arriving at Southampton with General Garibaldi and suite on board, April 3rd, 1864

62]

Waghorn had exhausted a large fortune inherited from his grandfather, a wealthy landed proprietor of Kent, " and subsequently his family fortune to the extent of £40,000 to £50,000, besides contracting large debts."

I have no other account of such an almost incredibly large private fortune being expended, and Waghorn himself made no mention of it in a petition he presented to the East India Company in 1848. He does, however, refer to his debts, saying, " Your petitioner prays you to relieve him from the debts he was obliged to incur to a large amount, granting him a pension (not a donation) and in so doing you will have the recollection of your petitioner so long as it pleases God he should exist."

This petition was evidently successful, because it was Minuted by the East India Company Court of Directors on 12th April, 1848, that—" Adverting to the merits and services of Lieutenant Thomas Waghorn of the Royal Navy in the Establishment of Steam Communication with India, and to the great benefits which have been derived therefrom, Lieutenant Waghorn be granted as a further mark of the sense entertained by the East India Company of those services, an annuity of One hundred pounds (£100) subject to the sanction of the Board of Commissioners."

Waghorn in reply asked that he should be allowed to draw the first year's pension in advance, and on this being granted, he applied again in January 1849, asking that the Court of Directors would " as a further mark of their favour make him a pecuniary grant."

The grant was given in the form of an increased pension raising the amount from £100 to £200 a year " as a final grant by the Company in acknowledgment of his services." This further grant of the £100 annuity was also paid to him for the one year in advance.

It would appear that in addition to this pension granted in the last years of his life, Waghorn had also drawn half-pay for some years. O'Bryan's Naval Biography of 1849 says that he " was advanced to his present rank 23.3.1842 and has since been on half pay."

Unfortunately Waghorn did not live long to enjoy his pension, his worries and long-continued physical exertions evidently bringing him to a premature end. He broke down while endeavouring further to improve the Trieste route in 1849 and died on the following 7th January.

In the church of All Saints', Snodland, a little village in Kent where Waghorn lived for a time, is a memorial tablet extolling his enterprise in pioneering the Overland Route. His grave is in the churchyard, near that of a sister. Two other sisters went to Australia in 1849 and settled there.

The inscription on the stone in the Snodland Churchyard reads :

ERECTED
To The Memory of
THOMAS FLETCHER WAGHORN
Lieut. R.N.
Who Departed This Life
January 7th, 1850
Aged 49 Years.

Also of Harriett
Widow of the above,
Who departed this life
January 19th, 1856
Aged 54 Years.

CHAPTER ELEVEN

"Oriental" Extension—1840

LET me warn readers to skip or skim this chapter if they take no interest in, or pleasure out of, a purely business and financial story, in the effort to get a cash backing to "swing a big deal," the fight against time to find suitable ships out of the very few existing (or even laid down on paper) to fulfil mail contract undertakings. Yet, I may say that there is a very human side to this business story, because the "big deal" was only carried through successfully by the shrewdness and cleverness, plus the unremitting toil and worries, of a few men who took the big business in their stride without allowing the little or even pettifogging details to clog their steps.

It was not until well on in 1840 that the Peninsular Company, against severe competition, won their contract for the extension of their mail service to Egypt. It was only on 1st September, 1840, that the new service began (which was a curious although fortuitous anniversary to a day of the first mail service of the Peninsular Steam Navigation Company); and the Royal Charter of the Peninsular and Oriental Steam Navigation Company was only completed in December of that year.

But as early as 23rd April, 1840, at a meeting of Directors it was noted as "Agreed that the new Company be called the Peninsular and Oriental Steam Navigation Company and that the capital be fixed at £1,000,000—say 20,000 shares at £50 each."

Now, only the Minute Books of meetings and the Company's private records remain to show how much had to be accomplished between those two dates, and give a hint at the intensive effort by which the difficulties were overcome.

F

65

The first and the worst of these was in finance, and for a time it seemed that investors were to be just as chary of the P. & O. scheme as they had been so long of Waghorn's. The new mail contract required two large and powerful steamers being put on the run, and in the plan of running between Egypt and India, which was one of the terms under which the Charter was granted, this section also required vessels big and powerful enough to beat fairly and certainly that bugbear of the monsoons.

Willcox and Anderson were able to meet the first need by obtaining the co-operation of the proprietors of the Trans-Atlantic Steamship Company, the fusion of the interests of the two companies, and the inclusion of the Trans-Atlantic steamer " Liverpool."

The Peninsular Company was to receive shares for £140,000 in the new P. & O. in return for their steamers " Tagus," " Braganza," " Royal Tar," " Iberia," and " Liverpool "—the last of these being known later as the " Liverpool " simply, while the new Trans-Atlantic's became the " Great Liverpool."

The Trans-Atlantic Company were to receive £80,000 in P. & O. shares for their ship " and as an equivalent for their interests in their Company." The Peninsular also, in addition to their ships, took their payment as " including their goodwill in the Line and the heavy expenses incurred by them in opening the Peninsular Station." Those " heavy expenses " apparently included the £30,000 which Willcox and Anderson had lost, individually, in running the Line before the mail contract was secured in 1837.

The Chairman of the new Company was Sir John Larpent, representing the " Comprehensives " and " Precursors," as certain rival interests were named. Amongst the Directors were Willcox and Anderson (Managing Directors), Captain R. Bourne, and James Hartley—all representing the Peninsular Company, as Bourne had represented the Dublin Company in the Peninsular ; Francis Carleton (Managing Director) and Jos. C. Ewart, representing the Trans-Atlantic Company. Another Director, Charles Wye Williams, was also a Managing Director of the Dublin Steam Packet Company, as well as a notable naval architect and inventor. It was reported of the new

P. & O. "Bentinck" "that in addition to the extra fastenings and other improvements this ship, as well as all the vessels built by this Company since 1840, have had introduced into them the watertight iron bulk-heads first adapted to steam vessels by Mr. C. W. Williams, one of the Directors of this Company."

The three Managing Directors were appointed on terms which, although seemingly generous enough and offering large rewards, actually meant a loss of income for some years to Willcox and Anderson, because they were obliged to drop their own profitable Willcox & Anderson business.

The three, in return for their services in negotiating the amalgamation of the two companies and for their general agency and management under the control of the Directors, were given a life appointment and were to divide $2\frac{1}{2}$ per cent. of the gross receipts of the Company, and 5 per cent. of the gross divisible profits. This remuneration had to cover all costs of offices, staff, and every other item of management. The method of remuneration died with the three first Managing Directors, and had been voluntarily surrendered by Willcox and Anderson before their death.

Pedro de Zulueta is another name amongst those of the first Directors, and it is worth a side-glance to see why he was there.

The firm of Zulueta & Company, well and firmly established in London in those days as merchant bankers, shipping agents, and the like, continued in business until about twenty years ago, when it was wound up for family reasons. It will be remembered still by many who were familiar with the City up to the time of the War.

The family was originally Spanish Basque, but had settled in Cadiz when Pedro Juan de Zulueta became involved in political troubles and was driven to escape them and his country in 1823. He founded a profitable business in London, and after the Spanish Monarchy was firmly established, Pedro Juan became the first Count of Torre Diaz. He had previously been agent in London for the Spanish Government, and this no doubt had brought him in direct contact with Willcox and Anderson during the Carlist War, and later with the P. & O.

Pedro José—later second Count—joined the family business at the age of 16. He married a daughter of Willcox, and it is his name which appears as a Director of the P. & O., as it continues to do unbrokenly until 1855, when it changes to Count Torre Diaz, and as such until 1866, when he resigned from the Board.

This Pedro José had four sons and two daughters. One, Brodie Manuel, became third Count and the father of the present fourth of the title. The second son, Pedro Juan, was Secretary to the Spanish Embassy in London for twenty years. One of the daughters, Josefa, married in London Don Rafael Merry y del Val, and their two sons are the present Marquess Merry del Val, for many years Spanish Ambassador here under the Monarchy, and the Cardinal Merry del Val.

In addition to their acquiring the " Great Liverpool," the Company were soon in negotiation for the purchase of the " Oriental," which was then building at Glasgow, and, like the other big vessel, had been designed for the Atlantic trade. A Minute mentions an insurance of £60,000 to be effected on the " Oriental " as " the full building cost of the ship."

While the Directors were, on the one hand, contriving to finance such costly ships, they were also immersed in a multitude of small details. Even before the contract for the Egyptian service was secured, they were making enquiries into the needs and possibilities of improving the transit across Egypt, and deciding that a new iron steamer on the Nile was a first essential ; while investigating depth of water at low Nile, requesting a *firman* or permit from the Pasha to run there, considering offers and prices of coal stocks at Malta and other ports, the provisioning of the ships along the new route, picking and choosing agents at the new stations.

At the same time they were using every endeavour to induce investors in India to drop various steam communication schemes in which they had been taking part for years, and to transfer their money into the P. & O. They met with most disappointing and discouraging difficulties in this, and it was only with a hard struggle that these were eventually overcome.

There were at this time three, if not more, varied and more-or-less opposing supporters of different plans for Steam Communication, and some of these had put down either hard cash or firm promises of it to forward their schemes.

The East India Steam Navigation Company—generally known as the Comprehensive Company or " Comprehensives "—was one of the most active.   What they described as " comprehensive " was a system which would make Ceylon the central point of call to and from Egypt and Aden.   From there the steamer could run on direct or by branch liners to Bombay on the west, Madras and Calcutta on the east.   By this method all three main ports would be fairly and equally served.

The East India Company, on the other hand, fought for the direct line between Egypt and their pet port of Bombay.   This maintained their old " Gateway to India " privilege, although it meant that other parts of India had to wait either for their mails to be sent on by land " dawk " (which meant slow road transport), or wait a shorter or greater time to get them sent round the coast by whatever vessels might be available.   We'll see presently how strenuously the East India Company managed to hang on to this privilege for another dozen years.

The Bombay Steam Committee was a supporter of this policy, but did at least find funds to spend on the improvement of the desert route across Egypt, and under the superintendence of a Mr. Hill had a number of rest-houses built, which, although inadequate enough, were at least better than nothing.   This Mr. Hill will crop up again in the story of the " Overland Route."

Another lot, known as " The Precursors," appear to have been an offshoot or breakaway from the Comprehensives, but claiming themselves to have been the originators or " Precursors " of the Comprehensive movement.

When the P. & O. came into being, they were offered by the East India Company a bonus of £20,000 a year for five years if the P. & O. successfully inaugurated a service between Calcutta, Madras, and Egypt —which left to the East India Company their monopoly of the shortest and most direct route to Bombay which they were then covering with their own armed steamers.

How inefficient their steamers were has been instanced in the cases of the " Enterprize " and " Hugh Lindsay," but the Company failed to profit by those experiences, and at a much later date were continuing to build or buy most unsuitable steamers.

An extract from C. R. Low's *History of the Indian Navy* gives one instance, which, although amusing to read now, would have been less so to the unfortunate East India Company passengers of those days :

" In 1839 an unfortunate addition was made to the steam packets of the Service in the purchase of the ' Kilkenny ' of 684 tons and 280 horse-power, which had been employed in carrying pigs from Waterford to Bristol. It was considered that this vessel would be an acquisition to the Service, and from her fittings would be particularly adapted for carrying passengers from Suez to Bombay ; accordingly she was dispatched from Waterford, and by Government notification was received into the Service and after her arrival was given the grandiloquent name of ' Zenobia.' From the first she was a signal failure, as were some other vessels of the same type, all costing large sums to keep in repair, besides being totally unfitted for carrying passengers with any degree of comfort."

The P. & O Directors had relied on their ability to convince the various opposed interests that the new P. & O. services would wipe out any need for the other companies and committees collecting funds or devoting collected subscriptions to starting rival lines ; but it was a hard battle.

The old agitations and arguments revived. A great deal was said at many meetings and committees, a great deal more was written in pamphlets, articles, and letters to the journals both in England and India ; and the P. & O.—quite evidently seriously concerned by the lack of financial support from India—plunged into the fray, with Arthur Anderson foremost in the attack.

In a lengthy pamphlet written by him, he argued for the amalgamation of all interests and for their putting their cash into shares in the P. & O. or " Oriental," as the Company was generally called in the East. He vigorously stressed the fact that all the previous years of talk and all the ink spilt " had not so far resulted in the formation of one plank of a vessel, or a single pin of an engine," that the P. & O. was going ahead with the support of a mail contract in the Mediterranean and £20,000 a year from the East India Company, that, under their Royal Charter, ships were built or building to be on the Eastern station within two years, and that these were to be the largest, most luxuriously equipped, and most powerfully engined in existence. He wound up by emphasising that unity is strength, and exhorting, " Let Comprehensives, Precursors and Orientals pull together and pull strongly."

To skip a little ahead of this 1840 year of the P. & O. extension, I may mention that the Comprehensives did subscribe for 700 shares in the P. & O. (to their speedy profit) in 1840-1, with three of their representatives taking a place on the P. & O. Board. The " Precursors " set about the building of their own vessel, and although the P. & O. made them an offer to buy her at a good price (to be paid in P. & O. shares), this was at first refused, but was eventually agreed, and brought into the P. & O. fleet their steamer " Precursor," although it was not until 1844 that this ship, a fine vessel of 1,600 tons and 500 horse-power, was finally acquired.

But while all the high finance of expensive ship buying and building, calling up shares, borrowing on loan and promissory notes, and trading shares for ships was going on, the Managing Directors were, even before their Mediterranean contract was firmly fixed, planning for improved transit across Egypt, and bickering over such detail as buying a little £2,000 iron steamer for the Nile. This first steamer was the " Lotus," which appears to have been bought on the stocks as the " Dahlia " and then specially fitted for the service. Mention is made too of the appointment of her captain at £20 a month. This seems to be a high rate for those days, but good pay was apparently the rule in the Company's sea staff, as we may see from a return of the crew of one of their liners in 1839 :

Captain	.	.	.	.	.	£20	per month
Mate .	.	.	.	.	.	7	,, ,,
Second Mate	.	.	.	.	.	4	,, ,,
Chief Engineer	.	.	.	.	.	12	,, ,,
2nd Engineer	.	.	.	.	.	8	,, ,,
Firemen	.	.	.	.	.	3 5s.	,, ,,
Quartermasters	.	.	.	.	.	3	,, ,,
Seamen	.	.	.	.	.	2 10s.	,, ,,
Carpenter	.	.	.	.	.	5	,, ,,
Cook .	.	.	.	.	.	3	,, ,,

Not only were these high rates of pay for that time—especially for the Master—but there was an additional gain to the crews that evidently a large number of the ships kept their whole crews on board between voyages, as against the usual practice of paying off all hands at the end of a voyage and re-engaging them or taking on new for the next voyage.

Mr. Waghorn comes into this 1840 picture, too. In June a communication from him is Minuted on that subject of an iron steamer for the Nile ; and a few weeks later the terms of an agreement with him were drawn up and entrusted to Mr. Anderson to exchange personally in Egypt for a letter of acceptance of the terms.

The terms, summarised, were for the charter of a Nile steamer for a year ; for a contract with Mr. Waghorn for conveyance of passengers and luggage through Egypt, except for the desert route between Cairo and Suez, which was to be left to Mr. Hill ; and that Mr. Waghorn, as connected with a Company employed in conveyance of mail, " must rigidly abstain from forwarding any letter or dispatches by private express." The arrangement (of which terms were to be finally agreed in person with Mr. Anderson) was to cover conveyance of passengers and luggage, but allowed other charges to be made for food, hotels, and the like as settled between Mr. Waghorn and passengers. Whether this agreement was accepted by Waghorn is not recorded. I think he must have declined it.

I could go on for pages quoting extracts from the brief but illuminating records of that year of the blossoming forth of the Peninsular into the P. & O.—notes that range from the trivial of " whether a quantity of old furnace bars may be disposed of " or that Directors' names in the Prospectus should be in alphabetical order, to the bigger subjects of spending £50,000 on a new ship, or £26,000 on another's engines, and even such decisions as came to have due and important bearing on the work and well-being of a whole city, as when a decision came to be debated and made whether the liners should use Southampton or Liverpool as their port of arrival and departure.

The Directors throughout that year of 1840 were holding three and four meetings a week, and there was hardly one that did not call for some deeply important, as well as many trifling, decisions being made.

But at the end of it all, the extended service began, smoothly, punctually, and efficiently. The best and most gratifying proof of this was in the first Annual Report of the year's working delivered in November 1841—a Report of eight steamers (including two of about 1,600 tons) at sea and another two 1,600-tonners building for the Indian Seas ; and, most cheering of all, no doubt, the declaration of a second half-year's dividend of $3\frac{1}{2}$ per cent., making a dividend for the year of 7 per cent., a result declared then to have been " unprecedented in the lot of any steam undertaking at so early a stage in its proceedings."

Little wonder that amongst the votes " moved, seconded, and carried by acclamation " was one of thanks to the Court of Directors and Managing Directors.

CHAPTER TWELVE

First P. & O. in the East

AT first thought it might seem that the Government, in stipulating that the P. & O. under the terms of their Charter should open a service in the East between India and Suez within two years, had granted a liberal allowance of time.   The time was little enough, however, for all that had to be done.

It was not only that the first ship had to be built and the special engines made for her—both of these being the more serious in responsibility because they were largely experimental, no vessel of the size and power having been employed in Eastern waters.   The ship had to be got out to India over a route where there was no provision at the available ports (except Gibraltar) for coaling, and where in some cases even provisions and watering were unknown quantities.

Coal ships under sail had to be sent out to each coaling port to wait there for the arrival of the steamer, and agents had to go out well in advance of the first ship to make all arrangements for provisions and drinking water, so that there should be no undue delay on the steamer's arrival.   The same difficulties had to be faced when the steamer was out on the Eastern station, where in some ports, like Suez and Aden, there was not even water to be had.

But by the time the " Hindostan," the first P. & O. liner to reach the Indian seas, was ready to sail, all the advance arrangements had been well and truly made, and there was little hitch in them throughout the long passage out round the Cape.

The progress of the " Hindostan's " building and fitting had been closely watched and widely reported throughout this country and India.

As the tales spread of her size and engine power, the luxury of her fittings and appointments, so the public interest grew. Her departure from Southampton on 24th September, 1842, was regarded as an important national event. Every ship in the port and roadstead was dressed and gay with fluttering flags, and the warships manned their yards as she steamed proudly past.

It was felt that here at long last was a complete answer to that vexed and up to then unsolved problem of steam communication with India which for years had filled the journals and occupied months of sittings of Parliamentary Committees and bulky volumes of official Reports. Even by that time, the P. & O. on its Peninsular and Egyptian service had so proved their reliability, that it was felt now that their first steamer was outward bound for Indian waters, success was within attainment. Other attempts—by the " Enterprize " and " Hugh Lindsay " and other vessels—had failed, while many promoters of other schemes had not, as Mr. Anderson declared, " constructed one plank or engine pin " of a steamer.

The Company reaped their reward in two useful directions. There had been a steadily rising demand for their shares in India, and well over 2,000 had been subscribed for when the " Hindostan " sailed. At £50 a share this meant a welcome addition to the Company's funds.

Another gain from the ship's advance reputation was that she carried a full passenger list, except for a number of berths that had been reserved for a considerable party at Cape Town. It had previously been estimated that it would cost £5,000 to cover the outward passage of the " Hindostan " and the same a little later for the " Bentinck," of similar type.

Passage money in the former, however, brought in £6,250 (out of which, of course, had to be met cost of provisions and wines as well as other expenses) so that only a further £1,800 was required to cover cost of placing her on the station.

The Press of the day was naturally filled with columns of description of the ship and her accommodation with such words as " elegant," " genteel," " superb," " magnificent," and " commodious " rather heavily overworked. A summary of the description is worth giving to

75

indicate the arrangement of saloons and cabins, especially as this seems to have been unusual at the time, and to follow a plan instituted by the Company in the " Oriental," which was built for them, but not in their " Great Liverpool," which was first built for the Atlantic.

Up to then the normal plan of the main (saloon and cabin) deck, which was immediately under the quarterdeck in the after part of the ship, was to have the saloon in the centre, and the cabin doors opening out of it into the cabins along the ship's side. The cabins were ventilated and lit by the portholes, and the saloon by a close-set row of large stern windows and a skylight.

In the " Hindostan " this plan was changed round. A saloon was provided extending across the aft part of the ship and lit by side ports and stern windows. Out of her total length of 240 feet, she had along the main deck " a spacious corridor, 170 feet in length on each side of the ship." These corridors ran " between the ship's sides and the range of private cabins, forming, as it were, a street, having on one side the range of spacious side-ports and on the other the doors entering the private cabins, which are adapted to the accommodation of families, parties of friends, or single persons."

This idea of placing the cabins in the centre of the ship—so completely opposed to present-day demands for cabins which passengers prefer to be " outside," and with a port opening out of each—was that, being centrally placed, passengers would feel less any rolling motion, and that sleepers would be less disturbed because " the rush of water along the vessel's side will not, as in the usual plan, be heard close to the ear."

One point that " warm, cold, and shower baths also form an item in the comfort provided " must have had a marked appeal to those passengers by ships of the East India Company like that ex-Waterford pig boat.

The " Hindostan " made up a total of 150 berths, which only averages out at about £40 each for that total of £6,250 passage money, certainly not an excessive charge for a full ninety days of " board and lodging " and travel under conditions of comfort never previously known to the East.

The passage was from Southampton to Gibraltar, to St. Vincent (Cape Verde Islands), Ascension, Cape Town, Mauritius, Point de Galle (Ceylon), and ended at Calcutta. This took 91 days, out of which 28 were spent in port.

Coal ships had been sent out to each of the ports named, and when the steamer arrived off St. Vincent at dusk she fired signal guns and rockets until the collier waiting her arrival showed a light indicating where she lay, so that the steamer could anchor close by. Those signal guns led later to a strange accident.

An unfired blank charge was left in one of the guns, with a tompion plugged later tightly into the muzzle. There it stayed until the steamer reached Mauritius, when the officers of two H.M. warships there came aboard to inspect the new vessel, and asked to be allowed to see a firing lock of the guns which was a new invention. The guns were on the quarterdeck, pointing forward, and in trying the one with the charge still in it, it fired, blowing the tompion from the muzzle, smashing it to pieces, and sending the fragments in all directions. One lump struck a nurse who was airing an infant on the quarterdeck, others ripped the awning end-to-end, wrecked the companionway, and passed whistling over the forecastle-head and between the seamen lounging there.

The unfortunate nurse had her leg so badly fractured that it had to be amputated on the spot, but the surgery was successful, and she was carried on to Calcutta.

Another life was lost soon after leaving Ascension in a way which conveys strikingly the makeshift methods of steam-and-sail even in the most modern steamer afloat.

Approaching Cape Town, the coal was running short and the engines were stopped to let the ship proceed for a time under sail only. For sailing, the paddle boards or floats were removed, and to do this a man had to climb in underneath the paddle-box, the paddle-wheel being moved to and fro until he could get at the bolts.

This was safely done in removing the boards, manpower and tackle being used to turn the wheels. But when they came to be replaced, steam had been raised and was used to turn the wheel. The first turn ahead went too far and jambed the unfortunate fireman, and the reverse turn went too far, pinning him again. He was seriously injured, and died a few days later.

The 91-day passage out was considered highly satisfactory, and the more so because the ship had behaved well through some very severe storms and heavy seas. Sails as well as engines were used, of course, with favouring winds, the ship carrying a good full suit—all headsails to her long jibboom, square sails on the fore, and fore-and-aft sails on main and mizzen masts.

The P. & O. had built the " Hindostan " without any promise of a mail subsidy, and when she sailed had their next big steamer for the East under way, and were bargaining for the purchase of a third equally large and powerful, but a contract was not obtained until just before the " Hindostan " sailed. The East India Company had fought against such a contract, it was said, in the fairly certain assumption that such steamers could not pay their way in regular running without a mail contract. They had their own mail service between Bombay and Suez, and it was so bad that it is natural they would hardly want it to be shown up by more efficient vessels and management. But again public pressure, freely expressed by the Press and in merchants' memorials, won the day and a P. & O. contract was at last made in September 1842 for £115,000 a year, to run between Calcutta, Madras, Ceylon, and Suez.

The fears of the East India Company were soon substantiated when the new service carried mails over the much longer route to Calcutta speedily enough for letters to be there so far ahead of the mails sent overland from the steamers arriving at Bombay, that the letters could be answered in time to catch an outward mail which saved a month in the out-and-back transit.

The " Bentinck " went out in 1843. She was named after the great Lord William Bentinck, Governor of India, for whom the P. & O. must have had a natural regard, because he had been one of the most prominent in pressing for improved steam communication, and had urged the Peninsular Company to extend to India as early as 1837–8. It may be that it was his first urging which led Willcox and Anderson to turn their thoughts to the Indian service at a time when they were concerned with a route no longer than that to Gibraltar.

The " Precursor " was finally bought and sent out in 1844, and with her the Calcutta–Suez and Indian services were fully launched and running full speed ahead.   Between the P. & O.'s Eastern and Mediterranean services there was that barrier of the Isthmus of Suez with all its attendant complications of land transport which should have no real place in the business of a shipping company.

It proved to be impossible for the Company to leave this overland section of their trade to the handling of outsiders, because on the smoothness, cheapness, and regularity of its working depended so much of the advantages of the P. & O. service between India and England, and the attraction of passengers to it from the Cape route.   Even in periods when the Company had no actual direct control of the Overland Route, passengers poured in complaints of cost, discomfort, and everything else to the Company, and blamed its management for all their troubles.

But greatly as the Overland section troubled the management for the first few years, when these were in the main overcome, the barrier of Egypt to sea transit proved to be one of the greatest sources of profit to the Company, simply because they had the control of it, and reaped a full and due reward of that exclusive fast transport of passengers, mails, and goods between East and West.

The whole story of the Overland Route therefore must be an integral and important part of any history of the P. & O.

CHAPTER THIRTEEN

The Overland Route

THE Overland Route between the Mediterranean and the Red Sea is older than history ; and because the line of traffic and transport must always tend to the line of least resistance, the route used between the two seas in the time of the early Pharaohs came to be the one adopted by travellers both before and after Waghorn came on the scene to organise transport to conform with the needs of " modern " travellers and merchants.

One can go farther, and wider, in this similarity of the earliest known times and the first use of the route by British travellers.

In the beginning, merchants with their goods travelled from India by sailing dhows to Egypt, across the desert by donkeys and camels to the Nile, and down it in sailing boats to the Mediterranean. The journey across the Indian Ocean was made either way at the season which gave the help of the monsoon's favouring gales. That prehistoric method of crossing continues into the present day, and it was only last year that the P. & O. " Viceroy of India " came across a tiny dhow half-way across to India with her crew of two out of both provisions and water. The liner drew alongside, and, to the machine-gun fire of passengers' cameras, lowered as full supplies of food and water as the cockle-shell could carry, and being vehemently assured that the dhow's crew would not " abandon ship " and be carried on in the liner, the Captain left them and drove his liner on her way.

Nobody knows how many of those dhows still make the crossing each year, or how many fail to make it and simply disappear. They, how-ever, are carrying on the traditional journey made in the earliest times.

S.S. "CHUSAN," 699 tons.   Built 1852

Before Waghorn tried to systematise the route and speed up the transit across Egypt, there were a few hardy travellers who each year followed the ancient route and system of transport. They sailed by native craft to or from India, they landed in Egypt either at Cosseir on the Egyptian shore about 250 miles down the Red Sea south of Suez, or continued the sea passage to Suez.

If they landed at Cosseir they crossed the desert to the Nile about Luxor, and down river to Cairo and Alexandria ; or they continued the sea passage to Suez and across the desert from there to Cairo, where they took native sailing boats down to the river-mouth.

There was a double reason for the landing at Cosseir. Crossing from there to Luxor allowed the traveller to inspect the most ancient and famous of the ruins and monuments of Egypt ; and because the 250 miles from there to Suez by sea were often so beset by adverse winds that they took weeks to cover, it was quicker to cross from Cosseir and take to the river down to Cairo. In the reverse direction the crossing of the desert from Cairo to Suez offered swifter and easier transport than the slow passage up-stream to Luxor.

These ancient and prehistoric facts were so well proved true that the travellers of the 1820's and 1830's related them in their writings to the current journals, repeating exactly the reasons for landing at Cosseir or Suez which had been traditional for hundreds or thousands of years.

Even when Waghorn began to advertise his Overland Route services, he offered his clients the choice of the two routes and made provision for their transport by Cosseir or Suez. Reading now the experiences related by those early clients of his, we can only wonder that there was sufficient temptation even to the hardiest traveller to journey by the Red Sea route instead of the slower but much more comfortable or even luxurious ease of the East Indiamen round the Cape.

Travel books of the day, and even the instructions of Waghorn and Hill, who were at first rivals and later partners in the transit business, made it plain what travellers had to expect.

Those who were coming from India were warned to write some months in advance to Waghorn or Hill in Egypt, say what ship they would come by, and whether they would leave her at Cosseir or Suez. If the former, the agents sent a boat or boats up the Nile to Luxor to meet the party.

An agent of the transit company at Cosseir engaged donkeys and camels and Arab servants, charging the traveller a lump sum for the service. Arrived at the Nile, as much or little time as was wished could be spent inspecting the ruins and sights, and then the waiting boat drifted or sailed down to Cairo, where there were more sights to see, and a junction was made with any party which had come on to Suez and had made the desert crossing from there.

Before the P. & O. came along, the next stage down Nile was at first by native sailing craft, but later a tiny steamer (carrying about ten and said to be the smallest passenger steamboat in the world) provided transport rather more reliable than the sailing boats—unless the steamer ran on a sandbank, as it frequently did.

The boat, the " Jack o' Lantern," must have been rather cramped for her passengers, because the moving of one person was enough to trim the boat. She was of 6 horse-power (described by the wags as 3 donkey-power), and there is the testimony of many travellers that she was the home of every existing species of creepy-crawly vermin. The normal journey took a day and a night down to Afteh, a point on the left bank of the river, where a transfer was made to a canal running from there to Alexandria.

This Mahmoudieh Canal was a remarkable achievement of the autocratic ruler of Egypt, Mehemet Ali. It has been said that a previous canal had run there in ancient times, but if so no trace of it remained when Mehemet Ali began his work.

On it he put 200,000 impressed or forced labourers—or, less politely, slaves. He gave them no pay, the scantiest of rations, and not even tools of any sort. Their taskmaster drove them so vigorously, however, that with no more than their bare hands and little peasant hoes and hand-baskets to carry the soil out of the trench, they dug a canal 48 miles long, 18 feet deep in parts, and 9 feet wide in four to five months from the start of the work to the day when the last wall of earth was cut down and the waters of the tideless Mediterranean allowed to flow in.

At least 20,000 labourers died of starvation, overwork, and sickness combined. The number may easily have been greater, but the Pasha did not encourage the collection of such statistics, so that the actual figure will never be known.

The Canal, used for years only by natives and their sailing or towing craft, later became one link of the Overland Route by which thousands of P. & O. passengers crossed Egypt.

Travellers' books and the journals of those days gave the fullest advice and relation of experiences to those proposing to cross by the Overland Route. All laid emphasis on certain points. First each person must take a sufficiency of bottled water for the desert crossing, as much as four or five dozen large bottles for the Cosseir trip, taking about 5 days, less for the Suez–Cairo journey, which took a full day and night and a good part of another day. A supply of wine and moderate amount of spirits was also recommended.

It was usually recommended that Messrs. Waghorn or Hill should be employed to hire animals and servants, tents, and other needs. Native bread being uneatable, cabin or ship biscuits and rusks should be carried. Any boat supplied at Luxor should be sunk for two to three days under the eyes of the traveller, because only this offered a hope of killing or clearing out the vermin—some of which, however, would survive even this drastic treatment, so that the boat should be washed down once or twice a day with strong chloride of lime.

At Suez the accommodation was evidently rather dreadful. One writer, relating his experiences in 1841, said—" The wretchedness of Suez has often been described, but never in terms too severe : the hotels belonging to the rival agents, Mr. Waghorn and Mr. Hill, are both uncomfortable. In Hill's, the accommodation for a party is of the worst kind. The bedrooms are few, and the ultimate resort is the divan or a large cushioned seat of the dining room, and the cold night air from the desert freely blowing on the sleepers from numerous broken panes of glass."

Another traveller about the same date says the food obtainable all the way between ship and ship was impossible for any European to eat— the meat and chickens being incredibly tough and tasteless, and only the eggs eatably tender—if those boiled to leather or bullet consistency were resolutely rejected.

Across the desert from Suez the few rest-houses then existing " erected under the superintendence of Mr. J. R. Hill by means of funds furnished by the Bombay Steam Committee" could not be subjected to that drastic treatment of sinking under water for three days, and so were described in the veiled terms of politeness required of any writer in those days, but which our franker age would call literally and liberally " lousy."

Over the Mahmoudieh Canal passengers proceeded in a native " track boat " towed by horses. A trumpeter or horn-blower posted in the bows gave continual warning to the sailing and towing craft to clear the way, without any of them taking the slightest notice of the warning. The towing or track horses had to be halted, and the rope lifted over the mast of each sailing craft, so that the 48 miles of canal took anything from 12 hours upward to traverse.

If the native boat traffic was heavy, the transit passengers had every chance of arriving at the landing-stage for Alexandria after or near sunset ; and after another transhipment to donkeys or camels of them-selves and baggage, arrived at the city gates to find them inexorably closed against all pleading, persuasion, threats, or even—strangely in the home of " bucksheesh "—against bribes. In such case there was nothing for it but to resort to one of the low and villainous cafés and resorts outside the city walls, resolutely refuse to sit, much less lie down, and watch the locals lounge and scratch nonchalantly but non-stop.

Taking it by and large then, the Overland Route of those pre-P. & O. days did not present many attractions to travellers, and one of the first tasks to which the management set their hand was the effecting of such improvements as would remove or at least reduce the reasonable causes for complaint or dissuasion against the Route as must keep passengers from using it and preferring the longer, slower, but more solidly com-fortable passage by the Indiamen round the Cape.

Long before the P. & O. had their own steamers running in the East, they set about the beginning of improvements in the Overland Route which at last reduced the crossing to a minimum of time and a maximum of such comfort as could be provided.

CHAPTER FOURTEEN

Overland by P. & O.

AFTER the rush of work in the promotion of the P. & O., Anderson hurried off to Egypt to see at first hand what could be done to improve the Overland Route. The result of that visit was swiftly apparent.

The waterways' transport offered the first and speediest ways of improvement. The " Lotus " had already been sent out, and she was followed by the " Cairo," a larger and better boat for the Nile transport between Afteh and Cairo. Two packet boats and two luggage boats were ordered for the Mahmoudieh Canal, and the next step was to place a steam tug there to do away with the horse tracking or towing.

Anderson interviewed the Pasha, was favourably received by him, and obtained a promise that the Pasha would do all he could to improve the road over the desert—an undertaking all the easier for him because he had unlimited forced labour at his disposal. The Pasha also declared that he did not want to make the transit duty a question of money only, and in fact he was prepared to authorise the transit of goods for one year without charge and leaving it to the P. & O. to pay whatever sum might be considered fairly due.

This pleasant arrangement did not continue long, however, and was soon replaced by one under which the Pasha was paid $\frac{1}{2}$ per cent. on the value of all goods passing through, a charge only reduced to $\frac{1}{4}$ per cent. in 1854 when the dues must have been making handsome returns.

The " Cairo " was an unusual type of craft specially built for the Nile work. She was the lightest possible iron shell, 100 feet in length and 14 in breadth, the hull fitted with nothing but cabin space and engines. The latter must have been good for their day, because they gave a speed advertised as of " 12 miles per hour " in still water.

She had two sets of cabins below deck, able to accommodate about fifty, with separate cabins for ladies containing sixteen sleeping berths. On deck she was fitted with an overhead awning for shade during the day, and at night this deck provided extra sleeping space by rigging side curtains to enclose the whole deck. It was carefully explained in the official announcements to a British public unused to this idea of sleeping with nothing more solid than cloth walls and roof that this deck " in a climate like that of Egypt is very agreeable for repose during the one night on the Nile."

A further protection of the deck sleepers at night and loungers by day was that " A range of gang boards outside of the bulwarks enables the crew to pass from one part of the vessel to another without inter-mixing with the passengers."

Food, wine, and all refreshments were on board, and the journey took 15 to 20 hours, according to the strength of high or low Nile current, the " Cairo " being the more powerful and reserved for the up-stream run, while the " Lotus " ran down.

In rather pathetic competition with these comfortable steamers, the little " Jack o'Lantern " was still run by Waghorn & Company, or Waghorn & Hill. Waghorn was still persistently carrying on his travel agency, and from about 1841–2 there are increasing signs that he was developing a definite opposition or antagonism to the P. & O.

He evidently had resented the control which the Company was forced into exercising by the continual complaints of their passengers. In several of the Directors' Reports it is intimated that they were desirous of leaving the transit in the hands of those who might fairly feel they had a prior claim to it, and that they were trying to co-operate in improvements with " respectable parties who have come forward with the sanction of H.H. the Pasha to carry on the undertaking with every prospect of success as regards their own interests and of giving satisfaction to travellers."

But by 1842, the Company being still dissatisfied with the transit conditions, said they must, if improvement was not effected, take over the whole thing. This was apparently done in 1842 or 1843, and perhaps Waghorn felt himself aggrieved and injured by this action, to which, however, it is clear the Company was driven by the increasing volume of complaints and the firm belief that the Route was under P. & O. control, although the Company did all they could to correct this mistake.

Waghorn was then devoting himself to developing the England–Egypt journey under his agency's care by three routes—the first by Paris to Marseilles, the second by the Rhine and Danube to Trieste, and the third from Southampton to Alexandria by sea—the last being the P. & O. service.

In a booklet advertising his " Overland Route to India " of May 1844, Waghorn describes the three routes in detail. There appears to be little in the overland sections to attract any but the most energetic or haste-driven. On the Trieste route the itinerary was :

Ostend–Liège—by railway.
Liège–Aix la Chapelle—by coach.
Aix–Cologne—railway.
Cologne–Mayence—coach or Rhine boat.
Mayence–Basle—steamer.
From Basle, by coach via Zürich to Wallenstadt ; coach on and over the Alps to Brescia and Venice ; steamer to Trieste.

The Marseilles route required fewer changes perhaps, the route being by Boulogne, Paris, Châlons, Lyons, and Marseilles, about 150 miles being down the Rhône ; but it still required, on the road stages, the driving haste of the mail coaches with the briefest halts to change horses and let the passengers eat, by night or day, or the employment of a private carriage or post-chaise.

In this same booklet, Waghorn, in advocating his own cross-Continent travel agency, complains bitterly of the policy of the P. & O. in their refusal to carry the baggage of passengers who wished to travel across France and send their luggage by P. & O. to meet its owner at Malta. He declaims against this attempt to force travellers to take steamer all the way from Southampton. This may have been the P. & O. intention, or it may be that they preferred to reserve their available space (which was severely limited) for the convenience of their own passengers, rather than for those who went across France to Marseilles and on by Government packet or French steamer to Malta.

Lieutenant Waghorn also takes pains to point out that " We think it right to observe, *en passant*, that the Peninsular and Oriental Company have at present no control over the transit arrangements in Egypt," and that " The Egyptian Transit Company was established by H.H. the Pasha and have the entire transmission of mails, passengers, etc., in their own hands."

But by that time (1844) the P. & O. had made arrangements, in addition to running their steamers under the Pasha's *firman*, to take over the desert transit and rest-houses, and because " the rapidly increasing intercourse by this route to India having outrun the ability " of those who had been conducting it, " the result had been the formation of an auxiliary branch of the Company under the designation of The Egyptian Oriental Transit Company."

By 1844 very extensive improvements in the transport of passengers by the Overland Route had been carried out. Not only had the transit over the Mahmoudieh Canal been made more comfortable and speedy by the Company's steamers and over the Nile by well-found fast steamers, but the desert route had been improved to the greatest possible extent.

The rest-houses themselves had been enlarged, more substantially built, and furnished to a degree of comfort before unknown. The number of stations for the changing of horses and refreshment of travellers had been increased, new and better-class horse-drawn carriages had been put on with changes of horses every five or six miles, and in the mid-desert rest-house, where usually the night hours were spent, a good dining-room, competent staff of cooks and servants under a European superintendent and his wife, and clean bedrooms and beds were provided.

Those horse-drawn carriages might hardly conform to our present ideas and standard of travel comfort. They held six passengers, who sat, three aside, on narrow knife-board seats, knees closely touching knees, backs bowed to fit to the curve of the arched canvas cover or tilt.

The horses were high-spirited Arab steeds hardly broken to harness. The normal procedure was for the snorting restive beasts to be held by the head after harnessing with a groom to each until the passengers were aboard and the driver had his reins in hand. Then, at the word " Go " the grooms let go, the horses made a frantic leap forward and tried to race each other over the desert.

Leaving the towns like Cairo and Suez, a footman or two hung on to the back of the omnibus ready to come into action if the frantic horses ditched the vehicle ; but on clearing the town, the footmen dropped off, depending on it that the fiery Arabs had the whole desert before them to absorb their superabundant energy, and knowing that if they strayed far off the track they and the carriage wheels would sink deep enough in the sand to reduce wildness to the docility of comparative exhaustion.

Some of the passengers thoroughly enjoyed this circus act and wild horses racing ; others did not, and wrote the Company accordingly.

In 1847, the Pasha had been pressing for the P. & O. to sell to him their steamers on the Nile, because he wished to take over the transit arrangements as a Government concern. The Directors were reluctant to hand over the service, having some doubts as to how efficiently it would be carried out, but, deciding that it would be bad policy to refuse, at last consented.

Another great improvement effected was making a connection by locks between the Canal and the Nile. There was an embankment between the two which, although it covered a distance of only 200 to 300 yards, had necessitated unloading luggage from the canal boats, loading it on camels, unloading it again, and shipping it in the steamers —four handlings, which were the cause of frequent grumbles about broken and damaged packages.

With the locks, the canal boat could go right through to where the Nile steamer lay at a new jetty and transfer passengers and baggage straight into her.

In addition to the outlay of capital on the actual transport system to convey passengers and baggage, the Company also spent large sums in the development of goods traffic which was steadily growing, especially in the shipment of goods like silk, indigo, and specie which could afford the high rates required to cover the costly transmission across Egypt.

Before 1850, substantial and roomy warehouses and stores had been built at Alexandria and on the Canal ; wharves and cargo sheds and a coal depot were also established near Alexandria, and coal hulks, lighters and cargo-handling facilities provided. Similar facilities were at Suez, as well as workshops and water condensers. Until the condensers were set up, the only water in Suez had to be carried across the desert from the Nile.

When Mehemet Ali died, a deputation from the P. & O. went out to interview Abbas Pasha, the new Viceroy of Egypt, and found him willing or even eager to give all the support he could to the Route—as well he might with that $\frac{1}{2}$ per cent. *ad valorem* duty providing a steadily and heavily increasing revenue.

It was only the passengers and their baggage that travelled by the route described over the Canal, the Nile, and desert crossing. The mails went the whole way from steamer to steamer by donkey and camel back, and made the crossing in less time with relays of animals than the passengers took.

This faster transport of the mails at first led to some difficulty and a risk to passengers that they might find the East India Company mail steamer gone from Suez before they could arrive there, with the result that they had to remain in Egypt another month to connect with the next steamer to Bombay.

This exceedingly inconvenient practice was stopped after the P. & O. had their steamers running beyond Egypt, but the tradition of it lingered, and the Company had to obtain and advertise a guarantee from the East India Company, that they would keep their steamers waiting for 24 hours after receiving the mail from England for Bombay on board and were also permitted to do the same later with their own Calcutta steamers. Such a ruling was the more necessary, because the commander of the steamer was controlled in all matters of sailing times by the Admiralty agent on board, who had charge of the mails.

In 1842, the P. & O. issued official notices of the time taken in transit of mails and of passengers, to show that there was no longer any risk of passengers being held up in Egypt. The comparative times are worth mention.

The mails, with relays of donkeys from Alexandria to Cairo and camels across the desert, took an average of 64 hours, steamer to steamer. The Suez steamer had to wait 24 hours, giving passengers 88 hours to reach Suez and catch the steamer.

Passengers took, from Alexandria to the Nile, 12 hours, including transference of baggage from canal to river steamer. This was before the steamers went to the canal and while relays of tracking horses were stationed at seven points along the canal, making the journey in about 8 to 10 hours—not a bad speed for horse-towed barges, since the 8 hours meant an average of 6 miles an hour over the 48 miles. There were two barges about 60 feet long by 7 wide, one for luggage, the other for passengers, with deck cabins and ladies' room and food and drink provided. Later the steam tug cut the journey down to 6 hours.

By steamer to Cairo took 18 hours, and 12 hours were allowed there for rest or sight-seeing. Across the desert, with 12 hours for rest and refreshment, took 36 hours. The total time taken to do the 250 miles from sea to sea was therefore 78 hours, allowing a margin of 10 hours before the steamer sailed.

It is worthy of note that to-day a very large number of the P. & O. passengers cross between Cairo and Suez by the same old desert route, but that now they make this crossing by luxurious motor-cars which cover the distance in two to three hours, travelling over a well-made road. This gives passengers ample time for sight-seeing in Cairo while the ship goes through the Canal. The old dire necessity and discomfort of the desert crossing is now a mere pleasure jaunt.

In the same notice which gave this reassuring time-table the P. & O. had a note that " passengers proceeding to India are strongly recommended to make no payments in London on account of their transit through Egypt. . . ." This was an evident reply to the advertisements

91

and advice of Mr. Waghorn that passengers should pay £10 down in London on booking their passage, so as to have priority on his agency's services across Egypt.

Under the quickly improved conditions of transit, the passenger traffic grew rapidly. In the two years preceding 1840 (that is, preceding the P. & O. beginning their work in Egypt) there was a total of 234 homeward and 255 outward—under 250 a year, or 125 a year each way.

In 1841, the first year of the P. & O. operating, the number of passengers rose to 573, and in 1842 to over 800, although this was while the only sea service beyond Egypt was still in the hands of the East India Company with their highly unsatisfactory and uncomfortable service.

After the P. & O. had the " Hindostan " and other steamers on the Red Sea route, goods traffic also began to grow steadily. The goods carried were only of the high-class trade which could afford to pay the high freight rates necessary to cover transport costs.

The goods, of course, had to be carried by camel, and the train of these required for the transport of a single ship's loading rose to as many as 3,000 or even 4,000 animals. Even the coal for the vessels in the Red Sea went across Egypt by camel-back, because the normal practice of sending coal out to the Eastern stations by sailing vessels could not be followed at Suez or in the Red Sea because of that old difficulty of the adverse monsoons.

One of the most surprising and unexpected developments due to the greater comfort and convenience with which Egypt could be reached and travelled was the swift rise of tourist or pleasure travel, and of Europeans spending the winter season in Egypt.

The latter class grew so numerous that they became a source of embarrassment to the Company, because the visitors, spending weeks or months in Egypt, were naturally given a preference by the hotels to the P. & O. passengers, who only sought a meal and a night's bed, and were forced to put up with very inferior board and lodging. The P. & O. therefore opened an hotel at Cairo, reserving it almost exclusively for their passengers.

But even before this there was developing a tourist and pleasure or sight-seeing travel which we now call " Cruising," and it is on the best of authority the P. & O. can claim that as early as 1844 they had invented this incentive to travel, and had deliberately organised it as something quite apart from their main business of carrying passengers who made their journeys for reasons of business or duty.

CHAPTER FIFTEEN

The First " Cruising "—1844

THE mail contract of 1840 extended the service to Egypt and also stipulated for a semi-monthly service between Malta and the Ionian Isles, but the last proved so expensive to run and in making demands in excess of the contract terms that the Company obtained release from it in 1842.

They maintained a passenger and cargo service, however, from Malta to Athens, Smyrna, and Constantinople, and then on by Beyrout to Jaffa (from which Jerusalem could be reached by a horseback or carriage journey) and on to Alexandria. From there tourists visiting Egypt went to Cairo by the P. & O. canal and river steamers, and returning to England could reverse the former route, or go direct to Malta and Gibraltar.

This was the tour or cruise route the P. & O. set out to popularise, and in 1844 Thackeray, the novelist, made the round with shore excursions to Jerusalem and Cairo and the pyramids, just as whole shiploads of cruising passengers do to-day.

He was given a free passage by the management, and a very good return they got for it in the shape of a book which Thackeray wrote and published, first in one of the popular journals, and later in a book of travel, *The Irish Sketch Book : and from Cornhill to Cairo.*

Thackeray, although not then at the height of the fame he reached with his *Vanity Fair*, was a well-established and popular author. He had written *The Yellow-plush Papers* in 1837, *The Great Hogarty Diamond* (1837–8), *Paris Sketch Book* (1840) and *Irish Sketch Book* (1843). His account of the P. & O. cruise must have been an excellent

94

piece of publicity, and have done much to make the possibilities of such travel known to the public.

Thackeray tells at the beginning of his story how, dining with a couple of friends at the Club one night, he was urged by one of them to join his "family party" on a tour of the Mediterranean, so that this was not a case of a solitary passenger making an unheard-of type of journey, but rather of his joining in an organised excursion, or "cruise," as we should call it now.

Thackeray makes this still more plain in the Preface to his book, saying, "The Peninsular and Oriental Company had arranged an excursion in the Mediterranean by which, in the space of a couple of months, as many men and cities were to be seen as Ulysses surveyed and noted in ten years."

This is not the only free advertisement the author gave the P. & O. He dedicated his book "To Captain Samuel Lewis of the Peninsular and Oriental Steam Navigation Company's Service," and makes handsome reference to "the noble Company in whose service you command (and whose fleet alone makes them a third-rate maritime Power in Europe)." Throughout the whole of the book too he gives generous praise to the comforts and pleasure of a "delightful excursion" which he found "so easy, so charming and I think profitable—it leaves such a store of pleasant recollections for after days" that he urges "all persons who have time and means to make a similar journey."

The book, in fact, is a wonderful advertisement for these early-day P. & O. cruises, and if we might suppose that the author could be no less than enthusiastic in view of his frank admission that he had been given a free passage, we can also find that he did not hesitate to describe hardships and discomforts when he met them.

What he writes about some of the places where they had a run ashore (in quite the present-day cruise fashion of shore parties being taken round to see the sights) might have put possible cruising passengers off cruises for ever.

By far the greater part of the book is occupied with description of the places and people ashore, but there are some glimpses of board-ship life of that time which have an interest of their own. The first part of the cruise to Vigo, Lisbon, Cadiz, and Gibraltar was made in the " Lady Mary Wood," the next leg to Malta, Smyrna, and Constantinople in the " Tagus," and the rest of the tour to Jaffa and Alexandria by the " Iberia."

The author describes nothing of the return journey, breaking off from his description of Cairo and taking a sudden leap to the next point saying, " Another week saw us in the quarantine harbour at Malta, where 17 days of pleasant and quiet were almost agreeable after the incessant sight-seeing of the last two months."

There were a good many features of a cruise in those days which would certainly not be attractive to-day, that mention of imprisonment in the quarantine lazaretto being one of them. One of his fellow-passengers died there, and Thackeray's manner of telling this indicates that such a death was nothing unusual.

The breaks in the journey necessitated by the changes from ship to ship would also be little welcome in a cruise to-day, where passengers settle down in a ship as they would do in a home. And another detail of Thackeray's voyage would certainly never be tolerated nowadays. He describes how, on the stage of the journey to Jaffa, a swarm of passengers invaded the ship ; how the " decks were covered with Christians, Jews, and Heathens ; in the cabin were Poles, Russians, French, Germans, Spaniards, and Greeks ; on the deck squatted several little colonies of people of different race and persuasion."

He gives such a description of these passengers and their ways ; of their dirty, objectionable clothing and habits as to-day would put a finish to pleasure cruising. It is true it was only on this one stage of the cruise that he had to suffer such discomforts on board, although there were plenty of them ashore.

Although he does not go into much detail on the point, it is evident that he was only one of many engaged on this or some other cruise, parties being met or joined at various places. In the journey from Jaffa to Jerusalem, he was with quite a little party of 14 in all, including guides and grooms and servants, and the party included several ladies carried in litters suspended between two mules placed " fore and aft."

In Cairo again he met a good many visitors, and was one of a party

S.S. "HIMALAYA," 3,438 tons. Built 1853

of half a dozen from the hotel who made an excursion to visit the Pyramids. All these travellers seem to have been of the most aggressively English or British type, as Thackeray himself pretends to be at some points with his blatant " Rule Britannia " attitude, and in others is less consciously perhaps, but no less certainly so.

The catering on board was certainly British to the last degree. A sample Bill of Fare is a reminder of the huge meals people ate in those days, and certainly indicates that the hungriest passengers had nothing to complain of. Here is the Bill of Fare " From the Providor's Logbook "—the Providor being the Purser or Caterer.

Mulligatawny Soup

———

Salt Fish and Egg Sauce

———

Roast Haunch of Mutton
Boiled Shoulder and Onion Sauce
Boiled Beef
Roast Fowl
Pillau Ditto
Ham
Haricot Mutton
Curry and Rice

For vegetables there were French Beans, Cabbage, Boiled and Baked Potatoes; and for sweets, Damson Tart, Currant Ditto, Rice Pudding, and Currant Fritters.

The most staggering fact about this prodigious array of joints and fowls and all the rest is that apparently there was one cook to handle the lot, even although he had helpers in the galley, no doubt. Thackeray makes mention of " the cook of the ' Lady Mary Wood ' with tattoed arms, sweating among the saucepans in the galley, who used (with touching affection) to send us locks of his hair in the soup." Another mention is made too of the cook of the " Tagus "—" the cook of the ship deserting at Constantinople, his successor was some time before he got his hand in."

H

If the standard and scope of that sample Bill of Fare was maintained, the cook must have been a busy man; and if the steward's lads were "brisk in serving the banquet," it is little wonder that later they had to be equally brisk and "sympathising in handing the basin," or that at times there were "indescribable moans and noises issuing from behind the fine painted doors on each side of the cabin."

Perhaps it is even more remarkable to find that, as late as the 1880's, such a journal as the *British Medical* published a long editorial article, which not only recommended strongly the beneficial effects of a health or holiday sea cruise for sick or well, but drew particular attention to the cruises offered by the P. & O.

The article began: "The announcement by the Peninsular and Oriental Navigation Company of a new and low scale of charges for accommodation on board their magnificent ships has a special interest for medical men and their patients"; and after a long explanation of the advantages to be derived from a sea voyage with excursions ashore, it winds up with another reference to the Company by name, a mention of the fares charged—"About 25,000 miles for a hundred guineas"— and a recognition of "the importance of the step which the Company has taken in popularising ocean travel."

The whole article might be one written by the advertising department of a cruising liner company to-day, and I wonder what one of those companies would give to get such an editorial published now in the *British Medical Journal*?

When Arthur Anderson first founded his *Shetland Journal* in 1835, he issued a specimen number distributed free, so that possible subscribers might know the class of paper to be offered. In the first specimen issue of the *Journal* there was evidently a lack of material likely to interest readers in the Shetlands, and the Editor had to fall back on his imagination and fill up space with what he called "Sample Advertisements," explaining these in a foreword saying, "As a vehicle for advertisements, the proposed *Journal* it is presumed will be found useful. To complete our model sheet in this respect we have been obliged to insert a little fiction which we have headed ' Sample Advertisements ' to distinguish them from the one or two real ones."

There follows a notice headed " To Tourists," describing a mythical cruise of a mythical " Steam Packet Hyperborean " to sail from Scalloway to North Faroe and Iceland, proceeding by the west coast of Shetland and calling at Papa, Hillswick, the Dorholm, etc., " so as to give passengers an opportunity of seeing the most remarkable coast scenery in that direction, as well as to ascend Roeness Hill."

The further cruise is described as to Thorshaven, the capital of the Faroes, a stay there of two days to allow passengers an ascent of Schaelling Mountain, " from which there is one of the most sublime views in Nature," a call at Reikiavik, Iceland, to land passengers who might wish to visit the interior and the Geysers or Boiling Springs, Mount Hecla, etc.

The packet was then to proceed to the Faroes and Scalloway to pick up " such passengers as may wish to make the tour of Shetland only " ; and after this she would sail round the islands, calling at Lerwick and starting on another round of Scalloway, Faroe, and Iceland, " making the voyage to these places and the tour of Shetland every fortnight during the season."

The whole description of the tour might easily be one written for a cruise of the present day, and it seems clear that Anderson had very definitely in his mind the plan of organising regular tours or " cruises " when he or his company had the vessels available. This notice or " Sample Advertisement," it will be noted, was published before the Peninsular Steam Navigation Company was formed, and the mail contract obtained from the British Admiralty in 1837, so that Willcox and Anderson then had only a number of small sailing ships and a little steamer or two. It is, to say the least, remarkable that Anderson at that time should have had the vision to see so far ahead and to plan such a summer cruise to Iceland as the Company's liners were to make just a hundred years later.

I think it must be conceded, then, that Arthur Anderson was the originator of pleasure cruises on the lines we know now, and that the Mediterranean cruises of the P. & O. ships described by Thackeray were the first to be regularly organised.

There has recently been some discussion as to which company

inaugurated cruising under the present conditions of taking passengers on board, carrying them round over a given route, and calling at various ports and bringing them back to their point of embarkation.

Such cruises were being carried out by the P. & O. in their " Vectis " as early as 1904. In that year they made 10 cruises and 2 special trips. In the next year they made 12 cruises, and in the third year 10 cruises.

The cruises were of anything from 14 to 29 days. Some were to Spitzbergen ; others to the Baltic, to the Holy Land, to the Canaries and Algiers, to Constantinople, to the Adriatic, to Norway, etc., over much the same routes, in fact, as cruising liners cover to-day.

The passengers carried in the " Vectis " numbered anything from about 100 up to 180 on the different cruises.

A paper in the office records is headed—

" Summary of Cruises performed by P. & O. Steam Yacht ' Vectis ' "—

so that even this word " cruises " was in use by the P. & O. in 1904.

CHAPTER SIXTEEN

Early Indian and Far East Services

THE first Indian mail contract was confined to the Calcutta Service, but after the P. & O. had their " Precursor " in Indian waters in 1844, they put forward proposals to take over the Bombay–Suez service which had been retained by the East India Company, undertaking to replace the latter's 200-h.p. unsuitable vessels with new ones of 520 h.p., better accommodation, and reduced charges for passengers, and faster passages, all for a charge of £80,000, which was a reduction of £30,000 on the cost to the public of the East India Company running their armed packets. The cost of that service had been admitted by the East India Company, in a return to the House of Commons the previous year.

The East India Company fought this proposal, producing many arguments why their Marine must retain the Suez–Bombay service. They were allowed to do so, and the P. & O. was asked to tender for an extended service from Ceylon to Penang, Singapore, and China. They did this, at the same time submitting closely detailed estimates of costs on which their tender was based ; and after long negotiation, a contract was made for this extension.

The China mail was to be transhipped at Point de Galle (this being the port of Ceylon then, and for a good many years until Colombo replaced it in 1882) by a monthly steamer, the required time being 140 hours from Ceylon to Penang, another 45 to Singapore, and 170 on to Hong Kong.

The " Lady Mary Wood " had been sent round to take up the new service, and she was the first to go on the run. She arrived at Singapore on 4th August, 1845, bringing mails 41 days out from London, and 8 days from Ceylon.

The event was naturally hailed with great satisfaction in the Straits, and a Singapore paper, after declaring the importance of it, proceeded to venture a prophecy which would have been very quickly fulfilled if it had not been blocked again by that dog-in-the-manger policy of the East India Company.

Said the *Singapore Journal*:

" The American and West Indian Colonies have long had regular lines of steamers between them and the Mother Country ; and now in the East it only wants an extension of the chain to Australia to render it complete. This we believe will not be long withheld, the growing importance of the Australian Colonies and the advantages resulting to Government itself from quick and regular communications with distant possessions, will speedily bring about the accomplishment of this line."

The importance of such a further extension to Singapore was that it was expected the branch line would run from there, so that, as was pointed out, with the Dutch monthly steamer and possibly a line to Manilla, Singapore offered promise of becoming of greater and greater importance as a mail-ship station. The latter promise was to be fulfilled in swifter and greater measure than Singapore could then have dreamed ; but it belongs to the tale of the Bombay service how and why the expectation of the Singapore–Australia branch was long frustrated.

The next arriving steamer was the " Braganza " (also sent out from the Peninsular service), and she brought nearly 1,500 mail packets of letters and newspapers from Europe. The " Lady Mary Wood," on her return passage, carried 4,757 packets, 4,000 being for Europe and the rest for Penang, India, and Aden.

A year or two later a system of notifying business firms and residents that the mail was being closed at the Singapore Post Office on arrival of the liner caused some disturbance.

A signal was made from the Government Hill by running up the Red Ensign to indicate closing the mail for Europe ; and the China mail was signalled by hoisting a yellow flag.

The first time the yellow flag was hoisted, a report swiftly spread through the town that an Arab pilgrim ship had arrived with a bad outbreak of plague on board, and that this was the reason for the yellow flag, which then—as now—was the signal of quarantine, but in those days had a much more dread significance.

The infection of a port might mean its quarantine, and not only the plague risk to local inhabitants, but the certainty of most harassing and inconvenient quarantine confinement of passengers at other ports, as well as the diversion from the plague port of vessels which otherwise would have called there. The P. & O. was to suffer a minor crisis, years later, on account of just such quarantine delays and difficulties.

Anxious enquiries by the Europeans in Singapore failed to bring any explanation of the plague report, the medical authority saying that they had not had any notification of " plague," which was the general term applied to bubonic, or to cholera, yellow fever, or any other serious epidemic. Then enquiries in the native quarters brought the answer in a pointing to the yellow flag floating from Government Hill as the urgent signal of plague.

The China service was not carried out without a clash with " vested interests " such as had already been met in the case of the East India Company and their Bombay service. In China the difficulties were raised by the opposition of merchants and shipowners who had for generations been making large profits from the carriage of goods, and especially silks and opium, by swift-sailing " opium clippers " and private steamers.

The " hidden hand " of the opium interests was rather exposed in a number of complaints of late running by the P. & O. steamers, which in one instance of a passage in 1848 was reduced to a statement that the liner had been delayed between India and China through her being overloaded, the coal bunkers having been filled with opium chests, and the coal loaded on deck.

The charge was subsequently disproved after full investigation by the Admiralty ; but soon after another effort against the P. & O. for a time broke off a China service which they had established.

In 1848, the Company sent out a small steamer, the " Canton," of

400 tons and 150 h.p., to act as a branch or feeder steamer between Hong Kong, Macao, and Canton, and sufficiently well armed to defend herself against the pirate junks which infested the Canton River. She was placed on the service without any mail contract or payment, but sufficiently paid her own way as a feeder to the main liners.

Although then the smallest ship in the P. & O. fleet, and a baby compared to the 1,000 to 1,800 tonners they were then employing, the " Canton " became the more quickly popular after an early exploit in China waters.

In September 1849 she brought into sight the sailing warship H.M.S. " Columbine," lying practically becalmed with a number of pirate junks she had been chasing slowly but surely making their escape by the use of their long sweeps manned by relays of rowers from their heavy crews.

The " Canton " came up with the warship, threw a line aboard, and getting her under tow dragged her off in pursuit of the junks. After towing her to within effective range, the " Canton " cast off, and the warship's guns speedily reduced the pirates to wreckage or surrender.

The Canton and Hong Kong merchants were the more ready to trust their goods to the " Canton," not only because she carried guns and a well-armed crew as a protection against the pirate junks, but also because a steamer had the additional and almost unbeatable weapon of scalding steam to repel boarders. It only needed a hosepipe connecting up with the boiler to shoot out a jet of steam that no flesh and blood could face and live.

In 1849, the Company placed the " Lady Mary Wood " on an experimental service between Hong Kong and Shanghai, without any mail contract, but setting against that possible disadvantage the other possible advantage that she could run as and where full cargoes offered only, and need not run, full or empty, to mail contract sailings and times. But in this the Company broke in again on an established service of sailing clippers on the coast, and were for a time beaten by a neat trick.

The sailing ships discharged and loaded at Woosung, a port 13 miles from Shanghai, so outside the port limits and jurisdiction of the British

Consul. This exempted vessels using Woosung from Shanghai port charges, and because Woosung was controlled by Chinese authorities, certain exemptions of duties could be " arranged " by shippers without much difficulty.

The " Lady Mary Wood " made similar use of the Woosung port under the arrangement of the P. & O. agent at Shanghai. A merchant in Shanghai (who as the result of a later investigation demanded by the P. & O. turned out to be partner in an important firm of the sailing-ship owners) sent a parcel of silk from Shanghai to be loaded at Woosung in the " Lady Mary Wood " ; and this having been done, an information was lodged that she had evaded the Shanghai customs by loading Shanghai goods without paying duty.

The whole transaction had been so openly carried out that on the complaint, the Shanghai consul had no choice but to intervene, and the " Lady Mary " was fined 200 dollars and ordered not to use the port of Woosung again. The ship therefore had to pay heavy port charges and duties on valuable goods like silk, and the Shanghai and Hong Kong merchants naturally preferring to ship by the sailing vessels which evaded such charges, the steamer lost shipments until she could no longer pay her way.

The Company promptly withdrew her, and lodged a protest with the Secretary of State for Foreign Affairs. It is enough to say here that this protest, backed by the support of many merchants and residents, resulted in the Supreme Court reversing the decision and ordering the fine imposed on the " Lady Mary Wood " to be refunded ; but it took months to right this, and the service was suspended in the meantime.

In 1852, a new contract was made, and in the beginning of 1853 a fortnightly instead of monthly service began to India, the Straits, and China. For the Far East, one mail went straight through from Ceylon to Penang and onwards, and the second went to Calcutta and from there to the Straits and China.

In 1849, an agitation had begun for a mail service with Australia, and out of this came that old vexed question of the East India Company Bombay–Suez service. The P. & O. were anxious to undertake this, because they were convinced that with the bigger, faster, and better steamers they would put on the run, they would speedily increase both the passenger and goods traffic between Bombay and England which they were certain languished under the East India Company.

The P. & O. offered to undertake the Australian service and the Bombay service together, for the same amount as the East India Company were receiving for Bombay alone. The offer was favourably considered, and a powerful deputation of London merchants and Members of Parliament, knowing that the East India Company were refusing to give up their contract, waited upon the Government.

It was decided to represent the position fairly to the East India Company, but although this was done at a conference at East India House, it ended with the same stalemate as it had done so often before—in the flat refusal of the East India Company to surrender the Bombay service.

The war between the Committee and the East India Company moved next to Parliament, and in both Houses the subject was raised and the issue fought out. There was plenty of straight talking and hard hitting on both sides. Sir J. Hogg, Deputy Chairman of the East India Company, was an M.P., and he stood up strongly for his Company, urging that the Bombay service was a necessary part of the Indian Marine or Navy, because it maintained a steam fleet which could be used in war.

He was told that the service was costing this country £50,000 a year and India another £50,000, and that if this country's payment was to be considered as helping to keep up the Company's war Navy, our Navy Estimates for cost of the fleet in the East ought to be cut down by that amount.

Sir J. Hogg could see no reason why the P. & O. should be allowed to add to its already excessive profits by being given the Bombay service. Mr. Arthur Anderson (then an M.P.) retorted that Sir John had sat on a Commission the previous year, where it was shown that the P. & O. had made no such exaggerated profits as he now stated.

Another Member pointed out that the East India Company ships carrying the mails could carry only a few passengers and little merchandise; or indeed had barely room for the passengers' baggage.

In the Commons, the result was a blank, except that the East India Company had been told pretty plainly what the House and country thought of them. In the Lords, there was, if possible, even stronger protest against the service given by the East India Company, its cost, and the refusal to better it or allow others to do so. A former Governor-General of India said bluntly that he had recommended twenty years before that the Bombay Marine or Indian Navy should be abolished " as being inefficient and extravagantly expensive," and that it had no right to employ its ships on a postal service.

But all this, as well as the series of deputations to the Government and the East India Company, petitions to Parliament, and a correspondence which ran for many months between that Company and Downing Street, failed in the desired effect, and the East India Company carried on.

In 1852, however, the Government was free to enter into new contracts, and these were made with the P. & O., and included a bi-monthly line between England and Calcutta ; a monthly mail between Bombay, Ceylon, and China ; monthly between Calcutta and China, which gave a fortnightly mail to China ; and finally, a new service between Singapore and Australia, connecting at Singapore with the English mails.

The finishing blow to all the claims of the East India Company to be running an efficient steam service to Bombay was their loss of a complete mail which they had sent on in a native sailing dhow, having no steamer available to carry it on from Aden.

This was too much. By then steam had become so firmly established for the mails, not only with regular services all over the Continent and Mediterranean and the East, but also to Boston, New York, and the West Indies, that it was intolerable so important a trade as that between Bombay and Europe should step back into the " dark ages " of sail and the irregularity and chance of favouring winds—especially where those were so rarely available in the Red Sea.

The Bombay–Suez service was forthwith passed to the P. & O.

One surprising fact emerged from the Parliamentary discussions on this Bombay mail—that, great as the volume of traffic by steam and the Overland Route had grown in a dozen years, it had not merely been doing so at the expense of the sailing-ship trade round the Cape. There were then more ships on the Cape trade than there had been before the opening of the steam routes. The explanation of this apparent inconsistency was that the whole of the Indian trade had been vastly increased by the facility of faster and more regular mails, which had encouraged, promoted, and increased the whole traffic.

There are some other telling figures to show how the trade of India and the East had benefited under the advantages of the P. & O. services.

Before they opened their extension to India, the whole trade of the East with this country was put at £20 millions a year. In the operation of the Overland Route before the Canal was opened, the value of the trade carried over it rose to £40 millions a year. Up to the opening of the Canal it might be said that practically the whole of the steam communication with the East was in the hands of the P. & O., and the year before the Canal opened, the value of the Eastern trade was set at £110 millions.

In the thirty years, therefore, greatly as the Company had increased its own trade and traffic, their share was only a fraction of the increase which had been derived from the improved communications and which was enjoyed by the whole trading communities and peoples here and in the East—to say nothing of the vastly increased gain to the Exchequer in direct and indirect taxation.

CHAPTER SEVENTEEN

Early Ocean Steam Travel

Before leaving that first period of the P. & O. history, let me try to give (through the reports of contemporary writing and records) an idea of the life of the ocean traveller of that time.

I have quoted Thackeray's references to the food supplied to passengers and the dependence of the ship's company on the service, skill, and superhuman (or super-heated) efforts of a solitary sea-cook. " Feed the brute " well and satisfyingly was, is, and always must be a primary consideration of any liner company seeking to attract passengers.   The wants of passengers in those early days may be astonishing to us now, but after all, they were the common wants of those people who could afford to indulge in what we should call now the gross pleasures of the table.

The British traveller then (like very many now) only considered British dishes and cooking as good ; and had no time for foreign " kickshaws "—except that, in the liners of the P. & O., even in European waters, dishes of Indian curries (chicken, beef, mutton, vegetable, and fish), with all due and proper accompaniments of chutney, poppadums, and " Bombay duck," plain and Pillau-rice, were from the first regarded as one of the essential and never-to-be-missed courses.

This law, custom, or convention of the P. & O. curry dishes is about the only one I can find still surviving in the P. & O. from " A Hundred Years Ago " until now.

That English custom of regarding the joints of roast or boiled meat as the mainstay of a meal lingered on at sea long after the 'forties.

There is a hand-written Bill of Fare honourably framed and hung in the P. & O. office to-day.   It reads :

P. & O. S.S. " SIMLA "
15th day of January, 1862

Mutton Broth

Roast Turkeys	Boiled Legs Mutton
„ Sucking Pigs	„ Fowls
„ Fore Qrs. Mutton	Fowl & Ham Pies
„ Geese	Kidney Pudding
„ Ducks	Sheep's Head Braized
„ Fowls	Pig's Feet Stewed
„ Beef	Chicken Sauté
„ Haunch Mutton	Curry and Rice

Corned Beef

2nd Course

Fruit Tarts	Jam Tartlets
Black Cap Pudding	Sponge Cakes
Sandwich Pastry	Brighton Rocks
Apple Turnovers	Pancakes

Rice Puddings

All the joints and poultry were brought whole to the saloon and carved there ; and perhaps the best joke on such a list of solid foods is to find them described as " too recherché."   I quote from a Melbourne *Age* of 1866.

" The cuisine," said the correspondent, " is luxurious and abundant, although the Rev. Dr. Lang, from his place in our [Australian] Parliament admitted that the viands were too recherché for his taste. . . . The victualling, abundant and varied though it be, is the constant theme of criticism and animadversion—the abstemious finding fault with the quantity of claret and ale consumed, and the *bon vivant* exclaiming against the age (or want of age) of his favourite, and too much favoured wines. An amusing incident occurs to me. A South Australian squatter on board the —— between Aden and Suez, after partaking heartily of soup, fowl, turkey and ham, roast joint and preserved game, all with vegetables, and then pastry, cheese and dessert—the whole washed down liberally with some excellent wine—remarked, ' Well, when I do get ashore, I hope I shall find some food fit for an Englishman to eat.' "

This meal, you will note, was eaten " between Aden and Suez," a stretch of the passage which was usually expected to reduce appetites to a minus quantity, or to a longing for no more than iced drinks. But until the Company installed their ice-making plant at Suez, there was no ice on the passage from there, although there might have been as much as could be carried taken aboard at Calcutta.

Ice was to be had in India many years before the P. & O. went there. It was shipped to there in sailing ships, usually, I believe, from America, and was natural ice from the streams and lakes, solidly packed into the ships' holds between deep layers of sawdust, and on arrival in India was stored in thick stone-walled and -roofed heavily built structures.

But the small quantities for which there would have been room in the steamers would not last long, especially in the fiery furnace of the Red Sea and with the lack of mechanical means of ventilation of those days. The outer cabins had their port-holes and the saloon its windows, but no breath of air came through these when the ship was running with a wind of about equal speed to her own ; and even with a breeze blowing, it was usually a hot and clammy air that entered.

Until designers learned from experience, there was no adequate division between the heat of the engine-room and the passengers' quarters. A " draught " was created in the saloon by the use of an Indian punkah—a length of cloth suspended above the table, kept swinging by the rhythmic pull of a native punkah-wallah, and doing no more than fan the stuffy hot air to and fro.

With a following wind, the smoke from the funnels rose straight up and floated overhead in a smut- and cinder-dropping cloud, and the inside of the ship everywhere was like an oven. The only relief to be obtained was when the Captain turned the ship about and steamed into the wind for a few minutes so as to get a good sweeping-through draught.

The passage of the Red Sea was always the dreaded part of the passage even in much later years, and I have at first hand rather a good story of this from an officer now senior in the Company but then very junior.

His Captain had quite modern ideas on publicity values, and the benefits of editorial Press paragraphs and stories. On one voyage, the pressmen swarmed aboard as usual at an Australian port, and one of them, having heard some chance remark about the very trying heat in the Red Sea, sought the Captain for a " story " about it. The Captain, scenting a chance to get the ship and the Line well into the newspapers, gave the story with all the detail the reporter could wish. " Red Sea Inferno " headlines and liberal space duly rewarded the Captain's effort.

On the next two voyages, the Captain's tales and the Red Sea temperature went up and up ; and the Australian papers in each port gave more and more harrowing tales of fainting passengers, heat-stricken firemen, and collapsing officers. The Captain's satisfaction grew with the space measure he won in the Press.

But on his return to London, he found himself unexpectedly " on the carpet " at the office, was told plainly that his " publicity " was driving passengers to evade the Red Sea by travelling in rival liners round the Cape, and advised to keep the temperature and the tales more moderate in future.

From then on the Captain's Red Sea passages kept getting cooler and cooler, until his officers swore at last that one day he would be reporting icebergs sighted there.

There is another, and older, tale that the P. & O. in the Red Sea heat was responsible for the creation of the slang word " posh."

On the outward passage, the cabins on the port side got the early morning sun, but had the whole day to cool off. The starboard side cabins, however, had the full heat of the westering sun all the afternoon, and were like ovens by bed-time. On the homeward passage, of course, it was reversed, and the port cabins got the worst roasting.

S.S. "CEYLON," 2,020 tons. Built 1858

High officials and important dignitaries were accordingly given the preference of the cooler cabins to port on the outward and to starboard on the homeward passages; and this " Port Outward—Starboard Homeward " became shortened down to the initials " P.O.S.H.," and the favoured passengers were the " posh " ones.

That remark in the *Age* correspondent's comments on the abstemious finding fault with the quantity of ale and claret consumed referred to a practice which carried on from the first days of the P. & O. of including all drinks in the amount charged for fare. Free wines, beer, and spirits were always available, and on any special occasion champagne was also served.

It is possible this custom first came from the Peninsular trade and catering, and the normal practice of French liners to supply table wine —as they still do—without charge. Or it may be that it was adopted from the East India Company and their steamers whose passengers would travel P. & O. on this side of Egypt and, no doubt, expect their free drinks as beyond Suez.

The East India Company system was for a certain proportion of the passage money to be paid to the Captain for " table money," and out of this he had to provide food and drinks. He made a profit out of his table money, and, no doubt, the better the food and drink supply of his table, the more popular his ship, the greater the number of his passengers and amount of his profits.

An East India Company notice of about 1840, after quoting the fares for lady or gentleman, child under 10, child under 5, and under 1, added : " . . . for the above sums, the passengers are to be provided with a plain substantial table ; but no person is *entitled* to more than one pint of wine or one bottle of beer per diem."

Whether the children from under 10 to under 1 either had to take or leave it or whether their ration of wine and beer could be claimed by the parents is not stipulated.

Some time in the late 'forties or early 'fifties, the P. & O. put a stop to the free champagne, but the free wines, beer, and spirits continued. There was always a supply at hand on the sideboard or swinging trays, even after the stewards retired at night, and no doubt the drink item

I

must have been a considerable one in the expenses—although it must be remembered that drinks of all kinds were extraordinarily cheap in those days.

About the 'sixties, the Tee-total or Total Abstinence Societies began to raise objections to the system, and in 1866 some sort of enquiry was widely reported. It was then stated that in the P. & O. " last year, there were consumed 1,300,000 bottles of wine, spirits, beer, and soda-water on board all the Company's steamers." An analysis of the total reveals some indication of the tastes of passengers of that time.

Pale ale and porter were well at the top, with 524,250 and 166,109 bottles respectively; claret came next (123,059 bottles), then sherry (102,711), rum (65,192), brandy (62,222), port (29,366), gin (15,427), and whisky a mere 7,424 bottles.

These seem vast quantities of liquor, but in the same analysis we have 203,759 bottles of soda-water and lemonade.

In the same year the ships' companies got through over 11,000,000 lb. of solid provisions and 3,046,004 lb. of ice. If passengers ate 11 lb. of solid food to 1 bottle of liquor, including a large proportion of light claret and ale, the drink consumption seems less terrible.

In the enquiry referred to, however, these facts were not brought out, and the efforts of the abstainers were directed to exposing the evils of the system. A witness, asked if he thought " that the practice of putting an unlimited quantity of wine and spirits on the table leads to a great waste," answered " Yes," and that it did a considerable mischief in exposing to the temptation of drink those not accustomed to it, especially young people. No evidence was produced, however, of drunkenness or excessive drinking. The Total Abstainers might well and wisely have " rested their case " there, but, foolishly for their cause, went on to compare the costs of an Atlantic liner's fare without drinks and the P. & O., with free drinks, and attribute the difference to the P. & O. liquor bill.

Comparing the Atlantic lines' passenger fares with those of the P. & O., it worked out that the latter charged about 6s. per day more; and this was put down to the cost of supplying free drinks. Actually, of course, the difference was due to almost every other cause, such as the difference in the price of coal, which cost the P. & O. three or more times as much to deliver to their Eastern depots as the Atlantic liner paid for coals bought in England or America; and the comparative cost of provisioning the ships was equally, or perhaps even more, out of proportion.

This comparative cost of running a ship in near and far waters, and the trifling difference in fares due to the provision of drinks, is further borne out in that same article in the Australian *Age* previously quoted.

Says the correspondent: "It is a well-known fact that cost of living on board the Australian steamers is about three guineas a day, exclusive of wines and spirits, while the charges on the P. & O. from here to England are £2 4s. per day, wines and spirits included."

However, the agitation against the free drinks continued, until— no doubt to the ultimate profit of the P. & O.—the final knell of drinks included in fares was sounded in the Directors' Report of 1871, and its pronouncement that "in deference to what appeared to be the wishes of passengers, the Directors have discontinued the system of including the supply of wines, beers, and spirits in the charge for passage money."

One feature of ocean travel which was a commonplace and quite unavoidable, and one which must have often been highly objectionable, was the need to carry an extensive stock of "live provisions." If you look back at that Bill of Fare in the "Simla" for a single meal, you will get some idea of the number of animals required to provide all the fore-quarters, legs and haunches, pork and poultry of all sorts.

No more than a day or two's supply of dead meat could be shipped because it would not keep, so that all the rest—as well as a cow or two for milk—had to be carried alive until their turn came for the table. The practice in the P. & O. was to ship at Southampton the full needs in live-stock to last to Alexandria and back, simply because at none of the ports of call between could either animals or poultry be found of a quality satisfactory to the British passengers.

Even in the biggest of the liners of 2,000 tons and over, there was not room enough to escape the sounds and scents of the farmyard and slaughter-house. One passenger, during a spell of close and muggy weather, wrote that when he woke in the morning to the crowing of cocks, cackle of geese, bleating of sheep, and squealing of pigs, he was inclined to think he was asleep and dreaming he was on an English farm; but the illusion was soon dispelled, because the worst of dreams could not conjure up the villainous odour which assailed his nostrils from the nearby pig-pens and hen-roosts. It certainly must have been trying to squeamish ones, especially in very hot weather and with a roll on the ship.

All these animals required a great deal to eat until the time came for them to be eaten, so that each ship had to stow hay by the stack and tons of fodder for sheep and poultry, as well as water for the animals and the passengers. This, with the large quantity of fuel needed for the extravagantly coal-eating engines of those days and the space given to passenger's accommodation and baggage, left practically no room for cargo, and this was one of the main reasons why fares were so high and substantial postal payments were an essential to keep a line running on a regular mail service.

The amount of personal baggage carried by each passenger was simply staggering, and to a modern traveller would seem wildly and extravagantly unnecessary. But it was the rule or the fashion then and had to be catered for, and it explains why the P. & O. declined to carry from England to Malta or Egypt the baggage of Mr. Waghorn's passengers who travelled across the Continent to Marseilles or Trieste and by foreign lines onward.

I have here a list of 1850 kindly lent me by Thresher & Glenny, who were "East India and Colonial Outfitters, at the Sign of the Peacock, Strand, next door to Somerset House," as they still are. This printed list of articles recommended to intending travellers has set against each item the numbers which had been ordered by the particular passenger.

There are over 100 articles of clothing alone on the list. Those ordered include 48 Longcloth shirts and 24 Longcloth Full Front shirts, 24 Indian Gauze Waistcoats (nowadays "vests"), and 18 Nightcaps.

Then there are 72 Cotton Half Hose, 12 Silk Ditto, and 12 Woollen Ditto—or just under 100 pairs of socks.

What you might call "furniture" included swinging cot, hair mattress, feather pillow, ship couch or sofa, case of blacking, brushes, etc., footbath, tin can for water.

The P. & O. passenger at this time did not require the articles of bedding and such like, because these, as their advertisements stated, were provided to first-class passengers. But they were required by any who were proceeding beyond Egypt by the East India Company steamers to Bombay, because they did not provide such articles ; and the P. & O. warned Bombay passengers that they should take a valise of bedding for use on the Suez–Bombay part of the passage.

The P. & O. about this date allowed first-class passengers 4 cwt. of personal baggage each, and any extra was charged £1 per cwt. England to Alexandria, £2 per cwt. Suez to India, while any excess of 2 cwt. across Egypt cost 14s. per cwt. Moreover, no package would be accepted for the Overland Route transit if exceeding 80 lb. weight and measurement of 2 feet 3 inches, by 1 foot 2, by 1 foot 2. The weight and measurements were dictated by the size, shape, and weight of a package that could be slung on a camel's back. The amount of excess baggage allowed was strictly qualified by the stipulation that it could only be accepted at Southampton " should there be room in the vessel." Imagine the tragic case of the passenger who found at the last minute that there was no " room in the vessel " for his seventy-odd shirts, his 100 pairs of socks, *and his eighteen nightcaps* !

The traveller was also carefully instructed that he should pack all his luggage in trunks which could (and would) be stowed below in the baggage room, to which he, or she, would have access at fixed intervals —weather permitting ; and that immediate requirements for a week, or two or three, ought to be packed in a " carpet bag " which could be taken into the cabin.

Somehow, those normal travel necessities of nightcaps and carpet bags seem to carry one back farther even than the period of paddle-wheels and punkahs.

CHAPTER EIGHTEEN

First Australian Mails

I T was not until the end of 1852 that the first mail steamer, the P. & O. "Chusan," arrived in Australia, but the agitation for steam communication had been carrying on persistently from within a year or two of the establishment of the P. & O. Indian mails ten years before.

The subject began to be ventilated in Australia in 1843, and after various public meetings at Sydney and elsewhere, a submission was made to the Legislative Council of New South Wales in 1844, and favourable resolutions were unanimously passed. Similar representations were made in England by import and export merchants and others concerned with the progress of the Colonies.

This was before the demand for fast clipper ships to the gold diggings in the 1850's brought about those famous passages of 90 to 100 days between England and Australia ; and even in 1850 evidence was given at a Parliamentary enquiry that it frequently took ten months for the sender of a letter to receive a reply from Australia.

Such postal delays dragged out the actions of those concerned at the two ends, and it was not until 1847 that the Legislative Council of New South Wales granted a sum of £500 a month for three years to defray expenses of establishing steam between Singapore and Australia —the P. & O. extension to China being then a well-proven success.

This supported action which had been taken in London when, at a public meeting at the London Tavern in 1846, of which Sir George Larpent, Chairman of the P. & O., and a few others were the prime instigators, it was resolved to urge on H.M. Government that enquiries should be carried out into the most expedient ways of connecting with Australia by steam.

There were then, and for years after, opposing views on the route likely to prove the best. Some were for the Cape of Good Hope route, others across the Isthmus of Panama, and others by the Egyptian Overland Route.

The Admiralty advertised for tenders, and a number of these were submitted, some unfortunately of a purely speculative nature by parties without the vessels or the means to carry out the services offered. A Company which had made the lowest offer was accepted, but after months of negotiation, the accepted tenderers were found to be quite unable to carry out a contract, and their Company reached their only port—in the Bankruptcy Court. The whole thing fizzled out, and the project was back where it had begun years before.

The P. & O. had first put forward proposals in 1847, but these the Admiralty and Post Office set aside. In 1849, there were more public meetings, committees formed, and finally a widely signed petition presented to Parliament. Again tenders were called for by the Government, and again a number were submitted, including that of the P. & O.

But now there intervened that clash with the East India Company of which the story has been outlined in the chapter on the Indian and Bombay mails. The East India Company were then receiving £50,000 a year from the British Government for their Bombay–Suez service covering 70,000 miles. The P. & O. offered to carry on this service and also to run it on to Australia for the same amount—which meant a service over 332,800 miles for the same amount as was being paid for the 70,000.

It was certainly to the benefit of Bombay as well as Australia that a means of steam intercourse should be available for the growing trade between the two, but the East India Company clung stubbornly to their Bombay–Suez service, and once more the whole of the plans fell through, even after the most vigorous protests had been offered in both Houses of Parliament. It was then shown that imports from Australia were valued at £2 millions a year, and exports at an equal amount.

The proceedings in Parliament produced some interesting facts. In 1847, the longest passage between England and Australia was of 159 days and the shortest 99. The average was 121. In 1848, the longest passage was 159 and the shortest 94—the average being 119. In the ten years 1840 to 1850, 520 ships had sailed between England and Sydney, and most of them took 121 to 130 days to the passage.

Against this it was pointed out that, by any of the three routes proposed, a steam passage should be made with regularity in about 70 days.

A completely new reason for a steamer service in Australian waters came up out of the proceedings in the Commons and the recital of a piece of Naval history known, of course, to our Admiralty but not to the general public until it was brought to light ten years later.

In support of an argument for a steam fleet (which would be armed or equipped for armaments in accordance with Admiralty requirements, as all P. & O. steamers then were), an extract was read to the House from the report of Commodore Wilkes, leader of the United States Exploring Expedition in 1839.

The two men-of-war of the Expedition arrived off Sydney Heads at sunset, 29th November, 1839, and having a fair wind to enter the harbour, the leader decided to run in, although it was a dark night and he had no pilot. A light on the Sow and Pigs Shoal at first raised doubts, but on it being fixed where the light was, the leader, with the second ship following his signals, ran on in with the intention of making Sydney Cove. This was safely carried out, and in the words of the report :

" We quietly dropped anchor off the Cove in the midst of the shipping without anyone having the least idea of our arrival. When the good people of Sydney looked abroad in the morning, they were much astonished to see two unknown men-of-war, lying amongst their own shipping, which had entered their Harbour in spite of the difficulties of the channel, without being reported, and unknown to the pilots."

The quotation of this old report had a most marked effect on the House, and it was well rubbed in that what had happened in 1839 might easily be repeated.

When the East India Company, badly badgered by all the fuss about their refusal to support the Australian service by allowing the P. & O. to take over their Bombay service, retorted that the two services could easily be considered separately, the P. & O. agreed.

Their main purpose in pressing for a link-up of their line through Bombay with Australia was the hope of increased trade between the two places and the feeding of their main line with cargo and passengers. But they readily declared their willingness to start the Australian service without Bombay being included, and were prepared to open the service in consideration of receiving the amount of the postage paid on letters carried.

This, the Company's fourth offer, having been rejected or put off, the whole matter was again put to a Committee of the House of Commons in 1851.

At last, in 1852, a tender by the Company of 26th February was accepted for a service to begin in January 1853. It is worth a glance at the conditions under which the contract was secured and the difficulties deliberately put in the way by the Government.

Tenders were invited for five separate services, any or all of which might be taken as sections or parts or a whole. The intention was to have as many competitive offers as possible, and so force rival tenderers to cut their quotations to the lowest possible figure.

The separated sections were for services between :
1. England and Egypt.
2. Egypt and Calcutta and China.
3. Egypt and Bombay.
4. Marseilles and Malta (to connect with England–Egypt steamers).
5. Singapore and Australia.

The last was to be run every other month, so little did the Government then think of the requirements of an Australian mail; although one must again remember that this was before the gold-rush needs or possibilities had been developed.

Only two tenders were put in, and that of the P. & O. was finally accepted. Their contract for the whole of the five services was for £199,600, and their competitor, the Eastern Steam Navigation Company, asked no less than £166,000 for the Singapore–Australia service alone, while their tender for the only other section they offered to undertake was for *half* the India–China mail for £110,000.

The disappointed competitors endeavoured to raise an agitation against the preference given to " the powerful and monopolistic P. & O.," and petitioned for a Parliamentary enquiry—which would have made the third on the same subject of steam communication with Australia.

The Chancellor of the Exchequer refused flatly to recommend such further enquiry, giving as his reasons that the P. & O. tender, with known means to execute the contract, was at the rate of 6*s*. 6*d*. a mile, while that of the Eastern Company, with questionable means or ability, was for 8*s*. and 10*s*. a mile over the respective sections.

The new contract was to be for eight years and covered services :

1. Bi-monthly between Southampton and Calcutta.

2. Bi-monthly, Marseilles–Malta, to connect with England–Alexandria service.

3. Monthly to Bombay, Ceylon, Singapore, and China.

4. Monthly to Calcutta, Singapore, and China (making, with Bombay service, a bi-monthly one to India and China).

5. Every two months between Singapore and Australia by King George's Sound, Adelaide, and Melbourne to Sydney.

The Australian service was contracted to begin in 1853, but in May 1852 the Directors announced that they were at once sending out two steamers to inaugurate an experimental service for the purpose of learning as much as possible about the route before the actual contract began.

Before we come to this first service, however, there is an interesting story to tell of how the Singapore–Australia route came to be proposed and adopted.

In 1846, a Lieutenant (later Commander) Crawford Pasco, R.N., who had some years previously been engaged in survey work of the Australian coast in H.M.S. " Beagle " and other ships, was in Hong Kong during the China Wars. At the Club one evening he was chatting over with some friends the berthing that day of the P. & O. steamer, and Lieutenant Pasco offered some remarks on the feasibility of the P. & O. running a branch line from Singapore to the Australian ports, and on the help this would be to the growing trade of the Colonies.

Amongst the group of friends there happened to be the editor of the local newspaper, *The Hong Kong Register*, and having listened to Pasco's clear and well-informed opinions, he begged him to write an article for his paper. Pasco did so, and the article duly appeared over his name ; and there, apparently, the matter ended so far as the writer and editor were concerned.

Six years later, the fruit of that chance seed appeared. Pasco was then in London on sick leave, and was considering a voyage, preferably to South America, to recuperate. Hearing, however, of the P. & O.'s plans to send out their " Chusan " that year, he went to their office to book a passage in her. But his name was familiar in the P. & O. office, because that years-old article had been of the utmost help in planning the new service. He was asked to see the Managing Directors, and by them was invited to go in the " Chusan " as the guest of the Company. He did so, and later enjoyed again the hospitality of the Company on a visit to England and on frequent cruises in the Australian waters.

I should like to add that I have only recently obtained these details direct from Mr. Montague G. C. Pasco, of Queensland, a son of Lieutenant Pasco.

It is true that Lieutenant Pasco's article was not the first suggestion of this Singapore–Australia service. As already mentioned, it had been discussed in a London public meeting as one of three routes to Australia, and in 1845 there was that article in the Singapore paper hoping that the P. & O., having reached there, might soon be branching to Australia. In 1846 the P. & O. Directors at the Annual Meeting said that for some time they had been considering the possibility of further Far Eastern extensions, and referred to making provision for these " as well as that embracing the Australian Colonies."

But all these were vague generalisations or " pious hopes," and it was undoubtedly the Pasco article, backed with his knowledge, experience, and reasoning, which had the most marked effect on the P. & O. plans.

The "Chusan" was a new iron-built screw-steamer of 699 tons and 80 "nominal working up to 250" h.p., square-rigged on fore and main and with mizzen spanker, and, as her pictures show, carrying a good length of jibboom and full suit of headsails. Her armament was particularly noteworthy. She carried one long 32-pounder mounted on a Ferguson patent traversing carriage, which enabled the gun to be fired in any direction; on the poop a long 18-pounder on a similar carriage; on the top-gallant forecastle 4 broadside 12-pounder guns, and round the poop rail six swivel guns. Small arms consisted of muskets, pistols, pikes, tomahawks, and boarding pikes in profusion. In addition to all those, she was provided with apparatus by which steam could be brought from the boilers to direct against attackers trying to come to close quarters, or to make any attempt to board.

All this apparently excessive armament was designed as a necessary precaution against the swarming pirate junks and prahus of the China and Java Seas.

The "Chusan" sailed from Southampton on 15th May, 1852, met with pleasant enough weather on her way down to the Cape, but with winds too light and baffling to help her make an impressive passage. She spent eight days coaling at St. Vincent (Cape Verde) and Cape Town, and after leaving the Cape ran into very heavy weather, which on one day was so bad that she had to lie hove-to for 24 hours—a severe testing through which the little vessel came triumphantly.

She arrived off Cape Otway with a wind astern increasing to gale force, and, running under whole topsails and foresails, she was making 14 knots. She rounded Otway Light at 4 a.m. on 29th July in a heavy gale and tremendous seas.

Here an unfortunate casualty occurred, and for a brief few minutes had the ship in jeopardy of total loss on the very verge of her arrival at Melbourne.

Chief Officer William Bencraft had the middle watch from midnight to 4 a.m. Pasco had come on deck for the special purpose of getting a bearing at sunrise, and Captain Down took the chance to go below for a shave, leaving orders to furl the topsails. It was blowing hard and the ship was running at 12/14 knots, before the heavy following gale and seas. The men were aloft furling the topsails when one fell from the yard-arm overboard. Pasco flung a lifebelt after him, and a grating to follow it.

Bencraft sent word to the Captain and called away the quarter-boat. Pasco and Bencraft jumped for the boat, shouting for volunteers. McEwan, a quartermaster upon the topsail-yard, slid down a back stay and jumped into the boat, followed by three seamen. At a critical moment, as the boat was lowering away, a tackle jambed, and was only knifed through in time. In the heavy sea, the boat was nearly capsized, and then narrowly escaped being caught by the propeller. However, she managed to struggle clear, but so strong was the wind and so fierce the seas that it was only by keeping her as nearly as possible head to sea that she was kept afloat.

Bencraft and McEwan took spells in rowing stroke and baling in turn, while Pasco steered, and at last the missing man's hat and a lifebelt that had been thrown after him were found, but the man was gone.

The ship by then had been lost in the thick, and it was only after two and a quarter hours of hard struggle that the boat was picked up and the exhausted crew were rescued. Bencraft, in a note-book of his I have just read, says that Lieutenant Pasco was the only man of them able to get out of the boat, the others being " quite done up and had to be lifted on board like bundles of wet rags."

In the meantime the ship herself had been in serious danger. Brought up into the wind to get the boat away, Captain Down had jib and foresail and spanker blown away in shreds, and before the ship could be steadied, a succession of seas broke aboard, flooded below, and drowned out the fires.

Still under command of her remaining sails, she was nursed through the seas until the fires could be relit and the ship brought under power again. The Captain pushed her up to windward, at last sighted his boat, and was able to steam up, get her under his lee, and pick her up.

Lieutenant Pasco, immediately he got on board, stripped and had a stiff rub-down all over with copious brandy, and took the deck again to bring the ship in through the Rip. Captain Down, supposing he knew the entrance, allowed him to do so, but was greatly astonished to hear, when they were safely in and handing over to the pilot, that Pasco had never been through there before.

Bencraft slept until 8 a.m., and on waking found on his table a card pinned there with a beautiful jewelled pin. It was from a French passenger, and bore the simple words " Pour valeur."

This Bencraft had an adventurous career. He was a Midshipman, R.N., in the first China War, was then invalided home and joined the P. & O. as Fourth Officer. He was shipwrecked in the " Ariel " off Italy, and was in the " Great Liverpool " when, with 500 passengers on board, she went ashore off Finisterre. Fortunately, after striking a reef seven miles out, she was beached on the mainland, and all were saved except one woman, a child, and a native nurse.

When the tide receded, the mail room was reached by cutting a hole through the ship's side, and Bencraft volunteered to take the mails on by a little brig in an adjacent harbour. It was blowing hard, but with three of his own ship's crew and two of the brig's, Bencraft made Corunna, 75 miles away, just in time to catch the P. & O. liner which was sailing as the brig arrived. For this service the Company presented him with a sextant with a gold arc and full compensation for kit lost, and speedily promoted him to Third, Second, and then to Chief Officer of the " Chusan."

Bencraft made one voyage to Singapore and back to Australia, and then retired from the sea. But at Singapore he again distinguished himself in a daring act of life-saving. On a pitch-dark night, with intervals of dazzling and blinding play of lightning, Bencraft was asleep below, but was wakened by the thunder and lightning to hear a shout of " Man Overboard." The " Chusan " was alongside the jetty, and Bencraft, racing on deck and along to the stern, saw phosphorescent foam drifting astern.

He whipped a line about him and jumped over into the $4\frac{1}{2}$-knot current tearing past the ship, struck out for the splashing, and found himself within a dozen yards of the struggling man as his line brought him up sharply. He threw off the line, struck out again, and caught not one man (although he did not know it then), but two. He got a grip on one, was dragged down, came up still holding on, was sunk again by the drowning man, felt him grow lighter, brought him up again, and on the point of sinking for the last time was grabbed from the boat which he had called away before he dived over.

So fierce was the current that it took two hours' hard rowing to get back to the ship. The rescued man was a dock shipwright, who in a blinding flash of lightning had missed the gangplank. A steward, who was an expert swimmer, jumped over after him, but was drowned by the frantic struggles of the non-swimmer, who, after over an hour's work by the ship's surgeon, recovered.

For this act, and his boat work off Otway, Captain Down recommended Bencraft to the Royal Humane Society in England, from whom he later received the Society Medal for the bravest deed of the year.

Bencraft left the ship and the Company on the return to Sydney, declaring that he wanted a shore life. He obtained a post with the Sydney Gold Escort Company, later with the Sydney Water Police, and from this joined the New South Wales Steam Navigation and Pilot Board. He then went to the Melbourne Fire Brigade, from which he retired as Superintendent and Secretary in 1864, with a bonus of £600.

He married in Sydney in 1855, and I find in his " Log " a note that the cup ran for at the first race meeting held in Sydney was a silver pint pot which had been made from a set of spoons given as a wedding present to his wife, Anne. This cup she had made and gave to her husband in 1864.

On the conclusion of his services in Australia, Bencraft returned to England and lived in retirement in Devon, where he died in 1912 at the age of 86. I am indebted to a niece in Melbourne and to his descendants in this country for a reading of his notes on the facts I have given above.

The arrival of the " Chusan " naturally aroused the greatest enthusiasm throughout Australia. It was a long-delayed triumph for those who had fought for years for a regular steam mail, and the fact that, time and again, hopes had been raised by rumours and apparently authentic reports of a mail contract being concluded, and that nothing but contradictions had followed, made it all the more a matter for congratulation that the first vessel was actually there to start the regular service.

Melbourne did all that was possible in the short time of the steamer's stay to offer a welcome to the Captain and his ship's company. It might seem now rather an incongruous part of the city's hospitality that it included putting an armed guard on board to see that nobody went ashore without a permit from the time of arrival up to the actual sailing, but this is explained by the common difficulty of arriving ships that their crews promptly deserted to join the gold rush. It meant that often a ship lay at her anchorage for weeks and months seeking vainly for a crew; and it was to prevent any such interruption of the new mail service that the precaution of the armed guard was taken.

A subscription dinner or supper and dance was held, and all the civil, military, and naval officials with the leading citizens were present to offer congratulations and good wishes to Captain Down. A medal of Victorian gold was struck later and presented to the Captain.

Captain Down returned the City's hospitality when the Governor, with various officials and leading merchants, were entertained to a champagne lunch on board and shown over the ship.

There is an amusing climax, or rather anti-climax, to these enthusiastic welcomes offered to Captain Down in the shape of an advertisement in the *Argus* of 4th September, 1852. It read:

" The party may keep the Pilot Coat and Goloshes advertised for yesterday if he has a fancy for them provided he forwards to the owner the letters contained in the said coat to the Port Phillip Club Hotel. The letters bear the owner's name and address."

The owner of the lost coat proved to be Captain Down, but whether the coat was recovered or whether it had been stolen by a mere vulgar thief or had been " collected " by a keen souvenir hunter does not appear.

Having arrived on the Friday, the ship was ready for sea and cleared on the Sunday morning for Sydney. She had brought a dozen passengers from England and carried on ten to Sydney—including Lieutenant Pasco. An advertisement by " J. B. Were & Co., Agents," gives the fares to Sydney as £10 10s. First Class, and £6 6s.

S.S. "BRITANNIA," one of the Jubilee ships, 6,500 tons. Built 1887

Coaling at Aden

second, " With provisions and bedding " ; and the freight on gold dust $\frac{1}{2}$ per cent.

The " Chusan " arrived at Sydney on 3rd August, and dropped anchor at 10.30 p.m. off Moore's Wharf.

As in Melbourne, the Press reported the event as of the greatest importance to Australia, and the Chairman, at a banquet later on, declared that the two great features of Queen Victoria's reign were the discovery of Australia's seemingly boundless gold-fields, and the establishment of steam communication with Australia.

Various plans were discussed for honouring the event, but eventually the Melbourne one was followed of holding a subscription supper and ball. There was a good deal of heart-burning over this decision, various " Letters to the Editor " complaining bitterly that this was a snobbish arrangement, because it confined the privilege of attendance to those who could afford the 25s. for a ticket. " An Australian " besought the Editor, to " raise with me an earnest and indignant voice against aught less than a public holiday " ; " A Merchant Taylor " wanted a meeting called of merchants, traders, and shopkeepers to make plans for a regatta and regatta ball ; and another supported the latter proposal, adding that the regatta should be held on the day of the " Chusan's " sailing.

However, nothing came of the other suggestions, the ball was held at the Museum, the largest public room in the city, and was a tremendous success. The toast of " The Chusan " was drunk with acclamation to the strains of the " Chusan Waltz," specially composed and published for the occasion.

An advertisement by " Henry Moore, Agent, Moore's Wharf," gives the fares to Batavia as £45 and to Singapore as £50, and remarks that " this powerful steamer will not carry cargo " and so would avoid detention in intermediate ports for any cargo-working.

The *Sydney Morning Herald* of 1st September reported the departure of the " Chusan " the previous day, saying, " Upon almost every available point of the Harbour a group was yesterday afternoon assembled to witness the departure of this noble steamship which left her moorings at half past four o'clock, proceeded down the Harbour in fine style,

K   129

and as she rounded Fort Macquarie, dipped her colours to H.M.S. Acheron."

That note of her leaving her moorings, and other reports of anchoring " off " Moore's Wharf, marks a custom to which my attention has been called but for which no explanation has been forthcoming. Not only the " Chusan," but all other P. & O. liners for about thirty years after her, lay at anchor or moorings out in the stream, instead of coming right alongside the good deep-water wharves which were available.

Later, other Lines adopted the same practice, discharging and shipping cargo by punts or lighters, and advertising the hour on sailing day at which a tender would embark passengers at Circular Quay to be taken off to the liner.

Is it possible that this was a practice which grew out of early precautions against the desertion of seamen for the diggings, which was, in the gold-rush days, such a menace to regular sailings ; or that any of the large quantities of gold shipped was considered safer aboard a ship in the stream than within reach of thieves ashore ?

The first call of the " Chusan " at Adelaide was made on her way from Sydney and Melbourne on the 11th September, 1852. Great satisfaction was expressed there, because Captain Down had definitely settled what had previously been a doubtful point on whether a steamer could be brought safely in and anchored. Adelaide, however, was not continued as a calling port in the first contracts, and it was not until 1874 that South Australia secured what she claimed was a due recognition of her postal rights. For more than thirteen years she had to put up with the ocean liners passing without calling, both on the inward and outward trips, and although during this time the South Australians never ceased to urge on the authorities at home and in the Colonies the gross injustice done to them, they had to submit and make the best of a bad business by running their own Adelaide service between there and Albany to carry the mails. This branch service with King George's Sound was carried on from 1860 entirely at the cost of South Australia, and on it nearly £200,000 was expended.

It is worth mentioning that Messrs. Elder, Smith & Co., Limited, the present P. & O. Agents in Adelaide, will shortly be celebrating their

Centenary, the firm having been founded in 1839, three years after the proclamation of the State. This firm was first appointed agents of the Company when Adelaide became a port of call, and they have continued to act in that capacity ever since.

The route by West Australia to Singapore brought prominence, and a good deal of prosperity, to the little town of Albany, because their safe harbour of King George's Sound was made the coaling depot of the Company against all the angry protests of Perth and Fremantle, where public meetings and memorials to the Secretary of State to the Colonies made vain endeavour to remove this " slight " and " insult " to the capital city and its port. The blunt fact was that Albany offered a safe and sheltered harbour and Fremantle no more than an open roadstead, with every risk of westerly gales dragging a ship's anchors and driving her ashore.

The first arrival of the " Chusan " at Albany brought the usual round of a ball on shore, a reception on the steamer, and a trip round the harbour with the visitors. The mails for Perth had to be taken by packhorses or cart from Albany, taking 4 to 6 days to the journey. Albany continued to be the port of call for nearly fifty years. Fremantle built their breakwater and artificial harbour and officially opened it in 1897, but it was not until August 1900 that the mail steamers changed over to it from Albany. The first P. & O. liner to enter Fremantle was the " India," on 20th August, 1900.

A correspondent tells me that his maternal grandfather, Captain van Zuilecom, was the first P. & O. Agent in Albany. He was descendant of a Dutch family which first reached England in the Court of William of Orange.

In Melbourne the first P. & O. office was opened in 1853 by Mr. Dan A. Hughes, who had been some time in the accountants' office of the Company in London. He was followed out soon after by his father, Wm. John Hughes, who had been a banker in Dublin and an original shareholder of the Dublin Steam Packet Company. In Melbourne he obtained a grant of a river frontage later known as Hughes' or Spencer Street Wharf.

The " Chusan " was quickly followed out by the second screw

steamer to join the station, the "Formosa," of 675 tons and 80 h.p. (nominal, working up to 250). The latter arrived with mails from England at Albany on 23rd November, 1852, the "Chusan" arriving the same day from Singapore.

These vessels did not remain long on the run, but were soon replaced by others, larger and more powerful. In the list of the Company's fleet given in the Report of December 1852, the "Shanghai" (screw; 700 tons, 100 h.p.) displaces the "Formosa," which is shown on the Calcutta–China service. In the following year the Directors reported that, in consequence of a Memorial resulting from a public meeting at Melbourne asking for an improved service, the "Chusan" and "Shanghai" were being replaced by the "Bombay" and "Madras," of 1,200 tons and 180 h.p. each. The Fleet list of 1854 gives the "Madras" and the "Norna" (screw; 1,035 tons, 230 h.p.) on the Singapore–Australia service.

CHAPTER NINETEEN

The 1850's—A Difficult Decade

THE Company had to pass through some difficult and even critical phases in the decade of 1850–60, and they must have been some of the hardest and most trying years up to then encountered by Willcox and Anderson, then the Managing Directors with James Allan, who had been transferred from his Secretaryship to replace the third original Managing Director, Carleton, on his death in 1848.

There was first that minor but worrying " war " with the sailing-ship and opium interests in the Far East which had forced the withdrawal of the " Lady Mary Wood " from the Hong Kong–Shanghai service. We must try to visualise the increased difficulty of London management in such matters by remembering that there was no communication with agents at the other end of the world except by slow and infrequent letters. It took, for example, over a year for that particular incident to be cleared up.

No sooner was this settled than fresh troubles—and much greater ones—cropped up in a series of attacks on the P. & O., accusations of high-handed and greedy use of monopolistic powers, enormous and unjustified profits won at the expense of the country in the mail contracts. All this led to a Parliamentary Enquiry into the system of Mail Contracts in general and the P. & O. contracts in particular.

These repeated enquiries meant a consumption of time and energy in the provision of endless data, examination of accounts, furnishing of figures, facts, and statements required by the Government, presentation of books, correspondence, and vouchers, interviews and cross-examination of one or other of the Managing Directors by Government officials.

133

Keep it in mind that this was all personal business with which only the three Managing Directors could deal, and that every letter, every page of figures, had to be laboriously hand-written and copied.

It is enough to say here that the results of the Parliamentary Enquiry—or rather Enquiries, because there were two of them—resulted in a complete vindication of the P. & O. contracts, an admission by the Government that profits had been no more than moderate, and that the country had saved handsomely on the contracts.

Overlapping all this harassing performance was the need to give the deepest and most careful thought to the improvements that had in recent years been effected in steamer construction and propulsion. This was a matter that hit the Company in a tender spot—the pockets and dividends of the shareholders, or "Proprietors," who looked with a touching but somewhat trying faith to their Managing Directors to keep on earning the profits to which they were so well accustomed and which had meant a steady 6, 7, or 8 per cent. dividend per annum.

The Management was faced with the fact that their ships had dropped out of date. They had a whole fleet on their hands, which they knew only too well had to be replaced or brought up to date at a staggering cost. Wooden ships, it was evident, were less safe and less efficient than iron-built. The screw ship had also proved its superiority over the paddler for long voyages.

Somehow, or anyhow, the fleet had to be modernised and the running cost of ships so reduced as to justify the expensive replacement of the existing fleet. This decided, the further decision followed swiftly that old ships must be re-engined, converted to screw, or scrapped and replaced by new vessels.

This was in 1851–2, and while worrying over this problem, plus the Parliamentary Enquiry, the Company also had to deal with the protracted negotiations, refusals of proposals, renewed offers and considerations on the Australian mail contract. That contract secured, was followed by the comparatively easy routine matters of establishing the service, and planning the other details of the new contracts of 1852 for services of increased and extended sailings all over the East and to Australia—all, mark you, on eight-year contracts.

A first jar to the decision of the Management to replace their wooden paddlers with iron paddle and screw ships was the somewhat delayed but flat ultimatum of the Admiralty that they objected to the employment of iron steamships on the postal contract. This came well after the Company had placed firm orders for three large new iron steamers. The orders had to be compromised or delayed while the Company started slow negotiations to convert the Admiralty to modern ideas—apparently a much more tedious and prolonged performance than that to convert a steamer from paddles to screw.

On top of these internal troubles came another over which the Management had no control. The price of coal jumped, and a shortage of freighters so forced up rates that the cost of supplying Eastern stations went up 50 per cent. over the previous year's cost. This was in 1853, just a year after the Company had made their extended service contracts due to run for eight years ; and when every penny had to be economised in view of the urgent fleet reconstruction.

An approach was made to the Government pointing out these facts, and asking for some abatement of the obligations incurred as to the number of ships and sailings required, with a proportionate abatement of the contract payment. These requests met with a flat refusal, and the Company was left with the choice of failing their contract and suffering the penalties for so doing, or carrying on at a loss. They accepted the latter alternative, and set about all possible steps to economise and reduce costs while still fulfilling the strict letter of the contracts' law.

This was at a time when five new ships had been launched, and provision had to be made for their payment. The five included the famous " Himalaya," which was then not only by far the largest ship in the Company's service, but the largest and most powerful in the world. She was then the wonder of the shipping world, of 3,500 tons and 700 h.p., with screw propulsion.

She had been designed and built on the basis of the current cost of coal, and on the growing trade of the Company. By the time she came into service (1853) the price of coal had been increased by more than half, and passenger and specie carrying was falling out of sight through circumstances which were a result of world events that had nothing to do with ship construction or running and were literally "beyond control" or foreseeing. It was too quickly evident that the "Himalaya" would make losses instead of profits on each voyage.

The Crimean War came in 1854, and the urgent need to find freighter sailing ships for the Crimea pushed up to fantastic heights the cost of coal shipments to the Far East. This calamity to the Company (still bound by those eight-year mail contracts in the East and to Australia) was met to some extent by the energetic steps taken in London and by the agents in the East to open up new coal-fields which had been discovered in such places as Labuan and Formosa, and by the purchase of steam colliers to transport these supplies to the Eastern depots.

The Crimean War led to the rapidly growing demands of the Government for the requisition of P. & O. steamers as transports for which they were specially suitable. Although charter rates were paid for these, the payments fell far short of the sums the ships would have been earning from passengers and freight. Besides this, the mail contracts were only being carried through at a greater cost than the ships could earn.

More and more ships were taken over by the Government, until at last consent had to be given to a cutting down of the Eastern mail services and the complete suspension of the Australian. The Company was fortunate in being able to sell the "Himalaya" to the Government for £130,000—roughly her first building cost. The cash was useful at the time, but the Government made a very good bargain and buy, because the huge accommodation of the ship made her excellent for trooping, and she continued to serve faithfully and well nearly up to the end of the century.

The accumulated difficulties forced the Directors, for the first time in the history of the Company, to announce that they could not recommend a dividend, and no dividend was paid. At the same time the Directors, in a speech by Mr. Anderson, expressed the fullest faith in the future of the Company, declaring that, although some gloomy prophets were saying that the "Rising Sun" of the P. & O. was becoming a setting one, he did not agree, and he advised all owners of shares to hold on to them in anticipation of better times ahead.

That his faith was fully shared was quickly proved. In the following year (1855) the Company increased its capital by an issue of £1,000,000 in new shares. A first preference of purchase was given to the existing shareholders, and these immediately took up nearly 14,000 at £50 each, the balance being reserved for applications from Indian and overseas shareholders.

For the moment I pass over the particulars of the tremendous service rendered by the Company in the Crimean War, because this I propose to include in some separate notes on the early war services of the P. & O.

At the end of the war some of the older ships were sold as unfit for the mail contract needs, and one had been lost in a typhoon in the China seas before then. Four new ships, however, were built or building, and prospects began to look brighter.

Almost immediately, however, the Company was to suffer a setback of a kind new to them. The Admiralty wished to restore the suspended Australian mail, and advertised for tenders. The P. & O. expected a number of their ships to be released from the troop transport service, and had planned to sell off some of the older veterans of the fleet—including those early ships, the " Precursor," " Oriental," and " Hindostan." They were also re-boilering and converting to screw four other of their ships.

The Company, therefore, was in a strong position to tender for the Australian mail again, but were disappointed—to put it mildly—when the contract was given to a new company, the European and Australian Royal Mail Company. The terms required by the Admiralty for the contract were such as the P. & O. directorate simply would not undertake, their knowledge and experience of the Eastern trade having convinced them that the required undertaking of speeds with a sliding scale of killing penalties for failures in running to time, and much less remunerative premiums for mail delivery ahead of contract time, could not offer any prospect of making the service pay.

Willcox, Anderson, and Allan, who certainly knew as much of the trade as any men and who had their fingers on the pulse of finance and shipping generally, were very sure that the new company had secured the contract on terms they could not fulfil with a profit ; and, moreover, believed that the declared capital and ships available were far short of probable needs. They prophesied a short life and NOT a merry one for the European and Australian.

They were speedily proved to be right ; but this at the time did not soften the blow to the prestige of the P. & O. in a contract being given to a rival company. There were many dark and dismal prophecies in the City that the " monopoly " of the P. & O. in the East being at last broken, it was more than probable the " rising sun " had passed its meridian.

The facts that for the first time no dividend had been paid, that a large amount of new capital had been brought in, and that fares, which had only been lowered a few years before, had been lifted again to the old level, all naturally added to the dismal forebodings.

A final difficulty of this time was one which may seem hardly credible now to anyone who knows how firmly steam had established and was to continue its ascendancy. But in the later 'fifties that ascendancy and the proved superiority of steam over sail was suddenly challenged, and for a time quite seriously.

On the abolition of our Navigation Laws, which had prevented foreign ships bringing cargo to England, there was a sudden invasion of the magnificent American sailing clipper ships. In 1850, a whole fleet of these arrived in the London river with cargoes of tea from China, on which they had been paid freight at double the rates any British ship out there could obtain. These clippers had made the passage in a record time, which astounded our whole shipping world. Our owners and builders picked up the challenge, and for some years the rivalry and racing home with the first cargoes of the new season's teas attracted the attention of the whole world.

It was recognised that there were ocean stretches where light and baffling or adverse winds must so reduce the average time of a passage that steamers had the advantage. On the other hand, there were routes over which the clippers, hard or even recklessly driven night and day, could match and beat the steamer. Then and years later, when the steamers had been greatly improved and had higher engine power, it was not uncommon for a clipper ship to overtake and pass a steamer as if she were standing.

In those late 'fifties it seemed no more than plausible and reasonable that a compromise would be the most effective solution. Sail with favouring winds could beat steam : steam without such helping winds could beat sail. The conclusion was natural that, if the fast and powerful clippers, relying on huge spread of sails for their long runs, had small auxiliary engines to carry the ship through the Doldrums' calms or keep them going against head winds, such auxiliary steam would be best. These ships would have the great advantage, too, that for long voyages they would not have to sacrifice a very large proportion of their cargo space to make room for their engines and coal bunkers.

Old sail owners and companies and new companies began to build and run these auxiliary-steamships, and when that new Australian mail contract was advertised, it specially stipulated that service might be either of steamers or auxiliary-steam sail. Even in the ranks of the P. & O. Proprietors there were many who believed in the future of the auxiliary-steamships, and pressed their views on the Management. Some of the Directors were strongly inclined to support them.

The Managing Directors refused to be tempted from their path or their programme of fleet reconstruction. Their firm belief was that steam must win as no compromise could, and they pushed on with the building of new and more powerful steamers, re-engining and converting to screw the best of their others. Once more in the long run they were proved to be right, but for a time the issue seemed to hang in doubt, and the new auxiliary-steamships did well. It was one more difficulty to be faced and fought in that difficult decade.

The closing years of the decade saw the P. & O. troubles fading astern. Many fine large and higher-powered steamers had been put in commission, trade was recovering, the railway across Egypt—to the building of which the Company had given every moral and material support—had been steadily progressing and promised further to increase passenger and goods traffic by the greater and quicker facilities of the Overland Route, and to lower the cost of transporting supplies and coal to Suez.

The Management was entirely vindicated in their policy of refusal to accept the Australian mail contract under conditions and terms they were positive could not be made to pay. The European and Australian Royal Mail Company, formed in 1856, was practically insolvent within a year, although it struggled on for a little with the help of the Royal Mail (West Indies) Company, and an arrangement for the amalgamation of the two companies was almost completed when it was stopped by the Royal Mail shareholders.

The European and Australian went bankrupt, having lost the whole of their capital of £400,000, contracted debts and mortgages for nearly another £300,000, and with practically nothing to show for their expenditure except some depots in Australia, two or three ships mortgaged to the hilt, and others chartered with no cash to pay charter money. The unfortunate Company lost in all about three-quarters of a million sterling.

The mail contract was advertised again, and was secured this time by the P. & O., which had opened in 1858 a new line from Aden to Mauritius, and planned to make this a stage of the Australian run.

The new route, however, was not successful, and in 1859 the Company proposed to the Government to change the route to connect up with Ceylon, and this was duly adopted.

In 1859, the Company had a magnificent fleet of steamers, many of them new, and of over 2,000 tons and over 400 h.p. Out of a total of 55 liners on regular running, 38 were screw, as were two building—one, the " Mooltan," of 2,500 tons and 400 h.p.

The services were divided into sections in the fleet list that year. These sections were Southampton–Alexandria, Southampton–Peninsula, Marseilles–Alexandria, Malta–Corfu, Suez–Calcutta, Bombay–Suez, Bombay–China, Suez–Sydney, Hong Kong–Shanghai, Hong Kong–Manilla, and Suez–Mauritius–Isle of Réunion.

All this had been built up in little over twenty years from a few small paddle steamers with Gibraltar as their farthest port, and it can fairly be said almost entirely by the wisdom and efforts of the two men,

Willcox and Anderson. The two had steered the P. & O. through the stormy waters of the early years, of battle against political and commercial jealousies and intrigues, of technical shifts and changes in steamer construction and improvement; then, in the middle of their sure progress to final triumph and the certainty of an assured fortune for each of the two, they quietly and unostentatiously surrendered their fortunes, and formally made over to the Company the fruits and profits of their labours.

CHAPTER TWENTY

Two Fortunes Given Away

IN the middle and worst of that bad spell of the 1850's, Willcox and Anderson made an announcement at the General Meeting of the Proprietors which was described in the warmest terms by some of them as a piece of " munificent generosity," " unheard of," " unprecedented," and " really incredible."

It was all this, and to reduce it to plain words meant that the two voluntarily surrendered a very considerable fortune each, entirely for the benefit of the Company. To explain the full extent of their action, I must recall and amplify the terms under which the two and Carleton the other original Managing Director, made their agreement on the extension of the P. & O. in 1840.

Willcox and Anderson, almost entirely by personal effort and negotiation, obtained the mail contract for the extension of the service to India, the terms of the Royal Charter, and by bringing in the Trans-Atlantic Steamship Company (represented by Carleton) engineered the financial support and the only ships available and suitable for the proposed new service.

Willcox and Anderson, it must also be remembered, had been building up a shipping business for about twenty years before the first mail contract of the Peninsular Steam Navigation Company was formed, had earned and secured the backing of Messrs. Bourne of the Dublin Steam Packet Company, had first risked (and almost lost) their cash and their business in their founding of the Peninsular service, and then, with no more than three years of success behind them, risked everything again by throwing in all they had won to stake on the unknown possibilities of what the extended " Oriental " service to India might turn up.

It is true that the three Managing Directors, Willcox, Anderson, and Carleton, made conditions which proved highly profitable to them in the long run ; but it is no less true that the profits were earned, largely if not entirely, by the experience, energy, and ability of the three on behalf of the P. & O.

The terms were that the three were to receive $2\frac{1}{2}$ per cent. of the gross earnings of the Company, that out of this they should bear all the expense of management, including office rent, staff salaries, and everything else, and that the $2\frac{1}{2}$ per cent. also included all commissions on the carrying through of financial negotiations and agreements involving £1 million.

In addition to this, the three were to receive a further 5 per cent. on the net profits as available for division in dividends to shareholders.

Finally, the appointments and emoluments were to be for life, and the $2\frac{1}{2}$ and the 5 per cent. were to be divided between the three in proportion of one-third each ; and that as and when one or two died, their share should die with them—in other words, that when one died, his share did not pass to the survivors, but to the Company.

There are one or two other facts of importance in relation to the action of Willcox and Anderson in 1854. In the first years' working of the P. & O., they received from their Company under their agreement less than they had been receiving in income from their own Willcox & Anderson business ; in 1841 or 1842 they found their time so taken up by the P. & O. business that they reluctantly decided to close their own firm ; and it was not until after the extended mail contracts of 1845 to Straits and China that the Managing Directors began to catch up their losses in the Company's profits, because the expenses of management did not expand as did the increased earnings and profits of the Company. But even in 1848 an item of the accounts shows that the three only received £2,700 between them on their 5 per cent. commission.

Mr. Carleton died in 1848. Mr. Allan, Secretary, became Managing Director in his place, but did so on a basis of salary only.

In 1854, Willcox and Anderson announced their renunciation of the terms of their agreement, and voluntarily surrendered their emoluments under it. Willcox retired from the Managing Directorate, but expressed his willingness to take a seat on the Board or Court of Directors and continue to give all the help and advice he could to the Company.

Anderson wished to continue as a Managing Director, but gave up the $2\frac{1}{2}$ per cent. on gross earnings while retaining his 5 per cent. on net profits so long as he remained an active Managing Director—this offer being made at the time when no dividend was being paid, and therefore no 5 per cent. was payable to him.

In addition to this surrender, the two made another. In 1849, the Company had decided to cease payments of insurance on their ships to outside underwriters, and to found their own underwriting fund out of which to provide for losses or repairs due to accidents. Such a private or Company fund had not been included in the first terms of agreement with the Managing Directors, so that they were fully entitled to claim on whatever sums were set aside for this purpose as a part of the net divisible profits earned. In giving up their agreed commissions, the two said that they had never claimed on this insurance fund, and had no intention of ever doing so.

Even apart from this last item, the amounts given up by the two amounted to £8,000 a year in the case of Willcox and of over £3,000 a year in that of Anderson. Willcox continued to serve as a Director until the retirement of the Chairman, Sir James Matheson, M.P., in 1858, when Willcox was appointed Chairman. He continued in that voluntary capacity until his death in 1862, when Anderson succeeded him in the Chair, and occupied it until he in turn died in February 1868 in his seventy-seventh year.

Willcox therefore lived for eight years after the surrender of his emoluments, which by the time of his death would have increased considerably. It may fairly be estimated that in all the Company benefited to the extent of about £100,000 from his generosity.

Anderson gave up his $2\frac{1}{2}$ per cent. over a period of fourteen years, and again on a reasonable average this amounted to a total sacrifice of about £60,000. His 5 per cent. of net profit was at the time of his death bringing him in some £12,000 a year, but out of this he for many

S.S. " PENINSULAR," 5,294 tons.   Built 1888

144]

years had been handing over very large sums for the benefit of the Company and its servants, as well as to outside charities and foundations, especially in his native Shetlands.

On making their relinquishment, it was suggested to the Directors that some part of the benefits which the Company would attain should be devoted to forming the nucleus of a Provident and Good Service Fund on a contributory pension basis for the Company's staffs. The suggestion was later adopted, and the Fund, in recognition of the two benefactors, was named the Willcox and Anderson Provident and Good Service Fund.

Up to the time of Anderson's death, the Directors had from time to time applied some part of the commissions the two had relinquished to this Fund, and on his death it amounted to £50,000, although very considerable sums had been paid out of it in the interval.

After Anderson's death, the Directors announced that it was not proposed to continue payments to the Fund out of the earnings of the Company, beyond the interest to be obtained from the invested capital of the balance of £50,000 then in hand.

There are still two monuments to the memory of Anderson and his connection with the P. & O. in existence to-day. About 1859, a proposal was made that a part of the Willcox and Anderson Fund should be applied to the provision of schools for the children of officers and staff at Southampton. This was agreed, but it was found, on taking legal advice, that there might be some irregularity in applying any part of the Fund to such a purpose. Anderson was then in Egypt on a mission to the Pasha there, but on his return the difficulty was explained to him. He promptly took out a lease of a building site, had the school built at his own expense, and by deed of trust made it over to the Company. It first had accommodation for 700 children as well as a lecture room and other facilities for the use of young officers in port.

I recently had a letter from a retired steward of the P. & O. who had joined the Company as a lad in 1874. His father died in the Company's service in China, and the child received free education at the Southampton school, this being the rule in such case as the one-time pupil tells me, speaking of the " P. & O. School at Southampton." I

L

am told it is still known under that old name by some of the elders of that port.

The Norwood Technical Institute, London, has lately adopted a visible sign of its having been founded by Arthur Anderson. Hearing I was writing this history, the Principal of the Institute asked me if Anderson had had a coat or crest which included a design of a bent arm holding a battleaxe. He had found this badge in a carving on the staircase, and repeated both in stone over the door of the lodge, and in an ornamental iron screen of the garden.

Anderson never had any registered armorial bearings, and I could find no branch of the Anderson family that had any including this " embowed " arm and battleaxe. Thanks to Mr. Nicolson, the author of that book of Anderson's life, a solution was found in the fact that this emblem was, and still is, one generally regarded as the badge of the Norse vikings, and that it regularly figures in the decorations of a yearly celebration of the vikings in the Shetlands. Anderson, always proud of the Shetlanders' Norse ancestry, had adopted their badge.

The Institute (now under the London County Council) has now begun publication of a House Magazine, has given this the name of *The House Flag*, and displays on its cover the diagonally quartered white and blue over red and yellow of the P. & O. House Flag, with a circle inset bearing the " embowed arm and axe " of Anderson's badge.

A year after the generous yielding up of their payments, Willcox and Anderson were presented by the Proprietors and Directors with a set of silver plate each, suitably inscribed and valued then at £1,500 the set.

Anderson in his will bequeathed his set to the P. & O. Directors, and it is now housed at the Leadenhall Street office.

In 1868, with the death of Anderson, the last of the three original Managing Directors, the terms of remuneration by commissions on the Company's earnings came to an end. He was succeeded as Chairman by Patrick Douglas Hadow, who had previously acted with him as Deputy-Chairman.

146

CHAPTER TWENTY-ONE

Side-lines and Routes

IN recording the deaths of Willcox and Anderson I have gone a little ahead of the sequence of this History. Anderson continued in harness right up to the end, and apart from those problems of the "Difficult Decade" previously described, there were many others concerned with new or abandoned contracts and routes, and in arranging these the long experience and deep knowledge of Anderson were invaluable.

There were a number of what I may call "Side-lines," because they were off the main routes, and may now seem unimportant, especially where, as in quite a number of instances, they have fallen out of the recollection of the present generation, although I have found that memories of them can still be recalled by a few survivors of the old times, or have been preserved by descendants in notes and letters and "Private Logs."

I have mentioned that, when the Australian mail contract was secured again after it had been lost for a brief period to that unfortunate European and Australian Royal Mail Company, the P. & O. renewed it, running over a route between Suez and Australia *via* Mauritius. That route was only followed for a year or so, but the Mauritius line was continued for about eight years in all, from 1858 to 1866. It was carried on sometimes by two and sometimes by four medium-sized steamers, and for a time was extended to the French Isle of Réunion, under a small mail contract with their Government.

At least one notable passenger travelled by this line and left his recollections of it. Sir Walter Besant, in a little book *Bourbon Journal* —published, I believe, for private or family circulation and therefore not generally known—has written of a passage he made in the " Nepaul " in 1863 to Bourbon, as the Isle of Réunion was then called.

It is true he does not have anything very good to say of the " Nepaul " or the ship's company ; but because, reading both his lines and between them, I gather that he was not a very " good sailor " and suffered from the effects of a gallant if misguided endeavour to combine hearty meals and strong cigars with a weak stomach, we can hardly blame him for his rather unfavourable recollections. He tells, for example, how, " in spite of premonitary symptoms of antistatic action," he went down to dinner " to partake of the mutton," but only retained " a foggy impression " of the conversation.

He declared that the " Nepaul " rolled so atrociously that the only argument in favour of her recovering from each roll was that she had done so from the previous one. Actually, she had been rolling and recovering for some years, and continued to do so, bucketing round in some of the stormiest seas of the world for years after Sir Walter thought each roll was to be her last.

He tells how the surest way to rouse the ire of a P. & O. Commander was to suggest that there could be any ships or service at sea as good as the P. & O. ; and relates how a German baron, who dared to suggest at dinner that some good might be said of a rival foreign line, was very properly and thoroughly snubbed by the Captain for expressing such a heresy.

Besant made plaintive comment on the lack of table napkins—" A man of cleanly habits who has the misfortune to wear a beard is put to serious inconvenience with the soup, to say nothing of the gravy, when the ship rolls."

Judging from his portrait and his expanse of moustache, whiskers, and a beard as big as a breastplate and bushy as a privet hedge, he would have needed relays of bath towels rather than napkins.

By odd coincidence the only other personal notes I have read about these Mauritius ships also refer to the napkin question. The writer was talking to an Indian passenger, who told him, " I knew that you and the purser were gentlemen before I spoke to either of you, because you both use napkins at dinner."

148

The writer in this case was making the passage to Australia, and he mentions that, after two days' coaling at Mauritius, their ship (the " Benares ") sailed with every possible corner crammed with coal and with 250 tons on deck—a " necessary nuisance " because of the distance to King George's Sound. Heavy head winds prolonged the passage, and it took 15 days to get there.

Another forgotten side-line which had a career even more brief was one between Hong Kong and Manilla. It was begun in 1857 under a contract with the Spanish Government for a mail twice a month each way. This was a period, however, when the Customs, port, and other officials of Spain—especially those a long way from home—were left to make up arrears of pay as best they could locally ; " arrears " being a polite term for pay they might never see and hardly expected, and bribery and corruption being the known and recognised method of supplying the deficiency. The foreigner, of course, was natural and fair game to be exploited.

The service therefore came to an end in less than two years, on finding that the line " was not susceptible of development " owing to " local restrictions " on non-Spanish vessels.

Amongst the earliest of the side-line services run by the P. & O. were the branch or feeder lines to Greece and Constantinople, and the running of these produced some striking evidence of the great value to the development of trade resulting from steam communication. The evidence was given in 1848 at one of those early official enquiries into the system of mail contracts.

When the mercantile community at Constantinople wanted the P. & O. to run a service to there, it was doubtful whether there was trade enough to justify the branch. A trial was made, however, and after six to seven years the figures of export and import trade for the year before the service began and figures for the last year available were compared. It was found that our imports had risen by £1,200,000 and exports by about £1 million.

Merchants who were asked for any explanation of this rise attributed it to nothing but the improvement in communication, the time of this having been cut down for the mails from 24 days to 13, and by an almost unknown time by steamers instead of sailing ships carrying cargo. The merchants said that steam allowed them to turn over their money many times more a year, gave them a certainty of time their goods would be on the market, and equal certainty of receiving goods out. Forty new firms of Levant merchants had opened in England in the six years.

This service to the Levant continued to run up to the time of the Crimean War, when it had to be dropped owing to the heavy requisition of ships for transport and war services.

This Constantinople service and at times others to Italian ports were run in conjunction with the " Peninsular Service " as it came to be called after the main and fast through run was established between Southampton, Gibraltar, Malta, and Egypt. The P. & O. services to Italian ports earned no mail subsidy at first, and in 1848 were discontinued owing to political disturbances and quarantine difficulties. Later on, in conjunction with the P. & O. Brindisi–Alexandria line, the service was extended up to Venice and Ancona on payments made by Italy.

The Brindisi route was opened when the Franco-Prussian War of 1870–1 interrupted the mail route through Paris to Marseilles. The improvement of the Italian railway route, and especially the opening of the Mont Cenis tunnel, expedited the Brindisi service to and from Egypt and beyond, so this became the permanent mail route for many years.

This, however, did not abolish the use of Marseilles as a port of the P. & O. or the agency which had been established there in 1852 when the new mail contracts were made for a service between Marseilles and Malta to connect with the Gibraltar–Egypt service, as well as those others to Australia and the Far East.

The firm of Messrs. Estrine & Co., Marseilles, are proud of the fact that they have held the agency continuously from that day until now, and are therefore amongst the oldest associates and representatives of the P. & O. Indeed, the firm can claim connection with the transmission of the Indian mails farther back than their appointment as P. & O. agents in 1852, and they also must be about marking their centenary in that work.

Estrine & Co. were first founded in 1815, and up to the 1850's were running under the title of Robert Gower & Co. The founder was a Welshman born near Cardigan in 1791, who took in as a junior partner a Mr. Albert Estrine, and on Gower's death the title of the firm was changed to its present one.

In the Estrine office there is a " museum " or collection of old prints and paintings of ships, documents and records, models and relics of the P. & O. which is certainly the most extensive and complete known to the Company. The firm still have the brass plate of their then new name—" Estrine & Co.—Late Robert Gower & Co."

When Mr. Waghorn began to run his mail services by the Continental routes, Robert Gower & Co. were his agents at Marseilles, and forwarded by express the mails handed in to them and marked " Care Mr. Waghorn." In those early days, the mail from London to Marseilles took over a week to the journey ; now the regular weekly " P. & O. Overland Express " leaves London about 2 p.m. on the Thursday and runs its passengers alongside the P. & O. liner waiting at the quay about noon next day.

In the Estrine collection is one of the first sailing lists from Marseilles under the new contract dated 7th January, 1853, and advertising the sailing of " Le pacquebot ' Euxine ' for Malta and Alexandria." The notice is headed :

Peninsular & Oriental Steam Navigation Company

Ligne du Levant et des Indes Orientales
Service des Dépêches
Transport de Voyageurs et de Marchandises entre

and it ends " *Pour Fret et Passages s'adresser à*

Robert Gower & Co.,
Rue Troisième-Calade,
Marseilles."

Another agency in which one family has carried on from the very earliest days of the Peninsular Steam Navigation Company is that of

Messrs. Smith, Imossi & Co., at Gibraltar. Mr. William James Smith was an agent of the City of Dublin Steam Packet Company in London, and when the Peninsular Company was formed, he was sent out to represent the Company at Gibraltar, which was then the terminal port of the mail. The son, the grandson, and now the great-grandson of that Mr. Smith have maintained the family connection ever since.

Trade with the Peninsular ports had been diminishing steadily for some years, until in 1862 there were only two steamers on it running to Lisbon, and the Post Office terminated the mail contract to there. The abandonment of the Peninsular Line or service was announced at the same General Meeting, in November 1862, as heard the announcement of the death of one of its original founders, Mr. Willcox.

CHAPTER TWENTY-TWO

Suez Railway and Canal

WHILE all the little side-lines were expanding and contracting, steady progress was being maintained in the improving and speeding up of the main routes. One of the most important of these was still the Overland Route.

The building of the railway was of the greatest service to the P. & O., and they did everything they could with moral and material encouragement to the Pasha of Egypt to forward the project, including loans and financial backing to an extent of about a quarter of a million sterling. The loans by the Company, I may add here, were all duly repaid, some of them at a period when the money was most useful to the Company.

Waghorn comes again into the story of the railway. He stated years later that in 1832 he submitted to the Pasha the advantages it would bring to Egypt if a railway were built across the desert from Suez to Cairo. He had been led to this idea, because he had found the desert so level.

In 1834, the Pasha had given the plan sufficient favour to instruct Galloway Bey to make a survey of the desert route and estimate of cost of a railway. The results were so satisfactory that Galloway was sent to England to purchase necessary materials and prepare his plans. Here, however, foreign politics intervened, and the jealousies and fears of different European Powers, that the railway might advantage one more than another, led to every effort and means being used to dissuade the Pasha from the project. These objections and further complications in Turkey were capped by the sudden death of Galloway, and the whole plan was shelved for years.

In 1851, the Pasha began serious preparations to start the work, but making the first section of it, not across the desert, but from Alexandria to the Nile. This part was completed in 1853 to the great satisfaction of the P. & O., because it did away with what they regarded as the most troublesome section of the whole Route, the landing of passengers and baggage at Alexandria, conveying them a mile or two to the Mahmoudieh Canal, shipping them in barges under tow, then transhipping again to the Nile steamers.

In 1855, the railway had progressed through to Cairo, and the next stage was begun across the desert. At the same time the electric telegraph was started across Egypt to replace the old system of semaphore type " telegraph " in use up to then. The work was completed at the end of 1858.

The railway, of course, belonged to the Pasha or to Egypt, and all transit fares over the route were charged by the P. & O. in passage money, but were paid over in full to the Egyptian Government. The charge was at first £15, then £12, and later £10, and to the many complaints made to the P. & O. of the charge being too high, it had to be explained for years after that the P. & O. had no share or part of the fare. After the Canal was opened, the rail fare across was dropped to £3 first-class.

The rolling stock when new met with warm approval from passengers. I have a letter by one who went out just as the railway was completing, and he declares the second-class carriages were equal to first-class in England, and the firsts " were the finest carriages I have ever been in." The speed, however, was only about 10 miles per hour.

The same passenger—he was one of the shore staff of the P. & O. on various Eastern stations for years—had a very different tale to tell about the railway only five years later, when he was home on a leave. " The carriages," he wrote, " which must first have been handsome first-class carriages, are filthy dirty and full of dust, their brasswork has never been touched since they came out, and all the baggage nettings are broken. Everything is slovenly, and you see a lack of energy in everything and everybody. It is a pity we cannot get the management of the railway into our own hands."

But if the P. & O. could regard with satisfaction the building of the railway, they might have been seriously alarmed if they could have appreciated the menace to their prosperity or even their existence in the growing plans for the cutting of the Suez Canal. But because there had been plans and proposals for a canal seriously considered from the time of Napoleon and all had come to nothing, it is not surprising that the P. & O. were not unduly worried by the first efforts of de Lesseps to form a Canal Company.

De Lesseps was first led to turn his attention to the canal project by the sheerest chance. In 1831, he was on his way to take up a Consular appointment in Egypt, and on arrival at Alexandria had to undergo a period of quarantine. To tide over his impatience and the tedium of his imprisonment, he was given a number of books to read, and these included the reports of a previous Egyptian Commission and the Memoirs of the engineer Lepère dealing with the possibilities of a junction between the Mediterranean and the Red Sea, and relating the story of the ancient canals and of various attempts in modern times to make a new one. Napoleon's had been the latest, but he had abandoned all hopes of a connection between the two seas on the report of his surveying engineers that there was over 30 feet of difference between the levels of the Mediterranean and Red Seas. The prospect of having to construct and maintain a system of huge locks was too much even for Napoleon, who had done so much in France to extend and improve her canal systems.

That mistake of Napoleon's engineers shelved the whole plan for a canal for years, until in de Lesseps' time a more accurate survey established the fact that the two seas were at the same level.

The old report which de Lesseps read while in quarantine so fascinated and impressed him that from then onward he kept in mind the possibility of reopening the waterway which he had been astonished to read had existed from hundreds to thousands of years before.

The earliest historical records of a " Suez Canal " had even at that time been discovered, although little interest was taken in this, except amongst a small circle of Egyptologists.

In the ruined temple of Der-el-Bahri, near Karnak, on the Nile, are certain carvings which date from XVIII Dynasty of Egypt of about 1500 B.C., and these show pictures and tell in hieroglyphics the story of a voyage of five ships from the Nile to the " Land of Punt," which was plainly shown to be some place well south in the Red Sea.

The pictures make it plain that the same ships made the whole voyage, and this in itself is evidence of a canal existing then, because there was no natural connection between Nile and Red Sea. Another picture confirms this in detail. The inscriptions record the return of King Seti I to Egypt from a campaign in Syria, about 1300 B.C., and the picture is of him approaching a fortified bridge over what is named " The Cut," and depicts an obviously artificial waterway with banks running in ruler-straight parallel lines and with the wavy lines and drawings of fishes picturing the water in the usual fashion of the Egyptian artists.

Other historians, from Herodotus down, recorded closings and reopenings of the canal, and a monument found between the Bitter Lakes and Timsah has an inscription by Darius—". . . in addition to Persia I conquered Egypt. I had this canal cut from the Nile to the sea which comes from Persia " (the Red Sea). Herodotus, who was in Egypt soon after the time of Darius, says the canal was wide enough to allow two ships to pass, and that it took several days to sail through it.

In the remote times the passage could be made, not only from the Nile to the Red Sea, but by natural and artificial waterways from the Mediterranean to the Red Sea. De Lesseps found the tale of this in the reports he was studying, and his own work later was to do much to confirm the route of at least one section of the waterway.

In the far-back period of say 4,000 years ago, the main stream of the Nile ran out near the present position of Port Said in a wide and slow-flowing river. Ships could sail and row up and down the river from the sea to about where Cairo now stands. From there a natural depression ran eastward to Lake Timsah, and this was artificially deepened into a canal connecting with the Nile.

From Timsah an artificial canal was dug across the desert over, roughly, the line of the present canal to about the position of Suez, although probably the waters of the Red Sea ran a good deal farther inland than now. The canals Nile–Timsah and Timsah–Red Sea may only have been navigable during the months of high Nile, but navigable they certainly were.

That ancient mouth of the river was slowly silted up by the mud brought down yearly by the floods and the sand thrown up by the sea throughout the centuries ; the waters spread and shallowed and found their way to the sea by the many mouths of the widening delta. The navigable stream became a miles-wide mud puddle during the time of low Nile, and a shallow sand-and-mud barred lake in high Nile— the Lake Timsaleh of to-day along the edge of which de Lesseps cut his first and easiest section of the Maritime Canal.

At the other, Red Sea, end, the wind-blown sands of the desert filled in " The Cut " much faster, filled it in and obliterated it, to be dug out and filled in at least three or four times in the centuries of recorded history.

De Lesseps pored and pondered over the old report with its mixture of history and pre-history, hieroglyphics and pictures of the monu- ments, theories and deductions of the Egyptologists, together with the cold figures and facts of the engineers' and surveyors' reports and estimates of sea and land levels, navigable depths, and possibilities of excavation labour and costs.

Out of all his reading and thinking, de Lesseps came to his con- clusion that there certainly had in ancient times been a waterway between the Mediterranean and the Red Sea ; and that what those primitive ancients had done, modern engineers could surely do again.

Over the succeeding years, while he continued his routine consular work, he never lost sight of his growing ambition to prove a canal feasible, and to find the means of making it. He took every opportunity to pursue his investigations and to seek out and plan the best route.

It was not until 1854 that he had his plans sufficiently in shape to put them before Said Pasha, but from him received the warmest encouragement and promises of all the help that could be given from Egyptian resources. With this support, de Lesseps went to Paris to enlist the backing of the French Government and to find the finance required.

From first to last the whole project was objected to by our Government and diplomatists, who used every public and private means at their command to squash the whole thing. It was feared that the cutting of a canal would jeopardise our maritime supremacy, and that if the Canal were in French hands (as it was planned to be), this would open to France a route to India which might be denied us in any war.

In 1858, de Lesseps opened the subscription lists for a Canal Company with a capital of 200 million francs. About half the amount was subscribed in France, about a quarter in the Ottoman Empire, and the balance in Egypt. The last were some of the shares which in later years were bought by Disraeli for the British Government in his famous and highly profitable deal.

Work on the Canal began in 1859, but it proceeded so slowly and against such difficulties of finance and labour that several times it looked as if the whole thing must collapse. The original capital was almost exhausted before anything more had been accomplished than the digging of a mere scratch over various sections, and the cutting of a fresh-water canal from the Nile to Lake Timsah—the " Lake " then being a dry sandy depression. In cutting this canal from the Nile, however, de Lesseps had overcome one major difficulty of supplying water to the labourers along the line of the projected canal, and he did so by re-digging that prehistoric canal by which the Pharaohs had sent their ships from the Nile to the Red Sea.

At a time when nearly half the original capital of the Company had been expended, a writer in a contemporary journal had some reasoned criticisms to offer from the description given him by an eye-witness of the work. He said that the Company was engaged in the cutting both of a Maritime Canal and of the sweet-water canal to bring drinking water from the Nile : between Lake Timsah and Suez, he said, nothing whatever had been done. At El Gizar a small portion of the Maritime Canal had been dug out to its full width and depth, but this being very slow work, a ditch had been made from El Kantara to Port Said, a distance of about 35 miles. This shallow ditch ran through Lake

Menzaleh, and the swampy ground there was dug out by the natives with their bare hands, the mud and sand just being scooped up and thrown out to the side. The ditch throughout was nowhere more than 22 feet wide and 4 feet deep, and it was pointed out that it could not be of any lasting nature. The writer sums up : " If more than two-fifths of the capital of the Company is expended in making a ditch 22 feet wide by 4 feet deep, over less than half the total distance, where will the capital come from to make a canal 182 feet wide by 26 feet deep, the whole distance from Port Said to Suez ? "

In 1862, a little channel was completed to carry the Nile water from Timsah to the Mediterranean, and in the next year another branch was completed, bringing the fresh water to Suez.

Said Pasha, who had been a warm friend to de Lesseps and had given him every support and many valuable grants of land and other concessions, died in 1863, and was succeeded by Ismail Pasha as Viceroy of Egypt under the rule of the Sultan of Turkey.

Said Pasha had promised all the native labour required under the old system of forced or slave labour, but this was withdrawn by Ismail Pasha, and new terms imposed with the approval of the Sultan, these terms reducing the number of labourers to be supplied, fixing rates of payment to them, and the handing back of land concessions granted by Said Pasha. The Sultan further declared that unless the new terms were accepted, work on the Canal would be stopped by force.

France rose to the urgent need, and further finance was found for the Company and help given in other ways. It is outside the scope of this P. & O. history to go into the full details of all the difficulties that were met and by one means and another overcome, but the repeated setbacks to the work, the bitter opposition of the British Government, the continual stream of hostile criticism poured out by the British Press, and the strong views of leading engineers that the whole plan was impossible and doomed to failure must have had a cumulative effect on the view of the P. & O. Directorate. Nevertheless, Arthur Anderson, in the last years of his life, was drawing up plans for ships that might use the Canal if it did at last succeed.

It is possible that the withdrawal of the forced native labour saved the project from failure by forcing the engineers to adopt mechanical devices and modern methods. The work up to then had been done almost entirely by primitive hand labour, the filling of little baskets by spade and hand-carrying these up the banks to empty them. The Mahmoudieh Canal, 50 miles long, had been successfully dug by exactly the same methods, and it seemed sufficiently reasonable that the 100 miles between Port Said and Suez could be dug in similar fashion.

By all sorts of shifts and stratagems of finance, by the use of dredgers and mechanical appliances and by the financial backing of the French Government, the work was at last completed in 1869, at a cost of nearly 433 million francs, more than double the amount originally estimated and provided by the first sale of shares.

The formal opening took place in November 1869, the P. & O. liner " Delta " carrying the official guests from Marseilles for the opening ceremony. On the 17th, 68 vessels of all nationalities made a procession, headed by the French " Aigle," with the Empress Eugènie on board, and reached Lake Timsah that night, went on next day to the Bitter Lakes, and on the 19th arrived at Suez.

On the evidence of a statement by Baron de Lesseps himself at a banquet in Paris celebrating the completion of the work, he said Lieutenant Waghorn had been one of the first to propose the Canal. In a reference to Lieutenant Waghorn, de Lesseps said, " He it was who first conceived the idea ; it was his indomitable courage and great perseverance, which led him on to prove its practicability . . . but he was in advance of his age, and the very plans that were scoffed at when first mooted were those which, in my position as the engineer of the works, have enabled me to carry them through."

Up to the actual day of the opening there were still many who prophesied that the Canal could not succeed, that it would silt up and cost more to keep dredged than revenue would provide, that ships must continually be going aground, and that the proposed scale of Canal dues would be prohibitive to regular and profitable trading.

In the first two years it certainly appeared that the main one of these objections must bring utter failure. In 1870, over 500 vessels passed through the Canal, but in that and the next year the working expenses

S.S. "CALEDONIA," 7,558 tons.   Built 1894

were more than the receipts could cover. In 1871, the Canal Company tried to raise a loan of 20 million francs, but completely failed to do so.

The Company had sold " the shirt off its back " in the way of disposing of land grants and other concessions, rights, and privileges it had first obtained from Said Pasha, and had spent the lot in getting the Canal through ; but if it could not keep the Canal open and had to allow it even for a year or two to be closed, there was little likelihood of other investors coming forward to reopen what had been proved a financial failure.

The Canal Company was faced with bankruptcy ; and it was only saved at the last moment by a sudden spurt in the traffic and the largely and rapidly increased revenue from dues charged on the ships passing through. By far the greatest number of those ships were British.

By 1872 the Canal was proved a final and assured success—a success, however, that threatened disaster and even ruin to the P. & O.

CHAPTER TWENTY-THREE

Canal and P. & O. Crisis

THE opening of the Canal and its proved success after a year or two brought crisis after crisis on the P. & O.

The value of all their costly establishments and organisation in Egypt was practically wiped out at a stroke. The huge fleets of ships suitable for European waters at one end and for the tropics beyond Suez had to be replaced by ships fitted for the through traffic. The competition of ships running through the Canal without having to bear any of the heavy " overheads " and onerous conditions of the mail service brought the P. & O. revenue down by a quarter of a million sterling a year to begin with and by nearly half a million by 1876. Finally, the Post Office insisted on the terms of their contract being observed, by which mails had to be sent overland and not carried through the Canal.

Glance first at the vast amount of capital the P. & O. had put into the development of the Overland Route up to the time the Canal was opened at the end of 1869. They had built and sent out their special barges and tugs for the Mahmoudieh Canal, and large and luxurious steamers for the Nile. They had laid out large sums in the improvement of the desert crossing, the building and extending of the resthouses and establishment of commodious hotels.

In addition, they had spent and lent heavily on the development of the railway and on facilitating the connections between it and the ships at both ends. They had built, staffed, and managed new lighthouses in the Red Sea—later taken over by the Egyptian Government, but used advantageously after the Canal opened by rival lines of steamers.

At Alexandria, the P. & O. had offices, warehouses, wharves, coal, and cargo storehouses, and a fleet of coal hulks, lighters, and tenders. Near Cairo they had a large farm for the production of poultry and eggs, vegetables and fruit for the steamers at Suez and Alexandria. At Zagazig was another farm for the same purpose ; and an extensive sheep farm had also been stocked and developed for years for the supply of better meat than could be procured from native-bred animals.

At Cairo there were offices and a large hotel provided specially for the use and convenience of P. & O. passengers after it was found that sufficient accommodation was not available for them in the winter season when visitors from England monopolised the other hotels.

The Company's establishment at Suez had grown to vast dimensions. For many years the only decently drinkable water had been supplied by their condensing plant, until the Canal Company's supply of water from the Nile was available, and because this was of very doubtful purity—to say nothing of taste—the condensers continued to be the main provider of drinking water and ice. A costly ice-making plant was in constant use. Stores had been laboriously built up and supplied with every possible need for repairs and maintenance of the steamers. Everything, literally, " from a needle to an anchor " was stocked in those stores. Finally, there were large workshops completely fitted up for the execution of repairs—most or all of the machinery for which had been transported piece by piece, carried, or dragged across the desert by camels. The Suez establishment also had coal stores and lighters and tenders to carry between ship and shore.

On the opening of the Canal, the capital invested in such establishments was a virtual " write-off," and instead of being capital " invested," virtually became capital " sunk."

This was bad enough, but there was worse in the need for the renewal of the Company's great fleet of liners. The temptation was to " renovate " or " reconstruct " them as cheaply as possible to make them suitable for the through service, but this easier way was rejected for the more expensive and boldly courageous plan of wholesale building of new ships. There was wisdom in this, as was soon proved. The Canal route quickly came to be used by a flood of new steamers built by owners for this particular trade in which they had not entered up to then.

163

For the P. & O. to have tried to compete against these with old and patched-up ships would have been disastrous, and as fast as their new liners were put on the run, passengers expressed their marked preference for them, and would wait weeks to get berths in one.

The development and proved economy of the compound engine at this time was another important and costly factor in the crisis. Even in ships running on branch services and not for some time wanted on the through run, it was evident that the new engines would pay in the long run; but this again meant the immediate and heavy expense of re-engining.

With all this loss and all the immediate expenditure to meet, the Company found its earnings falling in the most alarming or even disastrous fashion. For some time after the Canal opened the P. & O. income fell year by year at a rate of some £100,000 a year while actually carrying increased traffic and increased cost of it. A statement made to the Proprietors at the Annual Meeting in 1873 explains this seeming paradox.

In 1866, the Company carried specie—partly gold, partly silver—worth nearly £11 million, and by so doing earned about £230,000 in freight; but in 1872 carried nearly double the amount of specie and received for it only £60,000, or about a quarter the sum received for half the amount. In the year before the Canal opened, the carriage of 46,000 bales of silk brought in £110,000; but in 1871 an increased carriage of 50,000 bales only earned £44,000, instead of the £119,000 which would have been received at the old rate.

Added to these tremendous but unavoidable difficulties came a " last unkindest cut " from the Post Office, in their refusal to allow the Company to carry the mails through the Canal and their insistence on the letter of the law and the existing contract that the mails must go across by the Overland Route—unless the Company would accept a reduction of £30,000 a year on the terms of the contract, which still had a number of years to run.

The position under the contract was that what were known as the " heavy " mails—newspapers and similar packets—were shipped at Southampton and taken by the mail steamers right round to Alexandria, sent across by rail, and put aboard the other steamer at Suez. The express or letter mail went across Europe to Brindisi, by fast steamer on to Alexandria, and by rail to the steamer waiting at Suez.

The P. & O. did not propose to interfere with this express Brindisi mail, but asked that they should be allowed to carry the heavy mail from Southampton through the Canal. The Post Office raised all sorts of objections, some perhaps reasonable in the first year or two of the Canal's working and before it could be accepted that the Canal transit was safe and reliable. But even in 1873, when a regular stream of ships was passing steadily through without accident or delay, the Post Office still objected that a ship might ground and block the Canal, or for some other cause she and the mails might be delayed. Besides this, it was pointed out, the crossing by railway was faster than it was then by Canal.

The P. & O. offered to meet this last objection by speeding up the services to and beyond Egypt, so that delivery at all the terminal ports would be expedited by 24 to 48 hours. After interminable correspondence and discussions, the Post Office showed their hand more plainly by offering to agree to the mails going through the Canal if the Company would accept a reduction of the mail contract payments by £30,000 a year.

The Company, struggling against their almost overwhelming difficulties, dared not face this further cut in income, so the long-drawn haggling continued. It was now clear, however, that the Post Office was less concerned with the objections to mail carrying through the Canal than with the opportunity they had to force a reduction of terms on the Company.

There was the greater injustice in this, because some of the severest competition the P. & O. was then suffering was from the heavy postal subventions of other countries to their national shipping companies and the consequent ability of those companies to undercut ours in passenger fares and freights. The subsidised French, Italian, and Austrian Companies were all allowed under their contracts to carry their mails through the Canal, and it was naturally an attraction which drew passengers to those lines and away from the P. & O. that they with their baggage could go through without transhipment.

The P. & O. was then receiving an average of 4s. 2d. per mile over the routes, against which the French company of the Impériales Messageries, for example, was receiving over 20s. a mile. The P. & O. estimated then that their contract covered a fifth to a sixth of the cost of their ships' running; so that the French company was receiving a subsidy which bore practically the entire cost of running.

The Impériales enjoyed other advantages. Their Government had advanced a large proportion of the cost of building their ships, had undertaken to buy the ships if for any reason the service ceased; and, finally, had made the mail contract for a period of twenty years.

The insistence of the Post Office on the mails going overland was at last reduced to farce by the P. & O. dropping the mails at Alexandria, steaming through the Canal, and then picking up the same mails at the other end. This continued until 1874, when a revised contract allowed the mails to be carried through—but only on the Company accepting an ill-afforded reduction on the contract of £20,000 a year.

It was not only in Egypt that the Company suffered a heavy loss in property values and an urgent need to cut that loss. Very large sums had been sunk in the establishment over the East of docks and repair works, these being a necessity to avoid the heavy expense of bringing ships home round the Cape for alteration and repair of vessels, improvement or replacement of engines.

The maintenance of coal depots and supplies had always been another heavy charge on the Company. An average of 170 sailing ships, manned by about 3,500 officers and men, was employed year in year out carrying coal to the Eastern depots. In addition to such ships engaged on charter, the Company had two of their own—the " Haddington " (1,460 tons) and " Indus " (1,319 tons)—which they had converted from steam to sail and used mainly for carrying out machinery and stores.

With the Canal available, ships could be sent home for overhaul or repair and out again much more cheaply. Other Companies entering the Eastern trade were in the same position, so that the bottom fell out of the value of the Eastern establishments, works, and machinery.

Another drastic change and loss forced on the Company by the new

Canal route was in the need to transfer their terminal port from South-ampton to London.

A large proportion of the cargoes carried were for London shippers, and when these found that other rival lines offered to load and discharge in London, they raised objections to the cost of rail carriage between London and Southampton, plus the damage and risk of damage to shipments in such carriage. The Company was told plainly by a large number of their regular shippers that they must be allowed to ship to and from London, or must transfer their trade. This applied to much, or even most, of the freight trade.

Another reason for the shift to London was that on the very much lower rates then (1873–4) being received for freight, the Company could not afford to pay the heavy dock and railway charges incurred at Southampton.

During the thirty-odd years the Company had been using South-ampton as their terminal port, a large and solidly established connection had grown up there with offices and wharves and warehouses, to say nothing of a complete colony of the Company's shore and sea staffs' families and homes and their " P. & O. School." It could not have been easy to wrench all this deep-grown system out by the roots and transplant it to London ; but the drastic ill required the drastic remedy, and the decision was taken.

The Post Office contract still required that the mails should be shipped and discharged at Southampton, and this necessitated a skeleton staff and establishment being continued there. Passengers anxious to save a day also preferred to use that port, so that the system adopted was for the liners to call at Southampton on the way to and from London, and to make London the terminal port for those passengers and shippers of goods who preferred to use it.

This continued until 1880–81, but when Southampton ceased to be the mail port after the Government made the Brindisi route the exclusive one for mails, the Company decided to drop Southampton as a port and by making Plymouth a calling port to allow passengers who wished to save the time of the Channel passage to do so.

This matter of the terminal port was only one of the minor difficulties following the opening of the Canal. After looking over the tale of that great and almost crashing crisis of those years, considering the good points with the bad, the complete upheaval of the former routine methods of working, and the swiftly piled-up trials and troubles, after reading the inside story of those years, I can only regard it as little short of a miracle of business management that the Company fought through all their desperate battles and at the end emerged with enhanced prestige and power, and with a fleet which again led the van in numbers and in quality. The P. & O. could continue to boast itself the greatest shipping company in the world, its fleet the largest and best afloat.

It is an old saying that "the need finds the man," and this was certainly borne out in the case of this emergency in the Company's affairs after the Canal opening. The two men who had so long steered the ship through storm and trial were gone, Mr. Anderson only a year or two before. Mr. James Allan, the third of those " three wise men " who had served the Company since its start, under the strain of those trying years at his advanced age, retired from the Managing Directorate early in 1872.

His place as Managing Director was taken by Mr. (later Sir) Thomas Sutherland. It was soon to be shown that again the need had found the man.

CHAPTER TWENTY-FOUR

The Need and the Man—Thomas Sutherland

Sir Thomas Sutherland, G.C.M.G., LL.D., M.P., Chairman of the P. & O., and Director of the Suez Canal Company as he eventually became, began his business life in 1852 at the age of 18 in the London office of the P. & O. " at the smallest salary given in the office," as he himself put it years after.

Two years later he was outward bound for India and China; within twenty he was back in the London office as a Managing Director, with long years of leadership and accumulating triumphs ahead of him.

I have not found any full-length biography of Sir Thomas Sutherland, and if none has been written, I can only say I am surprised, because from the generally known broad outline of his career, I cannot imagine more attractive material for a book of any man's life.

But striking and dramatic as were many of the points of his business career, I have found here and there oddments and incidents in his life even more colourful and stirring. For some thirty years of his later life, the Press duly outlined the main features of Sutherland's business life and progress as he made it—when he became Chairman of the P. & O., when he received his title, when his negotiations with Lord Inchcape resulted in the merging of the P. & O. and the British India Companies into the biggest shipping interests afloat; and, naturally, most fully of all when his obituaries had to be written.

But in all those reviews of his life I have found no mention of what to me were two main turning-points in his career, two opportunities which may have appeared to be trivial, but which I believe were so seized and turned to advantage as to make just all the difference.

The first of those turning-points was when the young and unknown Sutherland, aged 20, was sent out to the P. & O. office at Bombay. Bombay was then by far the largest and most important station of the Company in the East, with offices, docks, repair shops and works, and a commensurate staff or staffs.

Sutherland was sent out to join this large staff, but he had barely arrived at Bombay when he received orders which sent him on at once to China. The reason for these orders he was only to learn many years later. It happened that Mr. Bayley, one of the Managing Directors, was going down to Southampton by train, and in his carriage met a young man proceeding to Southampton on his way to join his ship for China in the Company's service. The two got into conversation on the day's journey it then was, and Mr. Bayley was apparently well impressed with the young man's personality, or wished to be friendly to him. He asked whether the lad would not rather be stationed in the bustling business and social centre of Bombay instead of in the unhealthy climate and quiet backwater of the China station. The young man naturally said that the Bombay station would be very much more acceptable, and Mr. Bayley told him that something might be done about it.

The result was that immediate transfer of Sutherland from Bombay to China. This may have seemed hard luck for Sutherland, but I gather from many letters of the Company's shore staff of those days that, little as he may have guessed it, Sutherland was being given a streak of luck and a real chance to make his weight felt.

Those letters make plain what was the feeling of the young and keen shore staff men in the Far East stations. They were hard worked, or even hard driven at times ; but they were, in perhaps a comparatively small way, important members of the staff and of the community. What they did, well or ill, counted for or against them in an Eastern station and office, and, eventually, in the London office and the reports which went before the " Court of Directors " and the Managing Directors.

On the other hand, the young man in the Bombay or Calcutta station was " small fry " indeed. However much or little he did, good, bad, or indifferent, was submerged in the reports of his department or his chief; and the chief, not the underling, got the blame or the praise.

For obvious reasons, the keen and competent young men preferred to be posted to the smaller out-stations, however less comfortable and pleasant the social life; and they dreaded and fought, by every possible or impossible means of social or business friendships, accident, and (last resort) doctor's certificate, against a shift to the important stations, where they would be merely submerged and lost.

Sutherland, knowing nothing of this major difference, was saved from being reduced to a cog in the big Bombay wheel, and given a chance to become a wheel in himself in China. This I count as the first, and perhaps the biggest and most important, chance given him.

He took hold of his chance with both hands. In the next dozen years he made himself a personage, not only in the affairs of the Company, but throughout the East. Again I must quote from letters of the colleagues of his day—entirely private letters written to the family at home, never intended for publication or circulation outside the little group of the family's friends and relations.

Says one of these letters: " Sutherland . . . I like him much . . . a thorough gentleman as well as a clever man and good man of business . . . eminently given to hospitality and will have everything in the best possible style. . . . His dinners are a by-word in Hong Kong."

Another writer: " Sutherland . . . a little king in Hong Kong and all over China both amongst the English and the Chinamen. Even the biggest Chinaman would ' lose face ' (what you would call standing or acceptance amongst his business circle) if he was not on good footings with the P. & O.—which out here means S."

Another and last, which rather sums up the position in the East in those days, the positions which Sutherland escaped and reached by that chance of being sent to China instead of Bombay: " I am doing everything to get sent to China under Sutherland and not to Bombay

171

under the mass of favourites there. Sutherland gives everyone a chance. We all know what he can do and does do. Let us hope they do not drag him back to London, where he would be lost in the herd, like me if I went to Calcutta or Bombay."

Fortunately for the Company, Sutherland was "dragged" back to London; but only after he had laid a foundation of experience and knowledge attained through years of hard labour as well as discomfort and danger.

In China then, enervating and debilitating sickness and protracted illnesses were a normal and expected commonplace. Every European suffered mildly or severely from the still baffling and mysterious "China fever," and there were few who could stand more than a few years without either dying of it or only escaping by being sent home. In those days there was no system of sanitation and no water supply, except from primitive and rather doubtful wells. The creeping and flying carriers of disease germs were even worse than in Egypt. Sutherland went all through this, maintaining an unbounded energy and activity. In addition, during the years he was in China, he had to face, with other Europeans of the small colonies there, dangers of physical violence from the native population.

He was about twelve years in China, and almost without interval we were then at war—regular or, worse, irregular war with China or Japan. In China, a price was almost permanently on the head of every European, the price being payable, cash down, on production of the head, irrespective of the importance of its late departed owner. For years Sutherland, like all others of the English community, always carried a revolver, slept with it under the pillow, and on going out to dine, took the revolver along to place ostentatiously under the chair, just in case their own servants took a chance to win the head money.

He, and other Europeans, went through a more trying ordeal when the Chinese baker made a wholesale attempt at poisoning all the white community he served.

About eight one morning a sudden alarm went round that Europeans were falling in the street or hanging to the doorposts retching and writhing in agony; and it was quickly plain that they had been poisoned. The breakfast rolls which had been delivered that morning were found to be so overloaded with arsenic that, fortunately, the poison had worked its own cure, the overdose causing quick and violent vomiting, which quickly and thoroughly got rid of the poison. Sutherland escaped all this, because it was mail day, and he had been hard at work in the office, hours before breakfast time. The baker was afterwards tried, but nothing could be proved against him, and he got off, although it is not surprising that his sale of bread went down and the demand for tinned biscuits went up with a rush.

Sutherland, in addition to his constant activities for the P. & O., found time to organise the Hong Kong and Shanghai Banking Corporation, to the great advantage of commerce between Britain and the Far East, and also to help with the forming of the Hong Kong and Whampoa Dock Company.

About 1859, he made a dash over to Japan, taking the only craft then available, one of the beautiful little heavily canvased and hard-driven opium clippers. This was when a commercial treaty had been made with Japan but had not begun to operate; but Sutherland was intent on surveying the possibilities in advance.

Japan then had been closed to the world for over two hundred years, the only foreigners permitted entry being a few Dutchmen, who were allowed to trade to the extent of loading two ships a year. The Dutch community consisted of half a dozen or so people with two or three bungalows and storehouses, all planted on a little peninsula at Nagasaki. The area of the whole settlement was about half the size of a football field, and the peninsula became an island each night when a drawbridge, which was always under a Japanese guard, was hauled up, so making sure nobody could pass on to (or off) the Dutch territory.

Sutherland stayed about a week, meeting the Dutch governor and " factor," and, through him, some of the Japanese merchants. It was not long before he was back, this time to investigate the possibilities of a mail line between China and Yokohama, and this started in 1864 with the purchase of a little 600-ton steamer, the " Corea."

It was many years later, in 1904, that at a General Meeting, Sir

Thomas recalled that he had been the main means of opening the trade with Japan and wondered if he had done a wise or a foolish thing. Japan was then, he said, a primitive country with no conception of foreign trade or commerce, but they had since learned so much that they had become one of our severest competitors.

His words then, over thirty years ago, were more truly prophetic than most would have believed. " Japan has been, and will be," he said, " one of the most determined competitors of the commerce of this country, and all Western countries, and Japan, by means of subsidies and bounties, by means of cheap labour—so cheap that we can hardly apprehend it—will strain every nerve whenever she has the opportunity to make herself felt in all the commercial markets of the world."

He went on to say : " You are aware of the fact that the Bombay mills have succeeded in completely ousting Manchester from a trade which she formerly enjoyed in exporting yarns to China. Bombay's success was so great that Japan took up the trade, and Japan is striving by every art to oust Bombay from the same trade from which Bombay ousted Manchester. It is our unhappy fate to carry cargo for those two opposed interests. We carry raw cotton from Bombay to Japan in order that Japan may cut the throat of Bombay. We carry cotton twist from Bombay to China in order that Bombay may cut the throat of Japan ; and in serving these two interests, I can only say that, to try and satisfy them only brings to me the sort of feeling of being between the devil and the deep sea."

What even Sutherland did not foresee then (1904) was that the day was to come when Japan, by means of other " subsidies and bounties," was to take both those carrying trades from the P. & O. and from British ships. From a speech by the present Chairman last year, I learn that in those days practically the whole carrying between India and Japan was by British ships ; and that now Japan has captured some 80 per cent. of the trade and is fighting hard to seize the rest. The former Chairman felt we were " between the devil and the deep sea " ; and the present Chairman tells how we are being driven off the deep sea—and this by means of those very " subsidies and bounties " which Sutherland prophesied were to be used to secure Japanese supremacy.

Sutherland was brought back to the London office in 1866. During his stay in China he made many visits of inspection to other stations, and had seen and helped the P. & O. trade to grow enormously. His continuous stream of reports and suggestions had greatly impressed the Directors, and especially Anderson, and it was evident that his knowledge of the East must be of incalculable value in Head Office. Anderson's good impressions were more than confirmed, and it was one of his last acts before his death to have Sutherland appointed Assistant Manager in 1868.

This was when the impending shadow of the Suez Canal was hanging over the very existence of the P. & O., and Sutherland, sure of the enormous changes it would bring to Eastern traffic, devoted himself to the work of preparing, and then of reconstructing affairs to meet the flood of competing shipping.

The Board appointed him Managing Director in 1872 with the two other veterans then in that service, James Allan and Henry Bayley. Sutherland was then well under 40, and although his ability was well known to the Directors, it must have seemed to many outside them that he was far too young for such responsibility. It was at this point that there arose a situation of internal or domestic politics in the Company which now would be too trivial, too tiny a " storm in a tea-cup," to be worth mention, but for the fact that I believe it gave Sutherland his next big chance, just as his first was unwittingly given him when he was sent to China instead of Bombay.

A certain Captain Bain sent to all the shareholders a couple of bulky printed pamphlets bringing every sort of accusation against the Managing Directors—charges of incompetence, roguery, cooking the accounts, buying ships and stores at excessive prices for inferior quality, taking secret commission, almost every business crime conceivable—altogether a total of 213 charges. He declared his intention, as one of the Proprietors, of calling at the next General Meeting for an enquiry into all the charges.

The charges were so sweeping, so detailed in statements of instances, dates, and figures, that it could hardly have been supposed they were all brought without some good reason or basis of facts of which the writer was in possession. Naturally, the Press gave full space to the sensational story, so that, again naturally, the General Meeting was packed to the doors. Captain Bain began by adding a further string of charges and a mass of figures to support them.

Sutherland, as one of the Managing Directors accused of all these misdeeds, was given the task of answering. I have read his speech in full, and imagine it must have taken two to three hours to deliver. It was packed with simple but clear and striking figures and irrefutable facts denying and disproving the charges brought. It was a masterly, a brilliant, speech, even reading it in cold print, and every sentence in it scored heavily.

Captain Bain, who was taking the responsibility of speaking, as was supposed, for a large body of shareholders of whom he was one, turned out to be holder of five shares, on which £10 each had been paid. He had held minor commands of two of the smallest ships in the Company's fleet; in 1865 he had married a niece of Arthur Anderson's, and for the next year or so had practically nothing to do with the affairs of the Company. Then, at Anderson's request, he was appointed an Assistant Director, mainly for the convenience of Anderson, who wished to use him as a sort of personal assistant.

After Anderson's death in 1868, Bain was sent on a round of inspection of Eastern stations, but his reports were so unsatisfactory, so full of charges and complaints without any evidence he could bring to support them when asked to do so, that the Directors decided he was useless on such work. He was then appointed to Glasgow to help superintend the large tonnage then building there. He refused to go, and then made it plain enough to the Directors that he supposed the mantle of his wife's uncle, Arthur Anderson, had fallen on his shoulders, and that he expected such an important position as would fit that belief. He also made it plain that he knew enough to make matters hot for the Directors and Managing Directors, and meant to do so unless he were given such an appointment as he thought right. Naturally, he was dismissed on the spot, although later he was allowed

SIR THOMAS SUTHERLAND, G.C.M.G., LL.D.
Managing Director from 1872
Chairman 1880–1914

to resign instead, whereupon he set about his agitation, his circulating of pamphlets and stories to the Press. All this Sutherland related briefly but crushingly.

The conclusion of Sutherland's speech was a last smashing blow. Two letters were read from Bain to the Directors, dated only a few months before the Meeting, and long after he had circulated his pamphlets. In these Bain made it perfectly clear that, even at the last hour, he was willing to drop the whole matter and, if he were given the appointment he wished, to act harmoniously with the management "notwithstanding what has taken place hitherto."

It is hardly surprising that at the Meeting he was laughed out of court; but it is surprising that 213 charges, made deliberately and clearly in cold print and backed with detailed figures, could have been so completely and glaringly refuted in the course of a single speech.

When the vote was taken, there were nine hands raised for Bain's call for an enquiry, against the whole forest of hands for the contrary vote. At the close of the meeting, one after another of the shareholders rose to congratulate Sutherland on his lucid speech and illuminating insight in every direction into the affairs and position of the Company. One, in calling for a special vote of thanks to Sutherland, remarked that the thanks of the Meeting were also due to Captain Bain, because his action had resulted in their discovery, not only of how great an orator Sutherland was, but also how voluminous and exact was his knowledge on every phase of the Company's business, at home and abroad.

This, in fact, was the dominating outcome of the whole rather childish business. Sutherland had made a mark with the whole of the Proprietary. After that day his opinions and guidance were accepted, as I do not believe they would have been without another score of years of experience. When the Chair became vacant in 1880, Sutherland was appointed Chairman, to the unqualified satisfaction of the Proprietors, although he was even then only 46.

He continued to act as Chairman for some thirty-four years, and very largely, or some would say entirely, owing to his brilliant leadership, brought the Company through one severe and even desperate difficulty after another.

CHAPTER TWENTY-FIVE

The P. & O. Jubilee

In 1887, the P. & O. marked its Jubilee, and at the same time that of Queen Victoria, by the visible sign of building four of the finest ships in the fleet, remembered to this day as " the Jubilee Ships "—the " Victoria," " Britannia," " Oceana," and " Arcadia," all of over 6,000 tons, and an advance of about 2,000 tons on their predecessors.

The Jubilee year, however, was also a milestone in the progress which had been made by the Company over the previous period of about twenty years under the entirely new conditions which began with the opening of the Suez Canal in late 1869.

I told in my earlier chapters how a hundred years ago and for a considerable time after, the success of the P. & O. was built and largely depended on its receipt of payments for carrying the mails.

For at least a quarter of a century the Company derived its income from the mail contracts, from passenger fares, and from the carrying of very small cargoes of luxury goods at very high freights. The ships then literally had no room to carry more than this after allotting space to passenger accommodation, coal, stores (including live-stock and fodder for them), and mail rooms.

That the payments for the mail contracts were not in themselves enough to make sure of success was proved in the disastrous experience of the unfortunate Eastern and Australian Royal Mail Company when it secured the Australian mail contract ; and when the Royal Mail (West Indies) line came to its rescue and tried to help carry on the contract, it too quickly found that the very heavy expenses of running services beyond Suez made it so hard for a service to pay its way, that they withdrew to their old Atlantic trade.

After the Suez Canal went through and it became possible to reduce the expensive Eastern establishments and to save the excessive cost of sending new ships out or bringing them home for repair round the Cape, the comparative value of the mail contracts diminished, until they produced only a fraction of the revenue. The ships had to rely more and more on regular trading and cargo-carrying, and I am told that, at the present day, there are times when the space occupied by the mails could be more profitably filled with cargo.

In the years after the Canal's opening, up to 1887, the renewal of mail contracts was only secured by the P. & O. against ever-increasing and stiffening competition from the numerous new lines that had sprung up and were running on all the services to the East and Australia, where previously the P. & O. had held a virtual monopoly.

With each renewal of a contract, the payments were reduced, and greater speed—which all means cost—demanded. Each contract had to be fought for, and most were won, not only by virtue of the lower tenders made, but by the equally essential fact that the Company's extensive organisation and the number of its ships employed all over the routes offered a more certain and secure service than other lines could do. In any case of a mail liner being damaged or delayed by uncontrollable circumstances, the P. & O. could always find or divert another ship to carry on the mails. Up to 1887, few, if any other, lines could pretend to do the same.

Some queer situations arose out of these contract renewals, as, for example, when the expiry of the Australian contract in 1873 led to a tangle of jealousy and squabbles between the Australian States, especially Victoria and New South Wales. The terms and conditions and a final compromise may all seem rather ludicrous now, but were certainly much more vexatious than amusing to the Company at the time.

The whole point was that New South Wales wanted to make Sydney the terminal (or at the very least the arriving and departing) port for the Australian mails; and Victoria wished the port to be

Melbourne. To gain this object, New South Wales fought for a service across the Pacific and America, and Victoria for one by the Red Sea and Ceylon.

Neither of the two States felt they could afford to bear the total cost of a mail contract, or even the Australian end of it with the British Government paying a part ; but neither would contribute to a contract which brought the mails by the other's port. The British Post Office sought in vain to smooth the difficulty by offering to bear the cost of transmission either to Ceylon on the one route or across the Pacific on the other.

The P. & O. sent out a representative to make an effort to reconcile the opposing views. He found them irreconcilable, and, in fact, Victoria appeared to think him a rogue and a fool if he believed there was a glimmer of sense in Sydney's views ; while Sydney supposed him a fool and a rogue if he saw reason in Melbourne's.

Victoria at last made an offer which, being the only one possible under the conditions, was therefore accepted. It was that £90,000 a year should be paid for the same monthly service as had previously received £120,000 ; but Victoria's most strict stipulation was that, under the new contract, the mail should be carried only as far as Melbourne, and Sydney therefore be left right out in the cold.

The natural result was that mails and passengers carried to and from Melbourne had to be transhipped there into a branch-line steamer which the P. & O. put on to carry them between Melbourne and Sydney. This contract was for six years, was renewed, and ran on until a new one was made in 1880.

There was another glint of humour in this new 1880 contract, because it was only made after the P. & O. had laid down a flat ultimatum which forced the two rival States into a more reasonable frame of mind to each other. While the former contract ran, every effort had been made by the Company to persuade the two States to compromise, but Sydney was still hankering to be the terminal port of a Pacific service and would not give way ; nor would Melbourne in the boycott of Sydney, which forced the delay and inconvenience of the branch line on Sydney.

The service had been a monthly one, and the Company offered to improve this to fortnightly if the States would agree. When they continued to refuse this offer, the P. & O. in turn refused to tender at all for a renewal of the monthly service contract, while at the same time offering a fortnightly one at £5,000 a year less than they had been getting for the monthly—but this on the strict condition that the mail liner was allowed to continue the voyage on to Sydney. With a good deal of grumbling, both States at last agreed to the very reasonable conditions.

The next Australian contract brought another difficulty, because this time the only conditions proposed by Australia were that the Company should carry on payment of so much per pound weight of letters and newspapers—the amount per pound being a good deal less than the postage stamps would bring in. The Company would not have minded this, but did mind setting the certainty of their heavy expenditure against the complete uncertainty of how many pounds of mail matter would be forthcoming.

They refused to consider a contract on such a basis, but offered one which was finally agreed after long-drawn negotiations, on the terms of an acceleration of $2\frac{1}{2}$ days on the previous 35 days between Brindisi and Adelaide for £85,000 a year for seven years.

The tale of these mail contracts may make dull reading for most, but I must tell one more relating to that which, up to 1888, still required that the Brindisi mail should be carried across Egypt by rail. Long before then, there was little, if any, saving in time over that taken by the ships going through the Canal, and in addition to the loss of time in transhipment between ship and shore at both ends, there were innumerable troubles for passengers over the quarantine regulations. The time of transit through the Canal had been cut down to 34 hours in 1887, mainly by the introduction of electric light allowing night travel.

The Company was at last able to persuade the Post Office to conclude a contract which allowed the whole of the mail to go through by the Canal, but only on terms which reduced payment for the India and Far East contract by about £100,000 to £285,000 a year. By this

1888 contract the Company had in ten years reduced the cost of the India and China mail by £170,000, and had greatly improved the times and other conditions of the service.

The twenty years between the opening of the Canal and the P. & O. Jubilee saw a complete revolution in the Company's trade. The main, indeed almost the sole, purpose and reason for the Company's existence and progress by the old Overland Route had been in the carriage of the mails and then of passengers. Cargo was a mere afterthought and secondary consideration, although it grew to be one enormously profitable to the Company for the good reason that only the highest class of goods able to pay extremely high freight rates could be carried.

When gold or silver was in transit, it was idle and earning nothing ; and the shorter the time it was in transit, the sooner it came into the hands of banks or merchants who could make it earn and pay interest— sometimes a very high interest. Even in the days of the crack Australian clipper ships, the best to be expected of them was a passage of 100 to 110 days. One of the most famous of them, with gold to the value of a million sterling on board, was over 120 days at sea. The mail steamer would have made the passage in half the time, or less. Shippers, therefore, found it well worth while to send specie by P. & O., even at high freight rates.

Such costly goods as high-class silks and indigo were also worth sending from China and India by the Overland Route, because it was certain they would be on the market so much sooner than if sent by sail round the Cape ; and the shipper received the large amount of payments, and could turn his money over again, months before he could do so if he shipped by sail.

For such high freight and luxury goods then there was practically as much traffic as the P. & O. could carry. Their rates certainly were heavy, but so were their expenses east of Suez. That their profits were not excessive is shown by the dividends for a number of years before the Canal opened being round about 6 and 7 per cent. per annum.

After the opening of the Canal, all this was changed, because an increasing number of steamers invaded the trade, offering to carry at much lower rates. Freight rates from Calcutta in 1869 were £10 to £12 a ton; and by 1887 they had dropped to 20s. and 30s. Similarly, and in the same years, rates from China and Australia fell from £25 and £30 to 25s. and 50s.; and from Shanghai and Japan £28–£33 went down to 30s.–40s. Specie rates that had been $2\frac{1}{2}$ per cent. of the value fell away to $\frac{1}{2}$ per cent. or less.

This meant that the Company, no longer having the monopoly in such traffic, could no longer run their expensive fast liners, with their very small cargo space, and carry goods at the new low level. They had to build their fleet to carry substantial cargoes of the commoner and lower-rated goods. The size of the ships rose to meet this need, and the fleet of 1869 with ships averaging 2,000 tons was replaced by 1887 with new ships of an average over the whole fleet of some 4,000 tons.

The speed of the ships and time of mail transport had also been vastly improved. Taking 1873 as a year when the Canal transit was well established, and comparing mail times then with those of 1887, show that the Bombay mail time was reduced from 23 to $16\frac{1}{2}$ days, Shanghai from $45\frac{1}{2}$ to $37\frac{1}{2}$ days, Melbourne from 48 to 35 days.

But although passenger fares, freight rates, and mail payments had shrunk, skilful management and prudent finance had so improved the fleet and increased the turnover, that in their Jubilee year the P. & O. was in a stronger position than ever.

In 1870, the year after the Canal opened, the fleet was of 43 ships of 80,000 tons and 5 building. By 1887, this had risen to a fleet of 50 ships, totalling just on 200,000 tons. During the previous ten years, over £3 millions had been put aside for new ships and £2,500,000 had been spent on them. In six years from 1875, debts of £800,000 borrowed on Debentures had been paid off. Over the ten years to 1887, the dividends paid amounted to an average of £6 12s. per cent. per annum.

The assets of the Company in ships (£2,102,000), graving docks, workshops and machinery, coal stocks, wharves, buildings, and land all over the world, with other items, were valued at just under £4 millions.

So the greatest crisis in P. & O. history that had arisen from the opening of the Suez Canal had been magnificently conquered by 1887, and indeed had placed the Company in a stronger and greater position than ever. Yet the Canal was to produce another crisis, and this time one which was serious, not only to the P. & O., but to the whole of British shipping and trade with the East.

CHAPTER TWENTY-SIX

A Proposed Second Suez Canal

EVERYBODY knows the story of the swift and statesmanlike action of Disraeli, in seizing the opportunity to purchase for the British Government almost half the shares of the Suez Canal Company in 1876.

It is less a matter of general knowledge now how, after this, there developed a situation of the highest national importance over the treatment of British shipping using the Canal, and that this culminated in a demand for redress and action so powerful that the British Government actually signed an agreement for the cutting of a second and all-British canal, with a cash guarantee of £8 millions to de Lesseps towards the expense of the work.

It certainly deserves to be better known than it is how important, or even vital, was the part taken by the P. & O. through their Chairman, Mr. Sutherland, which led to the abandoning of this rather crazy plan for a second canal, and the substitution for it of another and a formal agreement from which all British shipping has continued to benefit ever since.

The whole thing arose, in the first place, through the strong resentment roused on the Continent when it became known how Lord Beaconsfield had quietly " scooped the pool " by his sudden purchase of those shares in the Suez Canal which our Government still holds. The resentment rose to wrath and a fear that the British might seize complete control when we subdued Arabi Pasha and took charge of the Government of Egypt.

The European Powers adopted an ingenious method of asserting their rights in Egypt at the expense of Britain, and the tool used was an International Sanitary Council, which had been set up to assist and advise the Egyptian Government in matters of health and quarantine.

Prior to this, the quarantine rules had been fair, reasonable, and yet perfectly sufficient and effective. Now the Sanitary Board proceeded to institute rules which hit British shipping heaviest and hardest, because 75 per cent. of the ships using the Canal were British, and which also struck at the whole of British trade with the East.

Stupid and harmful as the new rules were, our shipowners and traders were powerless, because our one representative on the Board of twenty-two was overwhelmingly outvoted on any point by which he strove to protect British interests ; and our shipping and trade began to suffer an increasing and intolerable squeeze under the system.

The crux of the whole plan was that the Board had (or took) power to grant pratique, or clean bill of health and undisturbed passage through the Canal, to ships from whatever ports they declared free of plague or infectious disease ; or, on the other hand, could put crushing restrictions on ships from any port they declared quarantine.

Practically all ports in the East were made quarantine, and this hit even our Australian trade, as well as our Indian and Chinese, because ships from Australia touching at Ceylon or Aden (as they had to do if only to coal) came automatically under quarantine.

Under the new quarantine rules, ships arriving at Suez were told that they might not take a pilot on board ; but, under Canal Company rules, no ship might pass through without pilotage of a Canal pilot. The only way to get over this was for the ship to employ a launch in which the pilot went ahead, shouting and gesticulating his directions to the following ship.

It need hardly be said that this " pilot fish " system quickly brought about a series of accidents, collisions, and groundings, and such a chaos of confusion that it was a commonplace for quarantine ships to take 4, 5, and 6 days to get through, instead of the normal $1\frac{1}{2}$ days, and that some ships actually took from 10 to 15 days to the transit.

In addition to the tremendous loss such delays inflicted on the shipowner who had a week to a fortnight added to the ordinary costs of his voyage, a further expense was added—trivial in comparison to the cost of delay, no doubt, but by no means trivial in actual cash, and annoying in the extreme. The feeble little steam-launch from which the pilot directed the following ship had to be hired by the ship at a charge of up to 50 francs—say, £2—*an hour*, bringing in no small sum to the Canal Company when a ship took 240 hours or more to make the transit.

The P. & O. Company had a special grievance. Under the quarantine they were not allowed to land any passengers at Suez to travel by rail to Alexandria and there embark on the P. & O. Brindisi mail liners. This was the greater hardship on numbers of the Indian and Eastern military and civil community proceeding home on leave and naturally anxious to travel by the quickest route.

The Sanitary Board, however, finding their methods so successful, gave the screw an extra turn, and that turn was one too many to be borne by the worst sufferers, the regular British Lines.

Mr. Sutherland, as Chairman of the P. & O., took the initiative, and quickly rallied the support of all the leading Lines concerned. He headed a deputation to Earl Glanville, the Under Secretary of State for Foreign Affairs, and presented a case which was endorsed in every respect by the other Companies represented. He took the bold line of declaring that the Sanitary Board had no legal standing, that, having taken the opinion of the highest authority at law, he was assured that the Canal rules of the agreement of 1866 contained no clause under which such a Board could be constituted or could properly act.

He produced figures to show that ports like Aden and Bombay, which had been declared quarantine ports because of cholera there, had been suffering no epidemic of the sort ; that ships arriving with a perfectly clean bill of health were made quarantine ; and that, finally, for six months past the British representative had been consistently outvoted by representatives of Powers whose interests were insignificant compared to ours, or were actually non-existent.

This action brought quick results in the shape of instructions to H.M. Representative in Egypt to tell the Egyptian Government that the

British Government would not submit to the " arbitrary and capricious acts " of " an irresponsible body " ; and, in brief—or perhaps I should say at length—made it plain that the Egyptian Government must forthwith mend its ways and break its Sanitary Board's.

But by this time very strong feelings on the subject had been roused throughout our shipping and commercial community, our Press, and public ; and in France a counter-agitation was raised against what the French supposed to be an attack on them, and their Canal shareholders' profits. Under the pressure here, the British Government made an impulsive, and, as it appeared then, an impressive step. They let it be known that it would be better for us to own a canal through Egypt ourselves, and, rather foolishly as it turned out, without any consultation with shipowners or other major interests, made a formal signed agreement with de Lesseps to undertake the cutting of a British Suez Canal, giving him a guarantee of £8 millions to make a start on it.

This, however, was not at all acceptable to the shipowners, and certainly not to the P. & O., because it was certain it must take years to cut another Canal, that throughout those years their trade might be injured beyond repair, and also because there might be endless legal duels over the right of the Khedive to grant a concession for a second canal in face of some legally doubtful terms embodied in the original agreement with de Lesseps in 1866.

These squabbles had been going on through 1882 and 1883, and in November of that year, de Lesseps and his son came to England and, after discussions with Chambers of Commerce and various other bodies, had some private interviews with certain individuals of the Shipowners' Association.

To cut the story as short as I can . . . formal discussions were begun between the shipowners and de Lesseps, and protracted meetings were held day after day, and often late into the night, in the Board Room of the P. & O. offices. The final result was that, at last, terms were agreed, and a formal draft ordered to be drawn up. The conditions of this were enormously more valuable to us then (and now) than those into which our Government had so hastily entered with de

Lesseps, because the Government had merely promised their support and cash for the second canal, without any stipulation as to having any representation in the control of it or of the existing one which must continue for years to carry the traffic.

The terms hammered out in the P. & O. Board Room were practically those under which the Canal is run to-day—allowing seven British Directors on the Board in addition to the three already on it by virtue of the share-holding bought by Disraeli, a Canal Company office in London, and a British Committee meeting there with power to discuss and represent British interests.

Moreover, an immediate reduction was to be made in dues, such irritations as the Sanitary Board removed, and the Canal Company engaged itself to spend £8 millions on widening, deepening, and straightening the Canal—instead of that sum being provided by the British Government.

There was another clause of some importance, that the expense of freeing and refloating ships which went aground had to be paid by the Canal Company—an expense which had previously been borne by the unfortunate owner whose ship was stranded, and perhaps damaged, entirely through the fault of the Canal pilot the ship was forced to carry. Unfortunately for the shipowner, that clause no longer stands, although the Canal pilot is still compulsory.

It was fully recognised how important was the P. & O. Chairman's vigorous action, and the skilful, powerful, and yet diplomatic reasoning he applied in the de Lesseps negotiations. The success of those negotiations and the terms finally accepted by de Lesseps are the more remarkable when we remember that he, throughout them, was " sitting pretty," with an agreement in his pocket signed by the British Government for another canal and a guarantee of £8 millions to get on with it. It must be remarked that M. de Lesseps gracefully relieved our Government from an awkward dilemma by releasing them from his agreement.

It was in November 1883 that the terms of the agreement were drafted in the P. & O. Board Room ; and a year later, at a General Meeting of the Company, the proposal was made, to be carried out next year, to present Mr. Sutherland with Canal Company shares to the value of £7,200 as some recognition of his services in smoothing out the Company's trials and troubles in the Canal affair. The benefits his action had conferred on British shipping were recorded by the representatives of our shipowners when they voted him into the Chairmanship of the Canal Company's London Board.

CHAPTER TWENTY-SEVEN

Early War Services

IT might fairly be said that the Company was born out of the war services which Willcox and Anderson first undertook for the Queens of Portugal and Spain, and in which the " Royal Tar " and other chartered steamers took active part as warships.   From then on, the P. & O. has rendered full service in every war we have fought.

From the first founding of the Peninsular Company, its steamers were classified by the Admiralty according to the number and weight of the guns they could carry, and this not only continued, but was later supplemented by an Admiralty contribution to the cost of construction and fitting the ships with gun platforms and stiffening of the hulls to stand up to the firing of heavy guns.

As early as 1845 *Gore's Directory*, in an article on " The Power of the P. & O.," wrote :

" The P. & O. Company now have in service and in process of construction 36 steamers, 26 being sea-going and 4 for river service ; 14 of them are from 1,200 to 2,000 tons and of 450 to 520 horse-power, 12 of them from 500 to 1,000 tons and of 200 to 400 horse-power.   They are all of them capable of carrying armaments, the first 14 as heavy as any steam frigate.   No single Power in Europe, France not excepted, can boast of such a steam squadron as this single branch of British enterprise has produced in the short space of four years."

A first slight but significant indication of the advantages of steam for urgent transport came in 1848, on the outbreak of a rebellion in Ceylon.   The P. & O. " Lady Mary Wood " was then at Point de Galle, and she was immediately dispatched to Madras with urgent letters to the

Governor there, asking that one wing of a European regiment and one complete Native regiment should be embarked with the least possible delay. The " Lady Mary " returned with these troops fully equipped for the field, and it was said that the island had been saved from a serious spread of the rebellion by their prompt arrival.

The first serious test of the Company's resources in time of war, however, came in the Crimean War in 1854-5. In the early part of the latter year, the Government had taken up 11 ships, some of them the biggest and best in the fleet, and amounting to 18,000 tons out of the total of the fleet then of 51,000 tons.

It will be remembered that, in consequence of the withdrawal of ships from their regular services, the P. & O. had to discontinue for a time the Australian mail service—an interruption hotly resented in Australia then and for long after, because they blamed the Company for it. After the war help given by the Company, the Government played rather a shabby trick when new tenders were called for on the Australian mail, and the contract (given, as I have told, to the European and Australian Company) was refused the P. & O. for one reason amongst others, " That the Government would have to wait until this Company's vessels were released from the transport service, and that there would be a delay of several months before they could be got ready for the mail service."

This was one of the reasons given to the House of Commons in June 1856, although it must then have been known to the Government that, the war being well over, the last of the transport vessels were due for return to the Company as they arrived home in turn. The unfairness of this supposed reason was proved when the new Company's service started with their chartering of the P. & O. " Simla " and her sailing from Sydney in February 1857, this ship having been one of those engaged on the Crimean transport.

Much of the Crimean trooping was done by sailing ships, and, in winter weather especially, the troops who were accommodated as " deck passengers " had to endure real hardships, being packed like sardines below and battened down in rough weather, and expected to live on deck when they could.

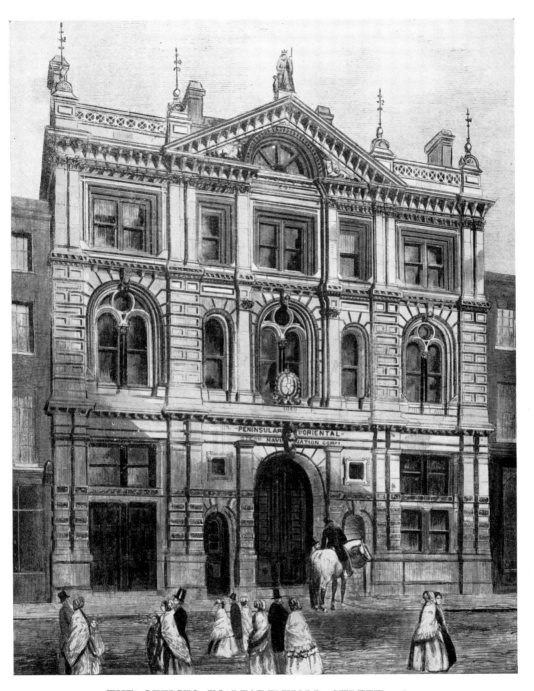

THE OFFICES IN LEADENHALL STREET, 1859
From an old print

The faster passages and better accommodation of the steamships employed was all the more appreciated by the troops, and the P. & O. carried 62,000 officers and other ranks, 15,000 horses, and a vast quantity of stores urgently required.

The next war service, although on a much smaller scale, was perhaps of even greater importance on the outbreak of the Indian Mutiny. One of the great fears in India was that the Mutiny would spread to Bombay and the West, and it was of the utmost urgency that reinforcements should be sent there. Two P. & O. steamers were sent from Bombay to Cape Town and to Mauritius, and hurried back with the 13th and 33rd Regiments to Bombay. At the same time troops were dispatched from England and Mediterranean ports, and, proceeding by P. & O. and the Overland Route, reached Bombay to strengthen the garrisons denuded of troops for the urgent needs of up-country. Between September 1857 and June 1858, the P. & O. took to India by this route 235 officers and 5,171 men.

The railway across Egypt was being built, but had still some 25 miles of the desert crossing to Suez to be completed. A personal account of how the gap was covered is given in some of a series of letters written by one of the P. & O. staff on his way to India, and lent to me now by a relative.

The writer, a Mr. F. H. Kendall, was a young man making his first trip to the East, so he naturally wrote of the sights and incidents which impressed him the more, as they were so strange to him.

He sailed in the " Ripon " from Southampton with a number of other passengers, in addition to 235 troops—a small number in a ship which was capable of carrying about 1,000 under ordinary trooping conditions. On arrival at Alexandria the troops were served out with long smock frocks and white linen caps, with long lappets to protect the neck from the sun, and immediately entrained.

The Nile was crossed by a floating bridge, which could be raised and lowered according to the level of the river water. The train crossed in sections, and while the troops waited they had supper, being (as Kendall wrote) " uncommon well fed with tea and coffee, Irish stews and all sorts of meat, bread, and vegetables."

O

The train went on about 5 a.m., and with only ten minutes' stop at Cairo, set out across the desert to reach the end of the railway about 10 a.m.

"Then came the fun of the day," writes Kendall, "seeing the soldiers all mount their donkeys. The officers showed them how to mount first, and the largest officer, a man about 6 foot 4 and stout in proportion, mounted the smallest donkey he could find and rode round amongst the men, much to their amusement. The donkeys are all very small and the men very large, and most could almost walk, although they were astride. The same unfortunate animals—unless they broke down, as several did—had to carry them the whole 25 miles to Suez, over a road where generally the hot sand was over their fetlocks. In England a man would be taken up for cruelty to animals if he rode one for a mile. Here they think nothing of it. There is even a man or boy to run behind each donkey the whole way and whack him along."

Kendall, with other passengers, went on ahead in "vans" drawn by two mules in the shafts and two horses ahead, and arrived at Suez at 3 p.m., the troops getting there at 6 p.m. and embarking at once in the "Pottinger."

There followed an incident, of which I have not read in any account of the Indian Mutiny. The "Pottinger" was a much smaller ship than the "Ripon," and a number of the men had to be accommodated on deck. After the comfort of the "Ripon" they did not like this, little guessing that before they had gone far down the Red Sea, any who were berthed below would be clamouring to be allowed to sleep on deck.

The men made the food served them for dinner a pretext for complaint, and when their officers examined it and had a number of casks of salt beef and pork opened for inspection and found to be in excellent condition, the men were told so. However, when the crew was ordered forward to get the anchor up, the troops rushed up, wrenched the bars out of the capstan, and threatened to throw overboard any man who tried to work the ship out.

The Colonel seems to have been a weakling, and feebly gave way, after begging the mutineers to "Come down now, men." He went ashore and made arrangements for the troops to be transferred to

194

another steamer lying there. This was done that night, and the
" Pottinger " proceeded next morning.

Some contemporary Press cuttings referred to this little mutiny, and
said that the regiment in India waiting these reinforcements was
determined to make it hot for the mutineers when they arrived. But of
what happened to them I have found no further account. Kendall
remarks that the men made a bad exchange, because the other ship,
although apparently larger, had no space on deck, so that the men
would have to berth below, and at that season (March) would be almost
stifled.

Some of the sea staff of the P. & O. were apparently not content
with their peaceful work of transporting troops to the Mutiny, because
in a history of *The Bengal Yeomanry Cavalry*, a volunteer corps raised
in Calcutta in July 1857, it is expressly mentioned that amongst the
volunteers were " midshipmen from the P. & O."

The Corps, which mustered 258 sabres, received the thanks of the
Governor-General for their distinguished service in fourteen engage-
ments. The mutineers called them the " Shaitan-i-Pultun " (Devil's
Own), a title which their historian says they well earned.

In the Persian War of 1857, four of the Company's steamers were
employed, and some were under fire. In those four years from 1853 a
clause in the Report of a Committee that year was remarkably vindicated, although few then supposed or admitted there was any sound
reason for it. The Committee was one more of those appointed to
enquire into the Contract Packet Service, and the frequent allegations
that it was costing too much. The Committee reported their views to
the contrary, and added : " Their [the Postal Steamers] advantages as an
auxiliary force will be very considerable. They will be available on the
breaking out of hostilities for the rapid conveyance of dispatches, of
specie, and to a certain extent of troops and stores. They may also be
expected to furnish the Queen's ships with men trained to steam navigation and possessing an amount of local knowledge which cannot fail to
be valuable in several ways."

The outbreak of the Crimean War in the following year more than
justified that opinion. It was to hold just as good in every war we have

195

known since, and in the Great War most of all. The words are no less true to-day, although in many quarters apparently forgotten, especially in regard to the reserve of trained men.

The four Jubilee ships of 1887 were fitted with gun-platforms and all material for speedy conversion to armed cruisers. This was largely due to a war scare that had arisen, and to the threats openly made by Russia in 1879 of the havoc that could be wrought amongst our merchantmen by the Russian " Patriotic Fleet " and by American privateers with Russian letters of marque.

There was another crisis with Russia in 1885, and a first precautionary measure for the protection of shipping in Eastern waters was the taking up of the P. & O. " Massilia " at Sydney and " Rosetta " at Hong Kong and their equipping as armed cruisers. The *Asiatic Quarterly* reported that these steamers were " fitted with guns and military stores, and were engaged in practising their guns before vessels chartered at Liverpool for the same purpose had taken their equipment on board." It may be added that all Indian natives of the crews on deck and below volunteered to the last man for war service.

Before this time, however, the P. & O. had given other demonstrations of the Company's value in war. In the Abyssinian War, six of their large steamers were employed on Red Sea and Indian Ocean transport work. The Company supplied 150,000 tons of coal from their Eastern depots to Government ships ; and lying off the practically waterless landing-place of the Expedition, the ships' condensers provided the army with 500,000 gallons of distilled water.

In 1882, the unrest in Egypt led to instructions from the Post Office to carry the Brindisi mails through the Canal instead of by the railway. When the Arabi Pasha troubles began, the P. & O. " Tanjore " was employed to lie off Alexandria as a refugee ship, and the Company had eight steamers on transport service for the Egyptian Expedition.

Two P. & O. liners were present at the bombardment of Alexandria that year, and I had a letter recently from a Mr. Treen, who after a lifetime in the Company's service, is now in retirement in Australia. Here is a summary of his recollections.

He was in the " Surat " when she, with China and Australian mail on board, and the "Ancona," with Indian mails, arrived at Suez. The Admiral of the East India Station would not permit the ships to enter the Canal, because Alexandria was to be bombarded next morning, but when an Italian gunboat offered to act as escort, the two were allowed to proceed.

The Italian led the way, followed by the P. & O. liners with their wheel-houses protected against possible rifle fire from the Canal banks by thick barricades of bales of cotton and silk. None of the ships met any interference, and when the two P. & O. reached Port Said, they proceeded round to Alexandria to find it in flames, but with four of the forts still firing. Action ceased at dark—if it could be called " dark " with the city spouting flames and soaring streams of sparks up to the glowing red-tinted canopy of rolling smoke clouds.

Next morning the warships moved in, cleared for action, to renew the bombardment, but before they opened fire the forts ran up white flags and surrendered. The Admiral detained the " Surat " to take his dispatches on to Brindisi, and when she had done so, she brought back from there Sir Henry Havelock Allan and General Graham, with staffs.

At Alexandria she found the troopships from home, and these proceeded by the Canal to Ismailia, where the troops were landed. Within 24 hours the " Surat " heard that the battle of Tel el Kebir had been fought and that Arabi Pasha was a prisoner. Treen concludes, " He was sent to Ceylon, and later I saw him there."

In 1884, when the Mahdi forces under Osman Digna were beleaguring small Egyptian garrisons, the P. & O. gave another example of how useful they could be in emergency—this time in a very small way which none the less was significant of the invaluable co-operation possible between an extensive organisation of ships and shore establishment.

The Government suddenly called on the Company to make the speediest arrangements they could for the transport of troops from Cairo to Suakim in the Red Sea. Instructions were hurried out to the Company's Egyptian offices, and when two East-bound ships arrived at Port Said, a mass of material and crowd of workmen were rushed on board, and while the ships proceeded through the Canal a feverish hustle of work on board converted the accommodation for the shipment of troops sent on by rail to Suez.

On arrival there, the ships were all ready, and within 10 and 16 hours respectively, of their arrival, the two were steaming at top speed for Suakim fully equipped, watered and provisioned for the 1,600 troops aboard.

After the Government bought the " Himalaya " from the P. & O. for trooping in the Crimea, they evidently found the advantage of keeping permanent troopers, and so ran the famous class of " Serapis " ships built specially for their regular trooping. For many years these troopers' names were household words throughout the Army. Built 1866-7, they were in regular commission until withdrawn in 1896.

Kipling made the names of two familiar to the present generation in his barrack-room Ballad of " Trooping " :

"The Malabar's in 'arbour, an' the Jumna's at her tail " ;

and another in " Soldier and Sailor Too " :

" As I was spittin' into the ditch
Aboard of the Crocodile."

But although these troopships were at first considered an improvement in the standards of comfort for the troops, they were continued in service well past their best days, and after great advances had been made in steamer construction and accommodation. They also became decidedly unpopular in Navy and Army, not for their own sake, but because of the system under which they were run.

They were run under the R.N.'s White Ensign, manned with Navy personnel, victualled, and kept up by H.M. Dockyards. The officers in them disliked the service, because they felt they were in a back-water with no chance of advancement in their profession ; and they were at constant feud with the military they carried and with the War Office.

The Army officers hated being placed under ship discipline, which required that perhaps their most senior officer had to take orders from

a mere midshipman or junior lieutenant. To the Army it was pre-
posterous that even a Colonel could have orders to his own men over-
ridden ; to the Navy it was even worse that any soldier, whatever his
rank, should be allowed any share in the control and discipline of the
ship's company.

Complaints grew too of the ships being extravagantly run and
out of date. At last the Admiralty called for tenders for troopships
which would be hired by the Government, but would be manned,
managed, and victualled by the owners. The P. & O. tendered, and
two of their ships, the " Victoria " and " Britannia," were duly taken
up on a six months' charter for the Indian trooping season of 1894-5.
The system of employing hired transports for the trooping season was
so economical and the comfort and health of the troops so satisfactory,
that the system has continued ever since.

At the same time the P. & O. in addition continued to have ships
taken up for trooping in the little wars like the China Wars, Ashanti
Expedition, and " side-shows " of the sort. During the South African
War of 1900–1902, the Company had nine ships running as transports
to the Cape, India, China, and the West Indies, and by the end of
1902 it was reported that 150,000 troops had been carried by the
P. & O. " with reiterated expressions of approval from all concerned."

The P. & O. has not for many years owned any troopships for charter to the Government in peace time, but in this last year of their
century they come back into trooping again on a contract signed in June
for the construction of a new troopship.

The new ship is to be designed and constructed in the closest co-
operation with the Sea Transport Department of the Board of Trade
and in conformity with all their requirements. She will embody all the
latest and best in the existing troopers with any extra refinements and
comforts experience of them may suggest.

She will be of about 11,000 tons, and will have accommodation for
some 1,150 troops on the main and lower mess-decks, as well as ample
and comfortable berthing in cabins and first-class public rooms for
officers, their wives and families.

CHAPTER TWENTY-EIGHT

Associated Companies

IN the present century, the first event of historical importance in the progress of the P. & O. was the purchase of the whole fleet, assets, and goodwill of Lund's "Blue Anchor Line," which for many years had been running steamers, mainly in the emigrant trade, round the Cape to Australia.

The first Lund who founded the Line did so in the period of the clipper ships in the China trade, which began with the repeal of our Navigation Laws and the rush of the American clipper ships into the tea trade in 1850.

Lund was owner of a London riverside sail loft at that time, and his first shipping ventures were in taking some shares in the clippers on the basis then in vogue of a ship being divided up into sixty-four shares. In the 1860's, however, his name appears amongst such famous clipper-ship owners and giants of the shipping world of that day as Jardine Matheson, Duncan Dunbar, Joseph Somes, Baring Brothers and John Willis, Shaw Maxton, McCunn, and Killick Martin.

Although the first China clippers ran out to China and back round the Cape, the demand for fast freight and passenger accommodation to the Australian gold diggings led to the usual run being made outward to Australia, then up to China to load with tea for the annual neck-or-nothing hard-driven " racing home the tea " to England.

The opening of the Suez Canal, by shortening the time of transit from China and lowering the freights, put the clippers out of that business, and Lund, like many others, turned to depend on the Australian trade out with emigrants and home with wool or other produce. As soon as steamers were made economically possible and payable on long voyages, the Blue Anchor flag device became as famous and familiar on their liners' funnel marking as it had been as the House Flag of the racing tea clippers.

In 1909, however, the Line suffered the loss of a new steamer in a foundering which is still counted amongst the great and totally unexplained mysteries of the sea. The "Waratah" was a new ship which had only made the one round voyage to Australia, went out again, and on the homeward passage simply disappeared. She had called at Durban, and was sighted by another steamer on her way round to Cape Town. When she failed to arrive, and days passed without word of her, there was a first-class sensation, especially in Australia.

It was supposed she might have met with some accident, an engineroom breakdown or something else that had left her drifting helplessly. Warships were sent out to scour the seas for her, all other ships passing anywhere near the place of her last being sighted made wider and wider divergences with picked men continually on look-out during the day, with rockets and blue lights blazing at intervals through the night. It was all to no purpose. Nothing, not even a scrap of wreckage, was sighted ; and so the "Waratah" took her place in the long line of ships posted as "Lost with all hands."

I was in Australia myself at that time, and I remember how profoundly the loss affected the whole community, how for days and weeks columns of articles and letters appeared in the Press, how it was argued whether the ship had been as seaworthy as was supposed. She was top-heavy, said some ; her cargo, badly stowed, had shifted and rolled her over, said others. Amongst the old salts and those steeped in shipping lore and tradition, as so many of the Australians are, the "Waratah" had just been a "hoodoo" or unlucky ship ; and the "hoodoo" theory spread from the lost ship to the whole Line. The longer the suspense and the sensation ran through the months, the greater grew the reluctance to ship in the "hoodoo" line.

I do not know how far the loss of popular favour and the reduced passenger lists induced Lunds to sell out. In 1910, the P. & O. bought out the Line, lock, stock, and barrel, and kept it in the same trade, but dropping the old name and running it as the "P. & O. Branch Line."

If any " hoodoo " theory induced the sale, it does not seem to have affected the purchase price, which could only be called a good and fair one. The Line owned five steamers, totalling about 30,000 tons, and they were taken over at their cost price, subject to an annual depreciation at the rate of 5 per cent. for every year they had been at work, making a total price of about £250,000. Another £25,000 was paid for goodwill and all trading rights.

The entry of the P. & O. into the trade round the Cape marked their first departure from their basic business of using the Red Sea route. The next association with another Line was a return to and extension of their long-established Eastern business when, in 1914, an agreement was concluded for amalgamation with the British India Steam Navigation Company.

There are some strangely marked points of similarity in the histories of the founders and founding of the P. & O. and " B.I.," as the latter has been known throughout the East for many years.

Both were founded by two partners who had little capital or influence, but steadily accumulated these by their own exertions ; both had to struggle against losses and difficulties in their early days, and Mackenzie and Mackinnon (like Willcox and Anderson) built up their shipping company to a position of the first magnitude, and lived long lives which ended with their management of one of the greatest shipowning firms in the world. A final similarity is that, when the time came for both pairs of partners to drop the reins, those were picked up by the capable hands of a man who, in each case, had entered the firm's employment as an unknown junior, had worked his way to the top by sheer ability and assiduity, and who carried their respective companies to still greater size and strength.

Robert Mackenzie was a young Scot who established a small general merchanting business in Calcutta, and requiring help in this, brought in a young man, William Mackinnon, from Glasgow. For the convenience of their business and shipment of their goods, they had to use what coastal shipping was available, until in 1854 the East India Company offered a contract for the carriage of mails, passengers, and cargo by steam between Calcutta and Burma.

Realising the shortcomings of existing traffic and the possibilities offering, the two partners sought and found sufficient capital amongst their Calcutta and Glasgow friends to allow a tender to be made, and, when a contract was secured, two small steamers, the " Baltic " and " Cape of Good Hope," were purchased. The Company was formed under the title of the Calcutta and Burma Steam Navigation Company, and a fortnightly service was started between Calcutta, Akyab, Rangoon, and Moulmein.

In this matter of mail contracts being a foremost part, or indeed need, of the British India business, there is another point of similarity to the early progress of the P. & O. which was largely founded on their mail contract revenue.

The British India from the first also made the mails a basis of their business, without which it is doubtful if they could have won through. The inefficient engines of those days required a heavy coal consumption, which was expensive in itself and more expensive in the ship's running, because it occupied so large a share of the cargo space. The British India was by no means the first to attempt running steamers in Indian waters, but others had lost heavily on the venture.

The " Cape of Good Hope," one of the two first British India steamers, was bought from a General Screw Steamship Company, which was one of several that had been forced into liquidation, although it started with a substantial capital, was founded by experienced business men, and was well and competently managed. Yet in the half-year before they wound up and sold their steamers, they lost £7,500, although their revenue in that time was nearly £55,000.

The Indian Mutiny brought profitable charters to the new British India—or rather the Calcutta and Burma Steam Navigation Company, as it still was—and two more steamers were added to the fleet. But losses at sea hit them hard—as you will remember it did the Peninsular Company, when they lost their biggest and best steamer in 1837. The " Cape of Good Hope " was sunk by a collision in the River Hoogly, and a new ship, the " Calcutta," went ashore on the Wicklow coast on her way out from the builders, and became a total loss.

Mackinnon returned to England, managed to raise further capital, bought one steamer, and placed orders for two more, and in 1862 was back in India with a project for the renewal of the existing mail contract and a new development of other lines of trade round the Indian coast, westward to the Persian Gulf and eastward to Singapore and the Malacca Straits ports.

The very boldness of these new plans nearly defeated their acceptance. Up to then no steamers had been able to maintain all-the-year-round coastal services against the strength of the seasonal monsoons. The Persian Gulf was so infested with pirates that regular trading was difficult and sometimes impossible, and the postal services had to struggle along under a system of being " farmed out " to local native chiefs, who only allowed the ports to be used in consideration of bribes or " tribute " payments, which, however, gave no guarantee of reliability or safety.

The pirates of the Singapore and Malacca Seas had a more forthright way of business. In all the bays and inlets along the coasts their swift sail-and-oar prahus lurked, ready to pounce out on any sailing vessel becalmed, or any steamer forced to stop to cool her engines or repair breakdowns. In such case out shot the prahus, crammed with men, urged to top speed by relays of rowers on the long sweeps. If they could surround their victim, they drove in from all sides, so that even a ship with guns could hardly stop the lot. Any prahus that got near enough showered " stink-balls " down on the deck, choking the defenders with thick, blinding clouds of smoke and fumes. Then from every quarter the attackers dashed in, and crowds of merciless brutes swarmed on deck shooting, stabbing, and slashing. That was usually the end.

Steamers were less liable to be becalmed, but engine breakdowns were not infrequent, and then the same programme was followed. Finally, even after the trick of coupling up pipes to the boilers and meeting the attackers with scalding steam and water which kept them from boarding, the pirates developed a new plan of attack. A number of them took tickets as coolie deck passengers, and when off an arranged part of the coast suddenly rose and attacked the ship's crew. It is an old method often quite successfully worked to this day.

204

Under these various difficulties and conditions the Indian Government naturally hesitated to make a mail contract which they had little reason to suppose could be carried out. Mackinnon and Mackenzie were determined that the mail contract was an essential to their new services, and at last, mainly through the warm support given them by Sir Bartle Frere, one of the Supreme Council of the Government of India, they obtained their contract on all the new services. The title of the Company was then changed to its present one of the British India Steam Navigation Company.

All the difficulties were successfully fought through, and when five steamers—two of them entirely new—were lost in cyclones, they were replaced, additional ships added, and the number of mail sailings increased.

In 1869, the Company was faced with one of the troubles which then, on the opening of the Suez Canal, beset the P. & O. Their older ships had to meet the competition of new steamers which broke into their trade with all the advantage of using the new economical compound engines. The British India had to re-engine practically their whole fleet, and their first ship to pass through the Canal into European waters was the " India," sent home with a cargo, but with the primary object of being re-engined.

A new service was started between England and the East, and another, which still continues, between London and East Africa.

In 1874, there appeared on the scene a Mr. James Lyle Mackay, a youngster sent out from London to the Calcutta office. It was an event of little importance then, but this was the young man who was to become Lord Inchcape, and to influence so profoundly the fate and progress of his own British India and also of the P. & O.

There is no need for me to describe here the personal story of the progress of young Mackay to his control of the British India, because this has only recently been fully told in the Inchcape biography by Hector Bolitho.

In 1881, a contract was made with the Queensland Government for a monthly service between London and Brisbane by the Torres Straits. For about two years the Line struggled against an insufficient traffic of cargo or passengers, but the regular running and low freight rates built the business to a paying basis.

A new complication cropped up in the jealousy and disfavour of the other States to the attraction being offered emigrants to the fertile Queensland areas. To meet any objections to non-Australian companies in the trade, the British India in 1886 acquired an interest in the Australian Steam Navigation Company, which, in amalgamation with the Queensland Steam Shipping Company, formed the Australasian United Steam Navigation Company, now a leading firm in the Pacific trade and one of the associated companies of the P. & O. and British India.

From the very first days of the British India, the most amicable relations prevailed between them and the P. & O., because the services of the two linked together to their mutual advantage. The British India ships acted as feeders to the P. & O., and in the reverse direction the P. & O. brought to and from India passengers and goods which could best—or in some cases only—be carried to ports served by the British India. I may add that the same position still applies to-day.

Even after the British India began their European lines, more or less in competition with the P. & O., the friendly relations and mutual helpfulness continued. It was a natural outcome that in both managements the thought must have occurred of a possible fusion, and as early as 1901 or 1902, Sutherland and Sir James Mackay (as Lord Inchcape then was) had some private and informal talks on the subject. Nothing came of these, however, not even a formal meeting and minuting of the proposals, because at that time Mr. Duncan Mackinnon was Chairman of the British India, and he was so satisfied with the power and standing of his Company and so proud of his Chairmanship of it that it was certain he would not listen to any suggestions for fusion with any company, however important and powerful.

These proposals were not revived until March 1914, when Lord Inchcape was Chairman of the British India, although it was curious that, quite two years before, there had been tales in the City that the P. & O. were planning great extensions and amalgamations, and, as a result, wild and unjustified speculations in P. & O. shares sent the price of them soaring beyond all reason. This continued for a time, although the P. & O. management offered the flattest denials to the rumours, and there were moments when the purchase of a block of shares rushed the value of stock up from £250 to over £400.

The negotiations between the managements of the P. & O. and British India continued from March to May 1914, with such complete secrecy that it fell like a bombshell on the City when the result was announced and the proposals for amalgamation were formally put before the shareholders.

Putting it as briefly as possible, the basis of the amalgamation was that the P. & O. exchanged Preference Stock to the value of £700,000 for an equal value of Preference Stock in the British India; and that the P. & O. gave their Deferred Stock for £638,133 in exchange for nearly a million of British India paid-up Ordinary Stock. In the joint Board of the associated companies, there were twelve Directors from the P. & O. Board and eight from the British India.

What this vast amalgamation meant I cannot explain better than in the words of the P. & O. Chairman to the Extraordinary General Meeting of the Proprietors called to confirm the provisional agreement. He said: " It means that we (that is, the combined P. & O. and British India) command the employment of a capital of fifteen millions sterling. It means that we command the employment of a tonnage of a million and a quarter tons, and this tonnage and this capital will be worked with a common aim and purpose for the prosperity of a great national enterprise."

The resolution in favour of the amalgamation was carried with only a single dissentient.

At this same meeting, Sir Thomas Sutherland announced his intention of retiring from the Chairmanship he had held for some thirty years, and from the unbroken and assiduous service he had given to the Company for over sixty years from 1852 to 1914. The changes he had seen in the Company and in the progress of ships and steam navigation can only be compared to the changes Willcox and Anderson had lived through; and, perhaps in less extreme degree as regards steam propulsion and shipbuilding, the experiences in the lifetime of Lord Inchcape from 1874 to his death as Chairman in 1932.

CHAPTER TWENTY-NINE

War Services—1914–18

On the outbreak of the Great War, the P. & O. and British India had about 200 ships at sea ; inside a couple of months, half of them were at sea again, but in the service of the Government, as armed cruisers, troopships, and transports of munitions, stores, and material of war. In the same two months had also begun the losses which, throughout the War, and especially in the unrestricted submarine campaign of 1917, kept piling up steadily in casualties to ships and men.

I could go on and fill this chapter (and others) with such figures and with reports of how this ship was lost and that one escaped ; and with tales of skilful and gallant Commanders of the Companies' ships who brought their ships through, or had them sunk under them and shipped out again as soon as they could get another command.

It would be impossible, however, in one short section of this History to tell the full tale of the share of the P. & O. and British India and their allied Companies in the War, and I think it may be more acceptable if I tell a few tales of experiences of men who are still " on deck " and known to the travelling public of to-day.

Actually, I find, in a glance over the records of some of these men, that between them they give us a good cross-section picture of the varied duties, perils, and experiences suffered by the Companies' fleets and personnel.

When war was declared, the " Mantua " was completing a cruise in the Baltic, and, warned by wireless of the danger of being cut off by the enemy, she made a full-speed dash for home waters. There is a persistent and oft-repeated story still told that, being short of coal and

S.S. "MEDINA," 12,358 tons. Built 1911

Leaving Portsmouth for the Indian Durbar with Their Majesties King George V and Queen Mary on board

being unable to risk any delay or danger of capture or internment in a foreign port, the engineers gutted the ship of any fittings below that would burn, and kept the fires going with them.

Captain E. P. Parfitt, R.N.R., now retired, was then in the " Mantua " as a young officer, but he can give me no confirmation of this story of fittings being used for firing. A possible explanation of this discrepancy has been given me—that an order to gut all fittings out of the ship being given the minute she arrived in port for her conversion to an armed cruiser, it was simpler to say nothing of this job being well begun before the ship reached port, with endless reports and explanations why.

Anyhow, the conversion was carried out at such speed that by the 13th August, the " Mantua " had been fitted with eight 4·7 guns, and was ready for sea as an armed cruiser with all her war stores on board. She survived the War, returned to the Company, and was only sold to the breakers in 1935.

Captain Parfitt left the " Mantua " and the Company's service for the Royal Navy (as so many others of the Companies' officers did, and more would have done if they had not been ordered to carry on the vital work of the fleet), and was in H.M.S. " Cochrane," and then the " Caradoc " of the Light Cruiser Squadron, which took her share with the Squadron in war actions, including Jutland. He will be remembered by many P. & O. passengers as commanding the " Moldavia."

What that operation was, of converting a liner to armed cruiser, I had very vividly pictured to me some time ago by another Commander of the P. & O., Captain A. W. Drew. He was in the " Macedonia " when war began, and she was converted to armed cruiser at the same time as the " Mantua," and in fact tied with her in that record of being ready for sea as an armed cruiser in 9 days.

The " Macedonia " missed the actions of the Falklands, but captured the store ship which had been supplying the German fleet, and although she was for some time busy hunting the enemy raiders then at sea, never met one. She did, however, meet the " Carmania," and heard how that ship, in a severe action with an enemy raider, had narrowly escaped destruction because she caught

P

fire through some of her wooden fittings having been left when she was converted to armed cruiser.

The " Macedonia " then had quite a quantity of similar wooden fittings in her, but on hearing what a danger they might prove, orders were given for a ruthless clearance. " Wrecking parties " were told off and armed with axes and crowbars. At first some of them could hardly bring themselves to use their weapons on the really beautiful panelling and furniture, but " orders is orders," and the wreckers went lustily to work. Huge plate-glass mirrors, costly panelling, stair-cases, carvings, beautiful furniture, decorations, and fittings were torn down, hacked to pieces, slung up in bundles on deck, and flung over-board. The interior was literally gutted to the naked metal bulkhead and floor plates.

Captain Drew stayed in the " Macedonia " through the War, and on return to the P. & O. after the War, served in the " Sicilia," " Razmak," and " Kaisar-i-Hind " as Chief Officer, and is now (at this time of writing) Staff Commander of the " Strathmore."

Mention of the " Kaisar-i-Hind " reminds me of the amazing escapes she had in the War. She only completed building in the first year of the War, and she had a speed of about 1 knot more than previous P. & O. liners—a fact which apparently saved her several times, because the German submarine Commanders aimed their torpedoes, calculating the interception angle on the known top-speed rate of others of the P. & O. fleet.

Captain John Murray Legg, who after the War commanded the " Mantua " for twelve years and now commands the " Ranpura," went through the War in the " Kaisar-i-Hind," and has kindly given me these notes on her escapes. The first attack on her was in the Mediterranean in 1916, when a submerged U-boat, evidently waiting to catch her dead abeam, loosed a torpedo which passed a long 100 feet astern. If it had hit, the submarine would have made a better bag than usual, because on board the " Kaisar " were Lord Chelmsford, Viceroy of India, his wife, four daughters, and his Chiefs of Staff.

The next escape was in June 1917, when again a U-boat fired a torpedo from somewhere broad on the beam. The U-boat Commanders had apparently been advised of the extra speed of the "Kaisar," but she was doing half a knot more than on the previous occasion, and the torpedo slid harmlessly past, although only 15 feet or so astern.

"Third time lucky" escape was only a month later, when, under a similar broadside-on attack, the torpedo passed so close astern that those watching its approach held their breaths, expecting to feel the shock and roar of the explosion as the bubbles were seen coming straight for the stern. This time the miss was by fewer feet than could be counted.

But the third-time-lucky escape was completely outdone by the fourth. This was just before the end of the War, and the ship was carrying over 3,000 troops and a crew of 500—a hopeless mass of men to have got away from a quickly sinking ship without terrible loss of life. This time the torpedo hit, and hit in the most vulnerable spot possible . . . but—by the Grace—did not explode ! On reaching port, it was found that the plates had been dented in a few feet forward of the fore stokehold, where an explosion would have wrecked the forward bulkhead and blown a yawning hole through into the engine-room and stokehold. It would inevitably have sunk the ship with an appalling loss of life.

For years after the War, whenever the ship went into dock for the repainting of her red under-water body, the damaged plates were painted a vivid green, and this was only discontinued a few years ago after the plates were replaced with new ones.

So far I have told tales of ships surviving the War and escaping attacks. There is, unfortunately, a long and more tragic tale of losses to tell, although even in these there is much, or more, in which we may take pride. The loss of the "Ballarat" is a fair sample which redounds to the credit of the troops on board even more than to that of the ship's officers and crew, as was very fully explained to me by the P. & O. officer who was there.

Captain Sheepwash, who after the War commanded the Branch liners "Benalla" and "Barrabool," was then in the "Ballarat." On the 27th April, 1917, she was nearing the English Channel with Australian reinforcements on board, when, without any torpedo being sighted, although it was broad daylight and there was an escorting destroyer near, and fifty men on look-out on each side of the " Ballarat," she was fairly and squarely hit by a big torpedo. The shattering explosion smashed one propeller and bent the other's shaft, destroyed the gun supports, and split the 6-inch gun on the steering house, broke away the main steam-pipe, brought down the aerials and buckled the watertight bulkhead between the shaft tunnel and engine-room. The ship began to fill at a rate that brought her perceptibly lower in the water every minute.

The signal for " Boat stations " was given, the troops quietly fell in, and in a few minutes twenty boats were away, rafts were dropped over, and troops transferred to them. Destroyers were seen racing for the ship, and these quickly picked up the men from boats and rafts. One destroyer ranged alongside, and the troops waiting their turn on deck were taken off in orderly batches.

The ship was desperately low in the water, and nobody knew the minute she would plunge under. The destroyer alongside was crowded with men, and the word was passed up that she could take only thirty more. To the troops drawn up in two ranks on the promenade deck, their Commander gave the order—" Thirty files from the right—right turn." Thirty *double* files obeyed the order, and, at the next, " Quick march," moved off.

A ship's officer saw the mistake, pointed it out—" You've sixty there, sir—two ranks of thirty." The Commanding Officer promptly shouted, " Rear rank—halt—front ! " and the thirty men, halted, quietly turned to their front and watched the others file off. Fortunately, a drifter came barging alongside, and over into her the rest of the Australians were hurried. The ship went down, but every man of the 1,750 on board was saved.

Another striking example of discipline drew a commendatory report from the Admiral of Patrols in the Mediterranean when the British India " Chyebassa " was torpedoed. The explosion tore a huge hole in the hull, and the boats were immediately ordered away with most of the crew, leaving the Captain and a few officers on the bridge, and the gun's crew standing by their gun.

The Royal Navy patrol ship dashed up, reached the boats, and was about to begin picking them up, when from the " Chyebassa " came a hail—" All boats return." Without hesitation, the boats pulled back, were hooked on and swung up, the men jumped aboard, and while some stood lined up on the boat-deck, the engine-room staff went below, and the ship began to steam slowly in towards the shore, about 20 miles distant.

Ship discipline of quite another sort was described to me by the Captain Sheepwash I have mentioned. At the close of the War he was in the " Borda " when she was repatriating 900 German women and children from Dar-es-Salaam. The women were of all classes, and those of the military and official caste were particularly arrogant and difficult to control. A German officer on board was told off to deal with the job, and told that as " O.C. Women " he would be held strictly accountable for their good order and discipline, with the full support of the Captain in any measure he might take, however drastic.

A first outbreak occurred when a German lady, who had demanded the pick of the first-class passenger accommodation as the wife of a Very Very High Official, lost her temper and flung a plate at a steward. She was brought before the " O.C. Women," who sentenced her to be moved from her cabin and quartered with the third-class passengers, the wives of workmen and private soldiers, and not to be allowed in the first-class accommodation, to meet or speak to her friends. The " Punishment " worked wonderfully as a cure and a warning to others, and there was not another single case of indiscipline on board.

In speaking of the discipline of crews under the severest strain, it must not be forgotten that in both the P. & O. and British India ships a proportion of the crews were Indians, that these were never behind in steady discipline, and that, like the white officers and men, they were always ready to go to sea again after escape from a torpedoed or mined ship. The Indians in the engine-room and stokehold in particular stood up without flinching to the trying ordeal of staying or returning below in an effort to bring a badly damaged ship to port or shore, not knowing the moment she might sink or be hit by another torpedo.

When the " Poona " was mined in the Channel, a gaping hole was torn under her forefoot, the forward well deck wrenched and buckled, and all deck gear forward of the bridge reduced to wreckage. The hull was also split by a long transverse crack that opened the deck plates and ran down the side to the water's edge. All hands took to the boats and were presently transferred to the patrol vessels that hurried in to the sound of the explosion.

The Captain and Chief Officer then returned to the ship and pulled round examining her. She appeared to be sinking by the head, but she carried a specially valuable cargo, and the Captain determined to make an effort to get her ashore. He, with his Chief Engineer and officers, went aboard the wreck again, and with them went six lascars who *volunteered* for the dangerous job.

Tugs were signalled for and came out, hawsers were passed, the crew called aboard again. White and Indian engine-room staff and firemen went below and raised steam, and, partly under tow, partly under her own power, the ship crept slowly, stern first, towards Portsmouth, the steam pumps running their hardest, but not quite coping with the inrush of water.

It was 40 hours after the explosion when the ship anchored at Spithead, and another 24 hours passed with a fresh wind and sea threatening a sudden end, before the ship could be towed into dock. Over three-quarters of a million sterling were saved by that feat, and it was only performed by the cold-drawn courage of the ship's company— white and Indian.

Captain Cotching, now commanding the " Rajputana," had a very similar experience when he was Chief Officer of the " Caledonia " in December 1915. Off Marseilles, the ship, with about 500 passengers on board, was hit by a mine or torpedo which blew in the whole bottom of No. 1 hold. The boats were sent away with all passengers and the crew, except for the Captain, Chief Officer, a couple of engineers, and a handful of the crew who stayed on board, kept up steam, and headed slowly for Marseilles. Tugs and tenders hurried out and picked up the boats, and an escorting destroyer circled round while tugs took hold of the ship and got her in. She was duly repaired and continued in service to the end of the War.

The war work of the Companies was not confined to the dodging or meeting of mines and torpedoes. For example, both P. & O. and British India ships took their share in the Gallipoli operations, from the landings right up to the evacuation. Two officers were in the same ship there—Captain J. A. Smith, who in 1935 was Staff Commander of the " Viceroy of India " and now commands the " Ranchi," and Captain H. R. Rhodes, now commanding the " Mongolia." They were in the " Kalyan " when she put two batteries of artillery ashore at Suvla Bay, and the ship, like most in the landing, was under heavy fire, was liberally peppered with gusts of shrapnel, and was struck in the funnel by a shell which passed plunging downwards and burst in the fiddley. The ship was full of ammunition, but luckily none of this exploded, and the damage was confined to the local effect of the burst.

Captain E. E. Starling, now Staff Commander of the " Strathnaver," was also at Gallipoli in the " Devanha," from which the 12th Battalion of the Australians was landed. The troops disembarked in the ship's boats, which were towed in by destroyers while the ship steamed close in to a point farther along to divert fire from the boats by making a show of attempting another landing. The troops were put ashore at Anzac Beach, and the " Devanha " people watched with feelings of mingled admiration and anguish the terrible toll being taken of the landing troops.

One of the ship's lifeboats is now in the Australian War Museum at Canberra, and her bullet-riddled and shell-splintered remains tell eloquently of what she and her men went through.

That same night the " Devanha " took off the first of the terrible flood of casualties, every man on board turning to voluntary duties of doctors' helpers. The ship was later made a hospital ship, and continued on that work right through to the Evacuation. She was the last hospital ship to leave Gallipoli.

Captain E. P. Lyndon (formerly commanding the " Ballarat " and " Mooltan " and now the " Strathnaver ") went from the P. & O. to the Navy in 1914, and was posted to the cross-Channel steamer " Folkestone," which, after a spell of mine-sweeping at Scapa Flow, was sent to the Dardanelles to sweep a channel clear for the attacking warships.

At Malta, the ship was fitted with steel shields over the bridge, and the ship's company had a chance to estimate the odds calculated by experts when they found the Navy men willing to bet anything up to 40 to 1 against the little ship getting out of the Dardanelles—if she were not sunk getting in.

Actually her first duty was to land 400 troops of the 9th Division from the troopship. This done, she hurried back for another load, vying with her sister ship, the " Hythe," in how many she could carry. The two of them, of about 500 tons, each actually carried in 1,100 men, packed in and on every part of the ship that offered foothold, or even handhold.

Lyndon also took part in landing the troops for the Suvla attack, and remained at Gallipoli until the Evacuation. After that, he was promoted from Navigating Officer to a command, and went on patrol duties in the Mediterranean. He believes his ship was the first to have initiated what came to be known later as the " Q Ship " plan of enticing submarines within range of guns concealed on an ostensible merchantman. He tells me that the ship was disguised as a peaceful trader, and that the crew of naval ratings were rigged out in all sorts of untidy costumes, with the Midshipmen dressed as girls. The guns were concealed, and all preparations made for dropping the disguise and opening fire on any deluded U-boat that came within range. None did, although one was sighted following for a time.

Other inshore excursions and landings were shared by five ships of the P. & O. and British India, which carried troops on the landing in German East Africa in November 1914. The first landing and attack was a failure, the troops were driven back, and the lifeboats of the transports manned by P. & O. and British India volunteers went in and helped take off the retreating force. The ships were also under the fire of shore batteries.

Other variations in war experiences of ships and men of the Company were " enjoyed " by Captain R. Harrison, D.S.O., R.D., R.N.R., at present commanding the " Strathmore " and Commodore of the P. & O. fleet.

Captain Harrison served through the War in the Royal Navy, to which he was called from the P. & O. in August 1914. He was appointed to the old cruiser " Sutlej," which, however, escaped that holocaust in which the " Cressy," " Aboukir," and " Hogue " were lost. From her he went to the " Conquest," of the Harwich Force, sharing the activities of that famous squadron and receiving the Reserve Decoration in 1916.

He was next appointed to the " Dalhousie," of the Indian Marine, and then to command of the gunboat " Cranefly " on the Tigris, and of the bigger " Mantis." He was given charge of the naval guns from the Tigris gunboats, and " navigated " them across Persia to the Caspian, a piece of arduous and exacting work which won him the D.S.O.

Since the War, Captain Harrison has commanded some of the best-known of the P. & O. liners, including the " Naldera," " Mooltan," " Strathnaver," and " Strathmore."

In the course of the War the P. & O. and British India lost 38 ships, some of them the finest liners in the fleets, leaving out others like some I have mentioned, which were mined or submarined and just dragged into port or on to the beach in time to prevent sinking in deep water. Up to the end of 1915, 42 P. & O. ships had been taken over from their usual work, but the mail services continued to carry on as best they might.

The mail-carrying work meantime had increased to an extreme degree, mainly owing to the number of letters and parcels dispatched to the troops in the East, Egypt, and the Mediterranean. The reduced number of ships were carrying at the end of 1915 more than ten times the amount of mail carried in the beginning of that year.

In the War years, the P. & O., under the Chairmanship of Lord Inchcape, continued the plans of expansion and association with other companies which began with the amalgamation of the P. & O. and British India. Since these are an important part of the P. & O. history, I have reserved them for another chapter.

CHAPTER THIRTY

More Associated Companies

IN the immediate years after Lord Inchcape's taking over the joint control of the P. & O. and British India, the activities which he displayed (apart from his great services to the Government and the country) and which left their most permanent mark on the P. & O. were in the extension of the Company's connection and the association made with one famous shipping company after another.

I list these briefly in their turn, to return presently to an outline of the history of each of the associated companies.

The first was the New Zealand Shipping Company, which with its subsidiary Federal Line was " brought into the fold " in 1916. In 1917, there came in the Union Steam Ship Company of New Zealand, the Hain Steam Ship Company, and the Nourse Line; in 1919, an interest was acquired in the Orient Line, and the bulk of the shares of the Khedivial Mail Company bought in. In 1920, the General Steam Navigation Company was joined up, and so renewed a connection which dated back to the earliest days of the Peninsular Steam Navigation Company, or rather the pre-Peninsular Company Willcox & Anderson days.

The New Zealand Shipping Company was formed, with a capital of £100,000, in 1873 by a group of merchants in Christchurch, New Zealand, who were dissatisfied with the shipping facilities of those days, and thought they might be improved by a line primarily serving their requirements.

At that time, there was a heavy demand for passages by emigrants to all the colonies, and the conditions under which some of the migrants were carried to New Zealand were not considered satisfactory or likely to attract the right class to that colony. In addition to this, the irregularity of shipping, and the number of cargoes ruined from damage by sea water and breakages, were other good reasons why the merchants should intervene.

The Company being formed, the next step was to send a Manager to London to open an office and arrange for the charter or purchase of suitable ships. The first four ships which the Company owned were bought, but four new ones were ordered to be built to the special needs of the trade. At the same time, others were chartered for the voyage, and in the first six months of the Company's existence, no less than 40 ships were sent out. In the first three years 150 ships carried out 20,670 passengers.

Some of those early clippers made great names for themselves and the Company, both for their speed and for the room and comfort in the accommodation. In 1875, the " Rangitiki " embarked 300 migrants at Plymouth, and made the passage from there to Lyttleton in 73 days, or 67 days from land to land. This was beaten in 1880 by the " Waimate," in 66 days from the Channel, a record which was not equalled in the thirty years from 1870 to 1900. Another vessel, the " Otaki," ran from Lyttleton to the Channel in 63 days.

The outward passages then were all made round the Cape of Good Hope, some of the ships never sighting land after clearing the Channel until they saw New Zealand or perhaps the coast of Tasmania. The homeward run was by Cape Horn, and the same routes are followed to this day by those vessels which do not use the Panama Canal.

The first frozen mutton was carried from New Zealand by sailing ships, many of the cargoes having to be frozen on board on account of there being no freezing works at the loading ports. Although the first shipments were not uniformly successful, they were, nevertheless, sufficiently so to encourage further attempts.

It was natural that the merchants and farmers of New Zealand who owned the Company were eager to persevere with the frozen-meat trade, because in it they saw a new market for their surplus sheep which formerly they could use to advantage only by boiling them down for the tallow in them.

When the Company was ten years old it owned 16 of the finest clipper ships, and was already launching out into steam. The first steamer chartered was the Clyde-built " Stad Haarlem," which took out 600 emigrants in 1879. In 1883, 5 steamers were running under charter, and 5 new ones were being built. The Company was the first to establish a regular line of steamers between England and New Zealand, and in 1884 a mail contract was secured and a monthly service was started.

The sailing ship did not yield to the new steamers without a hard struggle, and there are many tales told of the rivalry between the Company's crews in sail and in steam.

There is an interesting relic of those days still shown in the Company's house flag. The flag is white, with a red St. George's Cross, and a blue letter in each corner of the initials "N. Z. S. Co." Because in the early days the steamships carried practically as much sail as the sailing ships, and because when under canvas the funnel was often hidden, especially to anyone seeing the ship approaching bow on, a triangular pennant in red, white, and blue was flown above the house flag by the steamships.

Steam gradually replaced the whole fleet of sailing ships, but even after the latter had gone, the custom of flying the pennant, or " steam cornet " as it used to be called, had become firmly established, and because it had " always " been flown in steam, so it was continued and still is.

In the years before the War and the association with the P. & O., large additions were made to the fleet in vessels of 11,000 tons and over. These were passenger ships embodying the latest devices for comfort and safety, and at the same time new cargo steamers were built for refrigerated cargoes which continue to form an important part of the trade.

The Panama Canal was opened in 1914, and the New Zealand Shipping Company was the first regular line to adopt that route in November 1914. When the Company became associated with the

P. & O., it, together with its associated Line, the Federal Steam Navigation Company, Ltd., owned 28 liners totalling 220,000 tons. In recent years the two Companies have made marked progress in the building of fast cargo-carriers with motor engines. The latest of these, the " Orari," " Opawa," and " Otaio " of the New Zealand Line and the " Durham " and " Dorset " of the Federal Line, all of about 10,000 tons, have made some fast runs out by the old route round the Cape, and in 1935 the " Orari," on the homeward passage by Suez, ran from Fremantle to Hull in 30 days, calling at Aden to re-bunker Diesel oil and at Malta and Dunkirk to discharge cargo.

In 1929–30, a new and improved " Rangi " class was built and put on the New Zealand run by Panama. These vessels, the " Rangitiki," " Rangitane," and " Rangitata," are some of the finest and most luxurious of passenger liners, and have proved immensely popular with the travelling public.

Special consideration has been given to the needs of insulated cargo, the seven insulated holds having a capacity for about 150,000 carcasses of mutton. Oil engines are used for propulsion, and also for such auxiliary power as lighting requirements.

The New Zealand Shipping Company rendered notable service in the War, carrying a constant stream of troops and reinforcements to the various fronts, as well as food supplies so badly wanted in England. Heavy losses were incurred by ships running the gauntlet of submarines and mines, and the New Zealand and Federal Companies lost in the War 10 steamers of an aggregate 80,000 tons gross.

The " Otaki " will always be memorable in naval history for one of the bravest actions fought in the War. She was a comparatively small ship armed with a single 4·7-inch gun when she met the heavily armed German raider " Moewe." Captain A. Bisset Smith, of the " Otaki," refused to stop when ordered, and opened fire with his one gun. His ship was heavily out-gunned, but although she suffered serious damage from the enemy shells, being hit by thirty of them and set on fire, with four of her crew killed and nine wounded, she continued firing to the last, until the crew had to abandon their sinking ship. The raider also suffered, and a fire was raised which was only with great difficulty extinguished. Captain Smith went down with his ship, and a post-humous V.C. was awarded to him " for conspicuous bravery and devotion to his country in the presence of the enemy, when he fought a very gallant action against overwhelming odds and all but succeeded in destroying the enemy, finally going down in his ship with the British colours still flying."

The New Zealand Shipping Company now owns 16 vessels of a total 181,245 tons, and the Federal 14 of 142,293 tons, a grand total of 323,538 tons Gross Register. The Federal Line is a direct descendant of the old firm of Money, Wigram & Co., which through Wigram's former partnership with Greens of the Blackwall Yard, can trace a con-tinuous connection with shipping and the shipbuilding business to the times of Queen Elizabeth, and of Phineas and Peter Pett, who were amongst the first of the ship-designers capable of " building " a ship on paper first and then reproducing her on the stocks.

In 1805, the Blackwall Yard and business had come through a suc-cession of inheritance to the Greens, when Wigram bought a share, and the firm of Green & Wigram, while turning out a constant string of East Indiamen and Blackwall frigates, began to build Indiamen for their own private trading. Their first house flag was a red St. George's Cross on white, but because this was the flag of an Admiral of the Royal Navy, it was altered by placing a blue square over the middle.

When Green and Wigram dissolved their partnership, Wigram retained the old flag, and it is this which is flown by the Federal liners, with the device repeated on the funnels. The Line still continues to name its vessels after English counties, just as Green and Wigram did with their old Blackwall liners, in many cases perpetuating the most famous of those old ships' names.

The New Zealand Shipping Company and Federal Steam Naviga-tion Company, although under the same management, continue to fly their own house flags.

The Hain Company was brought into the P. & O. Group in 1917 on terms different from those usually followed under Lord Inchcape's methods. The method in most cases was that adopted in the fusion of the P. & O. and British India, under which the P. & O. made an exchange of shares to an equal or agreed value for shares in the associated company. This method, however, was varied in the case of the Hain Company, when their shares came into the market on the death of the Company's founder. The shares were bought in for cash with the fleet of 27 up-to-date cargo steamers having a gross tonnage of 108,707 tons.

The Company was founded in 1878 by Edward (later Sir Edward) Hain, a native of St. Ives, Cornwall. Until his death in 1917, the ships were registered at St. Ives, and all were given names beginning with the West Country " Tre-," like " Trevessa " and " Trefusis," a practice which still continues.

The Hain Steam Ship Company is engaged in general trading with modern steamers of 4,000 to 5,000 tons and two motor vessels of about 5,200 tons building.

The Nourse Line, with 6 vessels totalling 31,449 tons, was brought into association with the P. & O. and British India in 1917, because the vessels, specially built for the trade in the tropics, and having well-established connections in the East, fitted in well with the British India services.

The Nourse business was created by Captain James Nourse, who owned and commanded the sailing ship " Ganges " in 1861, and expanded by degrees to a fleet of over 20 fine sailing ships of from about 1,000 to 1,700 tons net register. They were employed in the Indian trade, mainly in the business of carrying Indian coolie emigrants to the West Indies for employment on the sugar estates.

Five years after Captain Nourse's death, incorporation as a Private Company was effected in 1903, and immediately thereafter began the disposal of the sailing vessels, with replacement by steamships built specially for the Company's regular trade from Calcutta and Rangoon to the West Indies and Cuba via the Cape of Good Hope.

From the first, Nourse had a general practice of naming his ships after rivers, mostly Indian or Irish, he himself being Irish of the Irish. Since the advent of steam, the names have been always Indian rivers.

The fleet consists of cargo vessels of 5,000 to 6,000 tons Gross Register, which trade regularly in the Company's service as described, the " Ganges " being specially constructed for the conveyance of Indian passengers to and from Fiji.

The latest vessel will be Diesel Doxford engined, to carry about 9,200 tons total dead weight.

The Union Steam Ship Company of New Zealand had its origin in a few small steamers of 300 and 400 tons, running between Dunedin and Port Chalmers, and in the Harbour Steam Company co-ordinating these services.   This Company was re-formed in 1875 under the present title.

The whole history of the Union is one long tale of an enterprise, initiative, and expansion which is the more amazing in the extent and rapidity of its growth when it is remembered that the business began as a purely local one with limited resources and apparently restricted opportunities.   The most active of the founders in 1875 was Mr. (late Sir) James Mills, who retained the leadership and control of the Company's destinies throughout his long life.   He died only last year in England.

For the first two years the Union ran only local coastal services, but in 1877 two steamers were bought and put on the " inter-colonial " run to Sydney.   A year later, the Union bought four more steamers and the New Zealand business from McMeckan, Blackwood, & Co. of Australia, then a well-known Shipping Company in Australia.   A new weekly service was opened between New Zealand and Melbourne.

One year more, and other vessels were being built and bought, including the " Rotomahana " of 1,727 tons, notable as the first steamer to be built of mild steel and fitted with bilge keels.   She was first placed on the inter-Colonial run, and it is safe to say that no steamer in Australian waters was more famous and more popular throughout her long life.   She was known as " The Greyhound of the Pacific," and was only sold for breaking up in 1925.

The Company has throughout its career been particularly noteworthy in its readiness to initiate or adopt improvements in shipbuilding, propulsion, and equipment.   Their first steel ship was followed by the " Manapouri," the first merchant ship to be fitted throughout with incandescent electric lamps ; and their " Mararoa "

S.S. "CARTHAGE," 15,000 tons. Built 1931

was the first vessel with triple expansion engines in the Pacific and to be seen in San Francisco.

The Union obtained a mail contract to San Francisco in 1885, and new services were being established with Fiji and other Pacific Isles. In 1913, the famous " Niagara " of 13,415 tons was built and put on the trans-Pacific run. She was the first steamer in the world to be granted a Board of Trade certificate for burning oil fuel instead of coal.

In 1925, the " Aorangi " (17,491 tons) was built, and was then the largest motor liner in the world, and the largest fastest Diesel-engined passenger and mail liner afloat. This was the Company's jubilee year, and in their fifty years they had expanded from their few small local traders to a fleet of 73 steamers totalling nearly 254,000 tons, an achievement remarkable in itself, but more so in the high standard, the outstanding quality, and fame of its fine ships.

The trade which the Union had initiated across the Pacific to San Francisco, calling at Honolulu, and which from 1885 had carried on a mail service jointly with an American line, was brought to an end in 1900. In that year the annexation of Hawaii by the United States brought those islands within the American " coast-wise " laws, which prohibited any but American ships from trading between American ports. The Union Company was therefore shut out of the run to San Francisco with a call at Honolulu.

In 1910, a new service was opened, substituting Tahiti for Honolulu as a calling port. The new trade, however, was small compared to what the Union Company had built up by the Honolulu route. The service was closed down in 1936.

In that year, the Union had a magnificent luxury liner built by Vickers-Armstrong. The " Awatea " is of 14,000 tons, with a speed of 23 knots, and her arrival in New Zealand after a passage out by Panama in record time was hailed with acclamation, and after she went on the New Zealand-Australia run, she was speedily christened " Queen of the Tasman." She is the fastest ship in the Southern Hemisphere, and there are, in fact, only two British ocean-going liners which beat her in speed—the " Queen Mary " and the " Empress of Britain."

In 1935, the Union Company established in New Zealand its Union

Airways, and daily air services were opened on a main line Dunedin, Christchurch, Blenheim, and Palmerston North, with connections to Wellington. The latest plans are for an extension of the services to bring in Auckland and Wellington via Palmerston North and New Plymouth, so that the main cities of both North and South Islands will be linked by air.

It is noteworthy that this development of the Union Steam Ship Company is the outcome of a remarkable piece of foresight on the part of the Management. As far back as 1913, new powers were taken to permit of development of air services at any future date, and it was under this power that the services were begun over twenty years later.

The Union Steam Ship Company, although now allied with the P. & O., is entirely under the control of its own Board and Management in its New Zealand Headquarters offices. The benefits of such local control were very markedly made plain during the War.

In August 1914, the first work undertaken by the Company was the transport of coal for the Navy in Australasian and Pacific waters. The most notable services, however, were the transport of troops, first of the New Zealand Expeditionary Force to Samoa, then of the troops to Egypt and the Western front, and even in later days the transport of American troops across the Atlantic.

Two liners were converted to hospital ships, another became a dispatch vessel in the Mediterranean and later a minelayer. The old " Aorangi " first served as a Naval store ship, and was finally sunk to block one of the channels at Scapa Flow. A fine passenger steamer of 15,000 tons was building for the Vancouver Service, but on completion was taken over by the Government, made a cruiser, and served as " H.M.S. Avenger " until sunk by a torpedo.

The Company's ships carried to the various seats of war 61,813 out of a total of 100,444 troops from New Zealand. They also carried 45,000 other troops and 47,000 sick and wounded in the two hospital ships.

It was not only in the provision of ships that the Company helped, because its expert staff of workers gave their services in converting and fitting the steamers, the victualling and provision of stores and all the multitude of detail inherent in a shipping business and rendered more difficult by the change to war conditions. The advantage of the local control and management was clearly stated by the New Zealand Minister of Defence in an acknowledgment of the Company's services. He said that his department had been very fortunate in having the Union Company located in New Zealand, an advantage that had been responsible to a great extent for the constant success of the service. " The Company," he said, " have assisted us in every way in securing and equipping transports and hospital ships . . . if such a Company had not been domiciled in New Zealand, there would have been great difficulty in maintaining regularity as regards the transport of our reinforcements."

In 1919, the P. & O. acquired the bulk of the shares in the Khedivial Mail Company. This Company was not, as many apparently suppose, engaged in the express mail service which had carried on for years between Brindisi and Egypt.

This Brindisi–Alexandria Line was one which the P. & O. made world-famous with their express liners " Isis " and " Osiris," specially built and placed on the service in 1898 with a great turn of speed. The efforts of the two to cut down the time of mail transit were not confined to the sea run, and an officer of the P. & O. who knew the service has told me how the race against time (and between the two ships) was counted from the minute the first mail bag came aboard at the one port to the minute when the last bag was over the side at the other end. Every available man was turned on to the job of getting the mails aboard or overside at top speed, deck-hands, stewards, and even firemen and engineers joining in as eager volunteers to hustle the mails into and off the ship.

As the last bags were flung aboard, the Captain was waiting on the bridge with his hand on the engine-room telegraph, and the engineers below with their eyes on the telegraph dial and a full head of steam to their hand. On the instant of the last bag falling on deck, clash went the gang-plank down on the quay, the hawsers cast off, and the signal " clanged " below and set the ship sliding out at swiftly gathering speed.

The " Isis " and " Osiris " continued on this run until 1914, when the Government made good use of their speed and handiness in taking them over as special dispatch carriers.

To return to the Khedivial Mail—the trade of the Company when the P. & O. bought its shares was of Turkish, Black Sea, and Eastern Mediterranean ports and by Egypt to ports of the Red Sea, and the intention was to use the ships as feeders from these ports to the P. & O. at Port Said and Suez.

The upheaval of warring political interests and revolutions in the Near East after the close of the War strangled the trade, and the Khedivial was a money-losing concern instead of profitable to the P. & O.

The shares had fallen to a value well below that at which the P. & O. had bought when Lord Inchcape, considering himself to some extent personally responsible for the buying of the shares, very generously bought them from the P. & O. at the price they had paid, bearing the resulting loss out of his own pocket. This was in the summer of 1924, and since then the P. & O. (again contrary to belief and many published statements) has had no connection with the Khedivial Mail.

In November of the same year the P. & O. acquired an interest in the General Steam Navigation Company, Ltd., and so renewed an old association which went back to the first chartering of some of their little steamers by Willcox and Anderson.

The General Steam can claim to be the oldest steam-shipping company to have run regular open sea services—as distinct from purely river and estuary services—and to have carried these on continuously from 1824 under the same flag and constitution.

Some little time before the Company was formed a few owners were running their own small steamers, most of them on the same run between London Bridge and Margate as the Company's fleet of " Eagle " pleasure steamers cover to-day, and one with a line between London and Scotland—the latter being, I believe, the first regular steam line over an open sea route.

The prospectus for the formation of the Company called for a capital of £2 millions in shares of £100 each and with an immediate call of £2 10s. per share. This was an enormous capital for those days (the P. & O., you may recall, for their plans of extension to Egypt in

THE RT. HON. THE EARL OF INCHCAPE, G.C.S.I., G.C.M.G., K.C.I.E., LL.D.,
R.N.R.

Chairman and Managing Director, 1914–1932

From a painting by Oswald Birley

1840 had a capital of £1 million), but it was certainly no larger than the plans of the proposed company required, the prospectus stating that their vessels were to trade with India, North and South America, as well as Continental countries, and any others thought advisable.

At the first half-yearly meeting it was announced that the Company owned 15 steamers and proposed to pay a dividend of 16 per cent. A sailing list of 1826 shows that the Company was running regular lines to Calais, Boulogne, Rotterdam, Hamburg, and Dieppe, and also down to Lisbon, Oporto, and Gibraltar. The regular daily service of excursion steamers down London river were continued, and one of the first steamers on this, the " Eagle Packet," is now commemorated in the magnificent fleet of " Eagle " pleasure steamers running down-river from the Tower Pier all summer.

The Continental trade was steadily increased, and in the 1880's was extended to Mediterranean ports. In 1836, the London and Edinburgh Steam Packet Company was bought with their entire property of 6 steamers and premises and warehouses at Newhaven and London. A more notable purchase was made in 1853, when the General Steam bought up the entire German Navy—or German Confederacy as it was then known—ships, guns, and stores complete included. The warships were converted to cargo-carriers and added to the Company's regular fleet.

Since the Great War the Company has adopted a policy of expansion and development in many directions, both in the United Kingdom and abroad, and is now represented by its own offices in all the main Continental ports. Throughout the depression the Company took every favourable opportunity of acquiring kindred businesses which were offered, thereby consolidating its interests.

In 1935, the Moss-Hutchinson Line was acquired with its 16 steam and motor vessels and a long-established trade with the Continent and Mediterranean. The Moss Line of Liverpool and Hutchinson's of Glasgow had been combined only the year before.

The Moss Company was founded in 1823 with sailing ships trading to the Mediterranean until they added their first steamer in 1850. In 1935, they were trading between Glasgow and Liverpool and ports extending from Casablanca to the Levant and Black Sea. The Hutchinson firm was formed in 1860 with services to Havre and Bordeaux, later extended to the ports of Western France, Spain, and Portugal.

The General Steam's most recent acquisition was in 1936 by the incorporation of the New Medway Steam Packet Company's fleet, including the famous " Royal Daffodil," which took part in the Zeebrugge raid, and on the deck of which the annual Zeebrugge Day Service is held to commemorate both the day and her share in it.

In addition to their extensive fleets and trade, the General Steam own wharves, docks, warehouses, repair works, offices, and other premises in ports of the United Kingdom and elsewhere. In London they utilise wharves and warehouses extending from just below London Bridge to about half a mile below the Tower Bridge, with loading and discharging berths in the very heart of the river traffic. At Deptford they still own workshops and wharf for ships under minor repair, their land there having been bought in 1825 just after the Company was formed.

The General Steam continue, in their fine block of offices overlooking the Tower of London, their separate management under their own Board and Chairman ; as in turn the Moss-Hutchinson Line carry on their business separately but in close association with the General Steam.

Taking all the associated companies into the count, the " P. & O. Group " now commands, in round figures, nearly £14 millions capital and £8,750,000 in debentures, with a tonnage of steam and motor vessels of some 1,950,000 tons.

CHAPTER THIRTY-ONE

Post-War Years

NATURALLY, the first efforts of the P. & O. after the War were the rebuilding of the fleet, the replacement of lost ships, and the reconversion of those returned by the Government from the stripped bare interior of the armed cruisers or the troopers' accommodation to the normal saloons, cabins, and comforts of a passenger liner. In addition, many of the ships burning coal were altered to oil-burning.

The energy with which the fleet was built up again can be told in a few figures. The Fleet List of 1919 shows a total of 44 ships (including Branch Line) of 345,000 tons, the biggest being the " Kaisar-i-Hind " of 11,430 tons. There were no less than 19 listed as " Building."

The fleet by December 1925 had risen to 60 ships, totalling 604,810 tons, out of which only 1 was completing building and the rest at sea. The fleet included 7 ships of about 16,000 tons, and 2, the " Mooltan " and " Maloja," of over 20,000 tons.

The rebuilding of the fleet was complicated by labour troubles, which made long delays in delivery. There were sectional strikes like the boilermakers'; and later the brief but expensively disturbing General Strike, the long Coal Strike, and, in Australia, the Seamen's Strike added to the troubles.

World conditions affecting trade and shipping were also disturbed in those post-War years. In Japan there were bad earthquakes, in China clashes of wars and political unrest; in Australia there were droughts, and when these had gone and conditions had so improved that about 1929 it was reported there were more sheep there than there had been for thirty years, drought in China, unrest and boycotts in

India, the collapse of the rubber industry pushed the balance down again.

The saving factor was that the Companies' interests were so widespread, that what was " lost on the swings " in one part of the world or one trade was at least to some extent " made up on the roundabouts " in some other direction.

In the first year after the War, the Company began, or rather recommenced, the extension of their office premises and property in 122, Leadenhall Street, which they had occupied since 1848, when the office was moved from 51, St. Mary Axe, where Willcox and Anderson had established their business. Naturally, the offices had extended as the P. & O. did, and the amalgamation of the P. & O. and British India in 1914 made it necessary that a much greater extension should be made.

The War stopped any building operations, but as soon as possible after, various adjoining offices and premises were acquired, either at the back of the main offices or on the Leadenhall Street frontage and round the corner in St. Mary Axe. In 1920, the rebuilding of the main front and the building of two additional floors to the main office began. This main building, where the entrance and courtyard of the P. & O. offices now stand, was originally the King's Head Tavern, where in the reign of William III Sir John Fenwick and his confederates met to plot for the restoration of James II. The name of the tavern was afterwards changed to the King's Arms, a coaching inn which in 1732 was the starting-point of the Romford and Colchester coaches. The present courtyard is on the site of one which is marked on a map dated 1677. The inn later became converted to city offices, and was pulled down in 1857 to be rebuilt as the P. & O. offices.

Other premises were acquired as opportunity occurred, one of these being the old and historic eating-house, " The Ship and Turtle."

The original tavern was known as " The Ship," and it is recorded as existing in 1377 in the reign of Richard II, the trustees being the proprietors of Rochester Bridge. It was extended in 1735, and for many years was managed by a succession of landladies famous throughout the City. The title was changed to " The Ship and Turtle " in

1847, and it became an important Masonic Centre, while the eating-house was famous for its turtle. In the clipper-ship days it was a highly popular resort of the famous clipper captains, and after the historic tea race of 1866, when three ships left their port in China on the same tide and after the closest possible race in which the ships frequently changed places in the lead, the same three docked in London on the same tide, 99 days out from Foochow, it was at " The Ship and Turtle " that the three Captains dined together to celebrate the greatest ocean race ever sailed.

In 1930 began the world depression, with the political and financial crises here which ushered in the " slump " of 1931. This was at a time when the Company was in the middle of further fleet extensions and improvements. Some of the older ships were being replaced by those of a larger and more luxurious type, necessitated by the demands of the travelling public and the need for the Company to keep abreast of the latest and best in ship construction, equipment, and engines.

In 1930, 6 ships, aggregating 84,000 tons, were under construction, and the " Viceroy of India " had been added to the fleet only the year before. In 1931, the " Strathnaver " (22,547 tons) instituted the new order of " Straths," with their departure from the traditional black hulls and funnels and buff or " stone " upperworks for the white hulls and upperworks, red boot-topping, and golden-yellow funnels. This, however, was not such a complete innovation or " revolution " as has been supposed, because in the " Ferry Service " between Aden and Bombay the white hull and yellow funnel colouring was known for many years from 1908, when the " Salsette " went on the run.

The P. & O. was hit by more than the depression following the National crisis of 1931 here. The Annual Report for that year makes grim reading of " China . . . serious floods in the Yangtse preventing Hankow business ; Straits and Ceylon . . . general depression . . . great fall in rubber prices ; India . . . suffering from unrest and the Anti-Foreign boycott . . . marked decrease in exports and imports," and a summing up of the general situation in a sentence : " In almost all the Company's trades there had been a decrease in shipments."

In common with so many National and Governmental and business circles, the P. & O. that year had to make a 10 per cent. reduction in all rates of pay.

In 1932, the Chairman and Managing Director, the Right Hon. the Earl of Inchcape, G.C.S.I., G.C.M.G., K.C.I.E., died, having been raised from the Viscountcy to the Earldom in 1929 in recognition of his great national work.

He was succeeded as Chairman by the Honourable Alexander Shaw, who from 1920 had been on the Board of Directors, and from 1927 had assisted Lord Inchcape as a co-Managing Director and Deputy-Chairman. He could hardly have taken up the Chairmanship at a more difficult and trying time.

The affairs of the Company under his Chairmanship are not yet far enough astern to be classed as " history," but there are one or two facts which will certainly take due place in the future history of the P. & O., and which therefore require recording here as a part of the closing years of the P. & O.'s score of " One Hundred—Not Out ! "

In the four years 1932, 1933, 1934, and 1935, the Company paid no dividend on its Deferred Shares—which is certainly an item of " agony prolonged " unprecedented in the history of the Company. But at the General Meeting in 1935, the Chairman closed his address by saying that he felt " rather like a man who has been steadily walking through a long dark tunnel, and who, although still surrounded by gloom, begins to see the glimmer of light ahead." Within a year, on 21st October, 1936, a wireless went out to all the Company's ships that the second half of the 10 per cent. cut in salaries imposed in 1931 was restored as from the 1st October ; and at the General Meeting on the 9th December, 1936, the Chairman announced that a dividend of 4 per cent. less tax would be paid for the year.

Again there is an item or two of current events rather than of history which yet ought to be included here in the tally of the last year of the P. & O.'s Hundred Year History.

In the Fleet List of 1937 there are 37 ships of an aggregate 478,494 tons under the P. & O. house flag. The associated British India has 110 ships and 664,910 tons—the largest fleet in the world under its own company or house flag.

One last, and if you like comparatively trifling, note which nevertheless will go down in printed and pictured history. In the Naval Review of this Coronation Year, the P. & O. " Strathmore" steamed proudly in the wake of the Royal Yacht and leaders of the Spithead " procession."

No choice of a liner to carry the Royal and Empire guests could have been more fitting. The " Strathmore" was launched by H.M. the Queen when Duchess of York; she was named for the vale of Strathmore, on the lands attaching to the Queen's family seat; and included in the " Strathmore's " saloon decorations is a portrait of the Queen as Duchess of York and a picture in tapestry of her old home, Glamis Castle, hard by the strath or valley of Strathmore.

1837—Queen Victoria came to the throne and the beginning of her long and glorious reign; and the P. & O. launched on its first Hundred Years' History.

1937—King George VI is crowned; and the P. & O. sails on its voyage into its second Hundred Years.

Surely the omens and auguries are inspiring and auspicious!

CHAPTER THIRTY-TWO

His Majesty's Mail

I HAVE written a good deal about the various mail contracts carried on unbrokenly by the P. & O. over the full hundred years ; but I have said nothing that can give an adequate idea of the steadily increasing bulk of the mails carried and the enormous extent to which the work has now grown.

It is, by the way, quite usual to hear or read of payments made for the carriage of mails as a " subsidy," but with the P. & O. it must be emphasised that this term is misleading, because actually the payments are made at no more than fair rates for space occupied, bulk carried, and service rendered, as if the mails were ordinary merchandise on which a shipper pays his freight.

This is on a vastly different footing from the sums paid by some foreign Governments to their mail companies, those payments often being wildly in excess of the service given.   One American company, running in opposition to British, has been reported, for instance, to have received payments 400 times greater than would have been earned at normal freight or poundage rates.

This can fairly be called a " subsidy," and the intention is a national and natural desire to build up a mercantile marine for their needs in peace and as a reserve of ships and men in war.

This country did the same from the first days of steamships, when it was necessary to subsidise steamers which at need would make valuable auxiliaries to the Royal Navy—as they have done consistently. The mail payments then were in no sense proportionate to the space occupied by the mails, and indeed that space in the first years of the P. & O. was negligible.

S.S. "STRATHEDEN," 23,500 tons. Built 1937

From a painting by Norman Wilkinson, P.R.I.

We get an indication of this in some of the contemporary accounts of shipping the mails. One writer describing the mails going abroad the ship for Gibraltar, comments on the number of mail bags shipped, and remarks that they looked so limp and empty that the poor little handful of letters in each must have felt quite lost in the space they had. He also wonders why there were so many bags for so few letters, unaware probably that there was one bag for each port, just as there are many bags for each port to-day.

Thackeray, in that *Cornhill to Cairo* book, also suggests how small the mail must have been for each port. He tells how at Vigo, a little boat rowed by three ragged lads pulled out to the ship, and how, "in the twinkling of an eye," the Admiralty Agent and Her Majesty's Mails were embarked. In the "Illustrations by the Author" this incident is pictured, and although this shows the boat, the rowers, and the Lieutenant in the stern, there is no sign of any mail bag, so that it can only have been a small one, perhaps in the bottom of the boat or in the sternsheets.

All the writers of those days refer to the Admiralty Agent and the solemn ceremonial with which he received and delivered the mail. These Agents were carried by the P. & O. in terms of their first contract of 1837, which required that each ship should be fitted with six 9- or 12-pounder guns, 20 muskets, 20 pistols, 30 rounds to each of powder and shot; and each ship had to carry an officer of the Royal Navy with his servant to be responsible for the proper care of the mails and observance of the contract terms.

A great deal of fun was poked at these officers, usually very elderly Lieutenants of the Royal Navy who were probably given this employment instead of being kept on half-pay without doing anything to earn it. Various accounts describe the various types—some cheery and good companions on board, others sullen, morose, keeping to themselves, and embittered by their failure to have risen above the lowest rank of officers in the Service after thirty-five or forty years mostly spent at sea in the Royal Navy.

When the mail was brought aboard, the Lieutenant stood stiffly at the gangway, dressed in full ceremonial uniform of long-tailed, gold-braided, brass-buttoned coat, very high and stiff white collar, glazed cocked hat with looped gold cord and sword complete. If the mail bag had to be rowed ashore, the Lieutenant accompanied it in the same full ceremonial dress, whether in the snow and rain of an English winter, or the roasting sun of an Egyptian or Indian port.

" Figures of fun " as so many made these officers out to be, however, they had certain responsibilities, and they appear to have controlled very definitely the movements of the ship so far as these affected the carrying or delivery of the mail.

A letter from a passenger in 1857 mentions an example of this. A messenger came to his ship from another lying off Suez, asking the Captain for certain provisions. The Captain, however, was getting his anchor up, and sent back an answer that, " because he was behind his time then, he dare not delay the ship, unless the Admiralty Agent would give him leave to detain the ship, which the A.A. declined to do, unless the A.A. of the ' Columbian ' (the other ship) would take responsibility for it." I have other instances of this recognised authority of the Agent to command the stopping or starting of the ship.

While this officer of the Royal Navy was on board, the ship was entitled to fly the long pendant of a man-of-war, and if the officer took the mail ashore in a boat, he flew a miniature pendant at the bows.

The Postal flag of the old sail packets was the Red Ensign, with a large white square in the centre bearing a design of a red-jacketed post-boy riding a white horse and blowing a horn—an odd device for a ship's flag. But the steamers had a special " Steam Postal Flag " of Red Ensign with large yellow anchor and crown over it on the red of the fly. This was flown from the gaff or a stern staff according to several contemporary pictures now in the offices of the P. & O.

These Admiralty Agents were carried right up to 1874, after which, as the " G.P.O. Records " office kindly inform me, " later contracts provided for the Master to take charge of the mails."

Those who have never seen a big liner ship her mails might suppose this meant the Master or Captain had to " take charge " in the literal sense of watching them in and out of the ship, like those Ancient Mariner officers of the Royal Navy. He may have done this when the

238

new rule began in 1874 ; but to-day he would need spare eyes in every pocket to keep one on each torrent of mail bags.

The Honourable Alexander Shaw, in his Chairman's address to the Proprietors at the General Meeting of 1935, gave some figures both of the amount of mail a liner carries and of the increase in recent years of the average amount of mail matter.

In the case of a steamer carrying mails for India, Colombo, and Australia, he said, on the average over 900 tons of mail are carried ; and on the previous Christmas the outward mail of the " Maloja " reached 1,285 tons of 40 cubic feet.

" In 1913," the Chairman continued, " the P. & O. Company's vessels carried outwards from Europe 334,658 bags of mail. In 1934, they carried 488,559 bags. So far from there having been a diminution in the amount of mail carried, there has actually been an increase of 46 per cent."

This, you will note, was " outward " mail. The figure has increased since then, and outward and homeward together would make round about a million bags a year.

It may be difficult to appreciate what such figures mean and the amount of ship's work they entail ; so let me try to give a quick sketch of what you can see every week at Marseilles, where the outward-bound P. & O. liner picks up her mails.

It is Friday night—ten, eleven, twelve o'clock. The liner lies alongside the quay, her massive bulk towering up into the darkness high above the quay. Here and there in the long tiering rows of port-holes, an odd one or two shines out in a bright round unwinking eye ; and from the upperworks piled deck on deck high above, a soft orange-yellow glow is reflected from the saloons and public rooms. The whole impression of the ship is one of ponderous weight and size, silence and stillness, of a mighty giant quietly asleep.

Down on the quay there is no darkness, no stillness. Looking down from the ship's upper deck, you see the quay as brightly alight under the arcs as if in the sun's glare at high noon. Little clusters of men are grouped at intervals along the quay—men that from the height above look like flies or ants ; and the thought of ants is strengthened by the steady processions that trickle across the quay to each group, turn and trickle back, all very exactly like little strings of ants in busy orderly process of running to and fro about their business.

Step down on the quay, and you find the " ants " are blue-bloused French porters carrying the mail bags from the train on the landward side of the quay sheds, and streaming back for a fresh load.

The train is a long and heavy one, consisting of mail vans only and crammed with the mail from London. There had been a similar train standing there in the afternoon with mails from Northern Europe—Holland, Denmark, and the North of France, and after it another with mail bags poured in to the main line from Germany, Switzerland, east and west of France. Before these, about noon, a train of another kind had rolled smoothly in to a halt—the " P. & O. Overland Express " with passengers who had left London about 2 p.m. the previous day and travelled across France in one of the finest luxury trains on wheels to-day.

But all those earlier arriving mail trains had been emptied and their contents safely stowed in the capacious mail rooms aboard—as other tons of the " heavy " mail were stowed in London a week before. The train with the mails from all over the United Kingdom is the last to arrive, and because the ship can sail as soon as the last bag is aboard, there is the more urgent need for speeding up the loading.

Hour after hour the bags pour from the train, cross the quay, and are dumped at one or other of those groups strung along the quay. In the centre of each group is a little table, and by it a ship's officer. Each bag is plumped down on the table in front of him, rolled over so that he can see it has not been slit or damaged, that the tied neck and seal are intact, that the label is of the right colour showing which hold it must reach for stowing and discharge at its proper port.

As each bag is passed, it is snatched from the table and heaved on to the growing pile heaped on a heavy net spread wide on the quay. As the net is filled, its four corners are picked up and hooked together, a dangling sling picks it up, and away aloft it soars into the darkness, to be swung in high above, and lowered swiftly down and down the yawning hold to the level of the deck and mail-room the labels say it must reach.

240

[Photo: Bertram Park.

LORD CRAIGMYLE, formerly The Hon. Alexander Shaw
Director from 1920
Managing Director and Deputy Chairman from 1927
Chairman and Managing Director since 1932

Hour after hour the work goes on—smoothly, steadily, and un-brokenly. For all the bustle and movement there is a strange and un-expected silence. There is no more than a faint rumble of wheels where some of the mails are trucked across, the soft shuffle of the porter's feet, the faint hiss or purr of hydraulic or electric crane hoisting and lowering the net-bags, the gentle puff and pant of the train's locomotive, a subdued voice calling a short order or direction.

In the later hours, the ship is full of sleeping passengers, and because of them, silence is the order of the night.

All this picture along the quay is one of modernity and mechanical efficiency—glaring arc lights, giant cranes with their long arms spiring up into the darkness, the strength and silence of the winches that whisk a ton of mail bags aloft as if it were a feather, the taxis and motor-cars bringing belated diners and sightseers from the town, all against that background of a twenty-thousand-ton liner packed with its mass of intricate main and subsidiary engines and its " floating hotel " luxury furniture and fittings.

But in the spotlight of the picture are those groups about the little table—the young officer scrutinising each bag, and between him and the spread net and mounting pile of bulging bags, a couple of Indians who represent the ancient, the human, factor. They are the checkers or tallymen, doing their work in exactly the same unchanging fashion as the foremen of the ancient Pharaohs or the Kings of India tallied their cargoes in and out of their ships.

The Indians are in their native dress—long belted tunics, turbans, tight-ankled trousers, and bare or slippered feet. By the side of one is a rack with bundles of white sticks or staves 2 to 3 feet long. In one hand he holds a bunch of these sticks, and as each mail bag passes him to fling on to the net, he transfers a stick from one hand to the other. At the tenth stick, he passes the bundle to the second man, who takes it, ties a knot in the cord or lanyard about his neck, and presently returns the sticks to the rack.

Primitive, even prehistoric, if you like ; but long since proved to be reliable and unfailing. The ship and shore officers alike will tell you they cannot remember when the tallymen made a mistake.

Out of this last little picture let me take a meaning and reminder.

Mail bags streaming across the quay to the ship, letters and passengers from anywhere in the Kingdom outward bound to scatter over the length and breadth of Empire from the Near and Farthest East to the Antipodes . . . and the stoutest, strongest, and longest-built Floating Bridge between East and West is still the P. & O.—the giant offspring liners of those pigmy steamers that sailed under the same flag one hundred years ago.

APPENDIX I

Peninsular & Oriental Company's Past and Present Fleet

Showing in chronological order the type and size of vessels employed in the Mail and other Services, from the commencement of the Company's operations in 1837 to the present time.

Name of Vessel.	When Built.	Gross Tonnage.	Material.	Propelling Machinery.			Steam Pressure in Boilers. lb. per sq. in.
				Paddle, Single or Twin Scr.	Description of Engines.	Indicated Horse-Power.	
WILLIAM FAWCETT . . .	1829	206	Wood	Paddle	—	60	—
ROYAL TAR . . .	1832	308	,,	,,	—	260	—
JUPITER . . .	1835	610	,,	,,	—	210	7
IBERIA . . .	1836	516	,,	,,	Direct Acting	180	7
BRAGANZA . . .	,,	688	,,	,,	—	260	—
Lengthened .	1844	855	,,	,,	—	—	—
LIVERPOOL .	1836	450	,,	,,	—	—	—
DON JUAN . .	1837	800	,,	,,	—	300	—
GREAT LIVERPOOL .	,,	1,311	,,	,,	—	464	—
TAGUS . . .	,,	782	,,	,,	Side Lever	286	10
MONTROSE . .	,,	606	,,	,,	—	251	—
ACHILLES . .	1838	992	,,	,,	Beam Engines	420	7
INDIA . . .	1839	871	,,	,,	—	300	—
ORIENTAL . .	1840	1,787	,,	,,	Side Lever	420	7
PRECURSOR . .	1841	1,817	,,	,,	,, ,,	500	—
LADY MARY WOOD .	1842	553	,,	,,	—	250	—
HINDOSTAN. . .	,,	2,017	,,	,,	Direct Acting	520	7
PACHA . . .	,,	592	Iron	,,	,, ,,	210	6
BENTINCK . .	1843	1,974	Wood	,,	Side Lever	520	7
DELTA . . .	1844	240	,,	,,	—	120	—
MADRID . . .	1845	479	Iron	,,	—	160	7
TIBER . . .	1846	762	,,	,,	—	280	—
ARIEL . . .	,,	709	,,	,,	—	300	—
ERIN . . .	,,	797	,,	,,	—	280	—
POTTINGER . .	,,	1,401	,,	,,	Oscillating	450	—
Lengthened .	1849	1,350	,,	,,	,,	—	—
HADDINGTON .	1846	1,647	,,	,,	,,	450	10
RIPON . . .	,,	1,508	,,	,,	,,	900	9
Lengthened .	1862	1,908	,,	,,	,,	2,000	23

Name of Vessel.	When Built.	Gross Tonnage.	Material.	Propelling Machinery.			Steam Pressure in Boilers. lb. per sq. in.
				Paddle, Single or Twin Scr.	Description of Engines.	Indicated Horse-Power.	
PEKIN	1847	1,182	Iron	Paddle	Direct Acting	430	—
INDUS	,,	1,782	,,	,,	—	—	8
Lengthened	1852	1,950	,,	,,	Oscillating	1,367	12
SULTAN	1847	1,090	,,	,,	Crosshead	400	8
Lengthened	1855	1,125	,,	Screw	Dir. Trunk with Beam	806	12
EUXINE	1847	1,165	,,	Paddle	Oscillating	1,069	6
MALTA	1848	1,217	,,	,,	—	—	7
Lengthened	1858	1,942	,,	Screw	Horiz. Trunk Direct	2,189	22
CANTON	1848	348	,,	Paddle	One Side Lever	150	—
BOMBAY	1849	1,195	Wood	,,	,,	450	7
VECTIS	,,	793	,,	,,	—	—	—
GANGES	1850	1,190	Iron	,,	Direct Acting	1,162	11
SINGAPORE	,,	1,190	,,	,,	Oscillating	1,122	13
SHANGHAI	1851	546	,,	Screw	,,	100	8
CHUSAN	1852	699	,,	,,	,,	80	—
MADRAS	,,	1,185	,,	,,	Beam with Gearing	754	10
FORMOSA	,,	675	,,	,,	4 Piston Rods, Vertical	80	12
BOMBAY	,,	1,186	,,	,,	Beam with Gearing	750	10
BENGAL	1853	2,185	,,	,,	,, ,,	1,084	12
CADIZ	,,	816	,,	,,	Trunk Geared	450	12
VALETTA	,,	832	Wood	Paddle	Oscillating	1,027	20½
VECTIS	,,	841	,,	,,	,,	1,058	21½
RAJAH	,,	537	Iron	Screw	Single Trunk Geared	120	20
TARTAR	,,	303	,,	Paddle	Trunk Geared	557	16
DOURO	,,	810	,,	Screw	Steeple Geared	554	11
NORNA	,,	969	,,	,,	,,	624	11
HIMALAYA	,,	3,438	,,	,,	Horizontal Trunk	2,050	14
MANILLA	,,	646	,,	,,	Trunk Geared	290	16
COLOMBO	,,	1,864	,,	,,	Beam Geared	—	14
Lengthened	1859	2,127	,,	,,	,, ,,	1,538	18·25
SIMLA	1854	2,441	,,	,,	Steeple Geared	1,766	16
OTTAWA	,,	1,275	,,	,,	Oscillating Geared	700	17
CANDIA	,,	1,961	,,	,,	—	—	—
Lengthened	1857	1,982	,,	,,	Trunk Geared	1,490	20
UNION	1854	340	Composite Iron	,,	Beam, Direct	227	12
NUBIA	,,	2,096	Iron	,,	Oscillating Geared	1,422	13
EMEU	,,	1,538	,,	,,	Beam Geared	300	—
SIR JAMSETJEE JEEJEEBHOY	1855	125	Wood	Paddle	—	36	—
ALMA	,,	2,164	Iron	Screw	Oscillating Geared	1,445	16
ALHAMBRA	,,	642	,,	,,	2 Piston Rod Geared	454	18
PERA	,,	2,014	,,	,,	Trunk Geared	1,373	19·5
AVA	,,	1,373	,,	,,	,, ,,	1,056	17
AZOF	,,	700	,,	,,	Direct Horizontal	348	20
CHINA	,,	2,010	,,	,,	Direct Vertical	1,488	20
BEHAR	,,	1,603	,,	,,	Direct Horizontal	900	20
COLUMBIAN	,,	2,283	,,	,,	Horizontal, 4 Pistons	2,116	25
ELLORA	,,	1,607	,,	,,	Direct Horizontal	1,055	20
ADEN	1856	812	,,	,,	Direct Trunk	954	21
ORISSA	,,	1,647	,,	,,	Direct Horizontal	950	20
GRANADA	1857	561	,,	,,	Direct Inverted	721	18
NEMESIS	,,	2,018	,,	,,	Trunk Geared	1,894	18
MALABAR	1858	917	,,	,,	Direct Inverted	724	12

Name of Vessel.	When Built.	Gross Tonnage.	Material.	Propelling Machinery.			Steam Pressure in Boilers. lb. per sq. in.
				Paddle, Single or Twin Scr.	Description of Engines.	Indicated Horse Power.	
BENARES	1858	1,491	Iron	Screw	Direct Inverted	1,373	16·5
SALSETTE	,,	1,491	,,	,,	,, ,,	1,550	16·5
NORTHAM	,,	1,330	,,	,,	,, ,,	1,514	20
CEYLON	,,	2,020	,,	,,	,, ,,	2,054	20
NEPAUL	1859	796	,,	,,	,, ,,	960	21
JEDDO	,,	1,632	,,	,,	,, ,,	2,059	18
DELTA	,,	1,618	,,	Paddle	Oscillating	1,612	20·25
MASSILIA	1860	1,640	,,	,,	,,	1,730	20
MOOLTAN	1861	2,257	,,	Screw	Invert. Tandem Comp.	1,734	27·5
POONAH	1862	2,152	,,	,,	,,	2,356	25
Lengthened	1875	3,130	,,	,,	2 Cyl. Inverted Comp.	2,590	65
CARNATIC	1862	1,776	,,	,,	Invert. Tandem Comp.	2,442	27
RANGOON	1863	1,776	,,	,,	,, ,, ,,	1,870	26·75
GOLCONDA	,,	1,909	,,	,,	,, ,, ,,	2,112	25·25
SYRIA	,,	1,932	,,	Paddle	Oscillating	2,602	27·5
DELHI	1864	1,899	,,	Screw	Horiz. Tandem Comp.	2,286	25
BARODA	,,	1,874	,,	,,	Invert. Tandem Comp.	2,486	27
COREA	,,	610	,,	,,	Direct Inverted	1,044	24
NYANZA	,,	2,082	,,	Paddle	Oscillating	2,304	25·62
MONGOLIA	1865	2,833	,,	Screw	Geared Oscillating	1,705	22·75
NIPHON	,,	695	,,	,,	Horizontal Direct	750	—
TANJORE	,,	2,263	,,	,,	Horiz. Tandem Comp.	2,090	25
GEELONG	1866	1,835	,,	,,	Direct Inverted	1,200	—
AVOCA	,,	1,480	,,	,,	,, ,,	1,014	23
MALACCA	,,	1,709	,,	,,	,, ,,	1,380	28
SURAT	,,	2,578	,,	,,	Direct Horizontal	2,516	26
Lengthened	1874	3,042	,,	,,	2 Cylinder Inverted	2,855	71
SUNDA	1866	1,704	,,	,,	Direct Inverted	1,342	26·5
BANGALORE	1867	2,342	,,	,,	,, ,,	2,255	22
SUMATRA	,,	2,488	,,	,,	,, ,,	2,277	25
TRAVANCORE	1868	1,900	,,	,,	Direct Horizontal	1,428	24
DECCAN	,,	3,429	,,	,,	Direct Inverted	2,584	23
HINDOSTAN	1869	3,113	,,	,,	Direct Horizontal	3,194	29
AUSTRALIA	1870	3,664	,,	,,	Inverted Compound	2,626	40
INDUS	1871	3,462	,,	,,	,, ,,	2,368	65·75
KHEDIVE	,,	3,860	,,	,,	,, ,,	2,695	67
MIRZAPORE	,,	3,887	,,	,,	,, ,,	3,182	68
PEKIN	,,	3,900	,,	,,	,, ,,	3,078	67·78
PESHAWUR	,,	3,900	,,	,,	,, ,,	2,962	66
HYDASPES	1872	2,984	,,	,,	,, ,,	2,052	70
CATHAY	,,	2,983	,,	,,	,, ,,	2,086	67·75
MALWA	1873	2,959	,,	,,	,, ,,	2,735	65·5
VENETIA	,,	2,726	,,	,,	,, ,,	1,944	71·75
BOKHARA	,,	2,944	,,	,,	,, ,,	2,037	70
ASSAM	,,	3,038	,,	,,	,, ,,	2,920	70·75
LOMBARDY	,,	2,726	,,	,,	,, ,,	1,713	63·5
ZAMBESI	,,	2,431	,,	,,	,, ,,	1,550	60
GWALIOR	,,	2,733	,,	,,	,, ,,	1,950	69
SIAM	,,	3,041	,,	,,	,, ,,	2,900	—
NIZAM	,,	2,726	,,	,,	,, ,,	2,246	59·5
ADRIA	,,	1,225	,,	,,	,, ,,	487	65
KHIVA	1874	2,609	,,	,,	,, ,,	2,100	70
TEHERAN	,,	2,588	,,	,,	,, ,,	2,016	70

Name of Vessel.	When Built.	Gross Tonnage.	Material.	Propelling Machinery.			Steam Pressure in Boilers. lb. per sq. in.
				Paddle, Single or Twin Scr.	Description of Engines.	Indicated Horse-Power.	
KASHGAR . . .	1874	2,621	Iron	Screw	Inverted Compound	2,101	70
THIBET . . .	,,	2,593	,,	,,	,, ,,	2,000	67
NEPAUL . . .	1876	3,536	,,	,,	,, ,,	2,870	56·25
KAISAR-I-HIND . .	1878	4,023	,,	,,	,, ,,	3,808	66·25
ANCONA . . .	1879	3,128	,,	,,	,, ,,	3,202	72
VERONA . . .	,,	3,116	,,	,,	,, ,,	3,302	69·5
RAVENNA . . .	1880	3,372	Steel	,,	,, ,,	3,342	72
ROHILLA . . .	,,	3,500	Iron	,,	,, ,,	3,386	80
ROSETTA . . .	,,	3,502	,,	,,	,, ,,	2,890	72
BRINDISI . . .	,,	3,540	,,	,,	,, ,,	2,742	69·5
ROME. . . .	1881	5,013	,,	,,	Tandem Invert. Comp.	4,677	89·5
Lenghtened .	1892	5,545	,,	,,	Triple Expansion	6,000	160
Renamed VECTIS .	1904	5,628	—	—	—	—	—
CLYDE . . .	1881	4,124	Steel	,,	Inverted Compound	5,240	88
CARTHAGE . . .	,,	5,013	Iron	,,	Tandem Invert. Comp.	4,600	90
SHANNON . . .	,,	4,189	,,	,,	Inverted Compound	4,400	85
GANGES . . .	1882	4,196	Steel	,,	,, ,,	4,400	83·75
THAMES . . .	,,	4,101	,,	,,	,, ,,	5,642	83·5
SUTLEJ . . .	,,	4,194	,,	,,	,, ,,	4,400	—
BALLAARAT . . .	,,	4,752	,,	,,	,, ,,	4,312	87·5
PARRAMATTA . .	,,	4,759	,,	,,	,, ,,	4,437	90
VALETTA . . .	1884	4,911	,,	,,	,, ,,	4,999	88·25
MASSILIA . . .	,,	4,908	,,	,,	,, ,,	4,741	85·25
TASMANIA . . .	,,	4,493	,,	,,	,, ,,	4,195	90
CHUSAN . . .	,,	4,636	,,	,,	,, ,,	4,143	89
COROMANDEL . .	1885	4,652	,,	,,	Invert. Triple Expan.	4,200	140
BENGAL . . .	,,	4,656	,,	,,	,, ,,	4,200	140
VICTORIA . . .	1887	6,522	,,	,,	Triple Expan., Dir. Act.	7,000	150
BRITANNIA . . .	,,	6,525	,,	,,	,, ,,	7,000	150
OCEANA . . .	1888	6,610	,,	,,	,, ,,	7,000	150
ARCADIA . . .	,,	6,603	,,	,,	,, ,,	7,000	150
PENINSULAR . .	,,	5,294	,,	,,	,, ,,	6,000	150
NANKIN ⎱ Purchased	,,	3,960	,,	,,	,, ,,	3,000	150
TIENTSIN ⎰by P. & O.	,,	3,950	,,	,,	,, ,,	3,000	150
PEKIN ⎰ in 1899	,,	3,957	,,	,,	,, ,,	3,000	150
ORIENTAL . . .	1889	5,284	,,	,,	,, ,,	6,000	150
BOMBAY . . .	,,	3,319	,,	,,	,, ,,	2,500	160
HONGKONG . .	,,	3,174	,,	,,	,, ,,	2,500	160
SHANGHAI . . .	,,	3,323	,,	,,	,, ,,	2,500	160
CANTON . . .	,,	3,333	,,	,,	,, ,,	2,500	160
ADEN. . . .	1892	3,925	,,	,,	,, ,,	3,000	160
MALACCA . . .	,,	4,045	,,	,,	,, ,,	3,000	170
FORMOSA . . .	,,	4,045	,,	,,	,, ,,	3,000	170
HIMALAYA . . .	,,	6,898	,,	,,	,, ,,	10,000	160
JAVA	,,	4,093	,,	,,	,, ,,	3,000	170
AUSTRALIA . . .	,,	6,901	,,	,,	,, ,,	10,000	160
MANILA . . .	,,	4,210	,,	,,	,, ,,	3,000	170
JAPAN . . .	1893	4,319	,,	,,	,, ,,	3,000	170
MAZAGON . . .	1894	4,997	,,	,,	,, ,,	2,500	160
CEYLON . . .	,,	4,094	,,	,,	,, ,,	3,000	160
CALEDONIA . . .	,,	7,558	,,	,,	,, ,,	11,000	165
SIMLA . . .	,,	5,884	,,	,,	,, ,,	4,500	170
NUBIA . . .	1895	5,914	,,	,,	,, ,,	4,500	170

Name of Vessel.	When Built.	Gross Tonnage.	Material.	Paddle, Single or Twin Scr.	Description of Engines.		Indicated Horse-Power.	Steam Pressure in Boilers. lb. per sq. in.
					Propelling Machinery.			
MALTA	1895	6,064	Steel	Screw	Triple Expan., Dir. Act.		4,500	170
BORNEO	,,	4,573	,,	,,	,,	,,	3,500	160
SUMATRA	,,	4,607	,,	,,	,,	,,	3,500	160
SUNDA	,,	4,674	,,	,,	,,	,,	3,500	160
PALAWAN	,,	4,686	,,	,,	,,	,,	3,500	160
INDIA	1896	7,911	,,	,,	,,	,,	11,000	170
CHINA	,,	7,912	,,	,,	,,	,,	11,000	170
CANDIA	,,	6,482	,,	Twin Sc.	Two Sets Triple Expan., Direct Acting		4,500	170
SOCOTRA	1897	6,009	,,	,,	,,	,,	4,500	170
EGYPT	,,	7,912	,,	Screw	Triple Expan., Dir. Act.		11,000	170
ARABIA	1898	7,903	,,	,,	,,	,,	11,000	170
ISIS	,,	1,728	,,	Twin Sc.	Two Sets Triple Expan., Direct Acting		6,500	160
OSIRIS	,,	1,728	,,	,,	,,	,,	6,500	160
ASSAYE	1899	7,376	,,	,,	,,	,,	6,500	170
SOBRAON	1900	7,382	,,	,,	,,	,,	6,500	170
BANCA	,,	5,995	,,	Screw	Triple Expan., Dir. Act.		3,500	180
PERSIA	,,	7,951	,,	,,	,,	,,	11,000	170
PLASSY	,,	7,405	,,	Twin Sc.	Two Sets Triple Expan., Direct Acting		6,500	170
SICILIA	1901	6,696	,,	,,	,,	,,	4,500	170
SOUDAN	,,	6,680	,,	,,	,,	,,	4,500	170
SYRIA	,,	6,660	,,	,,	,,	,,	4,500	170
SOMALI	,,	6,708	,,	,,	,,	,,	4,500	170
SARDINIA	1902	6,574	,,	,,	,,	,,	4,500	170
PALERMO	1903	7,597	,,	,,	,,	,,	5,000	185
PERA	,,	7,635	,,	,,	,,	,,	5,000	185
MOLDAVIA	,,	9,500	,,	,,	,,	,,	12,000	185
PALMA	,,	7,632	,,	,,	,,	,,	5,000	185
MONGOLIA	,,	9,505	,,	,,	,,	,,	12,000	185
MARMORA	,,	10,509	,,	,,	Two Sets Quad. Expan., Direct Acting		13,000	215
MACEDONIA	1904	10,512	,,	,,	,,	,,	13,000	215
POONA	1905	7,626	,,	,,	Two Sets Triple Expan., Direct Acting		5,000	185
PESHAWUR	,,	7,634	,,	,,	,,	,,	5,000	185
DELTA	,,	8,053	,,	,,	Two Sets Quad. Expan., Direct Acting		8,000	215
MOOLTAN	,,	9,621	,,	,,	,,	,,	13,000	215
DONGOLA	,,	8,038	,,	,,	,,	,,	8,000	215
DELHI	,,	8,090	,,	,,	,,	,,	8,000	215
DEVANHA	1906	8,092	,,	,,	,,	,,	8,000	215
NILE	,,	6,694	,,	,,	,,	,,	4,500	215
NAMUR	,,	6,694	,,	,,	,,	,,	4,500	215
NYANZA	,,	6,695	,,	,,	,,	,,	4,500	215
NORE	1907	6,696	,,	,,	,,	,,	4,500	215
SALSETTE	1908	5,842	,,	,,	,,	,,	10,000	215
MOREA	,,	10,890	,,	,,	,,	,,	13,000	215
MALWA	,,	10,883	,,	,,	,,	,,	13,000	215
MANTUA	1909	10,885	,,	,,	,,	,,	13,000	215
COMMONWEALTH *	1902	6,616	,,	,,	Triple Expansion		4,000	180

* Purchased by P. & O. in 1910.

Name of Vessel.	When Built.	Gross Tonnage.	Material.	Paddle, Single or Twin Scr.	Description of Engines.	Indicated Horse-Power.	Steam Pressure in Boilers. lb. per sq. in.
GEELONG .*	1904	7,951	Steel	Twin Sc.	Triple Expansion	4,150	200
NARRUNG .*	1896	5,078	,,	Screw	Quad. Expansion	3,000	200
WAKOOL .*	1898	5,004	,,	,,	Triple Expansion	3,300	180
WILCANNIA .*	1899	4,953	,,	,,	,, ,,	3,600	180
MEDINA .	1911	12,358	,,	Twin Sc.	Two Sets Quad. Expan., Direct Acting	14,000	215
MALOJA .	,,	12,431	,,	,,	,, ,,	14,000	215
BALLARAT .	,,	11,120	,,	,,	,, ,,	9,000	215
NANKIN .	1912	6,853	,,	,,	,, ,,	4,500	215
NOVARA .	,,	6,850	,,	,,	,, ,,	4,500	215
BELTANA .	,,	11,120	,,	,,	,, ,,	9,000	215
BENALLA .	,,	11,118	,,	,,	,, ,,	9,000	215
NAGOYA .	1913	6,854	,,	,,	,, ,,	4,500	215
NELLORE .	,,	6,854	,,	,,	,, ,,	4,500	215
BERRIMA .	,,	11,118	,,	,,	,, ,,	9,000	215
KHIVA .	,,	9,000	,,	,,	,, ,,	7,000	215
KHYBER .	1914	9,000	,,	,,	,, ,,	7,000	215
BORDA .	,,	11,118	,,	,,	,, ,,	9,000	215
KAISAR-I-HIND .	,,	11,430	,,	,,	,, ,,	14,000	215
KASHGAR .	,,	8,840	,,	,,	,, ,,	7,000	215
KASHMIR .	,,	8,963	,,	,,	,, ,,	7,000	215
KARMALA .	,,	9,098	,,	,,	,, ,,	7,000	215
KALYAN .	1915	9,062	,,	,,	,, ,,	7,000	215
NALDERA .	1918	15,993	,,	,,	,, ,,	18,000	215
PESHAWUR .	1919	7,934	,,	,,	,, ,,	7,000	215
NARKUNDA .	1920	16,227	,,	,,	,, ,,	15,300	215
NAGPORE .	,,	5,283	,,	Screw	One Set Triple Expan., Direct Acting	2,800	180
LAHORE .	,,	5,252	,,	,,	,, ,,	3,000	180
KIDDERPORE .	,,	5,334	,,	,,	,, ,,	3,000	180
JEYPORE .	,,	5,318	,,	,,	,, ,,	2,644	180
ALIPORE .	,,	5,273	,,	,,	,, ,,	3,000	180
PADUA .†	1912	5,907	,,	,,	,, ,,	3,600	206
PERIM .†	1916	7,648	,,	,,	,, ,,	3,500	200
MIRZAPORE .	1921	6,715	,,	,,	One Set Double Red. Geared Turbines	‡2,300	200
BALLARAT .	,,	13,033	,,	Twin Sc.	Two Sets Quad. Exp., Direct Acting	9,500	215
BARADINE .	,,	13,144	,,	,,	,, ,,	9,500	215
BARRABOOL .	1923	13,148	,,	,,	,, ,,	9,500	215
BALRANALD .	,,	13,039	,,	,,	,, ,,	9,500	215
BENDIGO .	,,	13,039	,,	,,	,, ,,	9,500	215
MOLDAVIA .	,,	16,436	,,	,,	Two Sets Double Red. Geared Turbines	‡13,250	215
MONGOLIA .	1923	16,504	,,	,,	,, ,,	‡13,250	215
MALOJA .	,,	20,837	,,	,,	Two Sets Quad. Expan., Direct Acting	16,000	215
MOOLTAN .	,,	20,847	,,	,,	,, ,,	16,000	215
RAZMAK .	1925	10,602	,,	,,	,, ,,	12,000	215
CATHAY .	,,	15,104	,,	,,	,, ,,	13,000	215
COMORIN .	,,	15,116	,,	,,	,, ,,	13,000	215

* Purchased by P. & O. in 1910.   † Purchased by P. & O. in 1920.
‡ Shaft horse-power.

Name of Vessel.	When Built.	Gross Tonnage.	Material.	Propelling Machinery.			Steam Pressure in Boilers. lb. per sq. in.
				Paddle, Single or Twin Scr.	Description of Engines.	Indicated Horse-Power.	
RANPURA . . .	1925	16,585	Steel	Twin Sc.	Two Sets Quad. Expan., Direct Acting	15,000	215
RANCHI . . .	,,	16,585				15,000	215
CHITRAL . . .	,,	15,100	,,	,,	,, ,,	13,000	215
RAWALPINDI . .	,,	16,500	,,	,,	,, ,,	15,000	215
RAJPUTANA . .	,,	16,500	,,	,,	,, ,,	15,000	215
VICEROY OF INDIA .	1929	19,648	,,	,,	Turbo-electric	*17,000	350
SOMALI . . .	1930	6,809	,,	Screw	Quad. Expan. + Bauer-Wach	7,000	230
SOUDAN . . .	1931	6,677	,,	,,	,, ,,	7,000	230
STRATHNAVER . .	,,	22,547	,,	Twin Sc.	Turbo-electric	*28,000	425
CORFU . . .	,,	14,251	,,	,,	Geared Turbines	*14,000	425
CARTHAGE . . .	,,	14,304	,,	,,	,, ,,	*14,000	425
STRATHAIRD . .	1932	22,544	,,	,,	Turbo-electric	*28,000	425
STRATHMORE . .	1935	23,428	,,	,,	Geared Turbines	*24,000	425
ESSEX . . .	1936	11,063	,,	,,	Diesel	13,500	—
SUSSEX . . .	1937	11,063	,,	,,	,,	13,500	—
STRATHEDEN . .	†	24,000	,,	,,	Geared Turbines	*24,000	425
STRATHALLAN . .	†	24,000	,,	,,	,, ,,	*24,000	425
CANTON . . .	†	15,500	,,	,,	,, ,,	*18,500	425
Troopship . . .	†	—	—	—	Diesel	—	—

* Shaft horse-power. † Building.

Peninsular & Oriental Company's Past and Present Fleet

Silhouette sketches showing the change in design from 1837 to the present time.

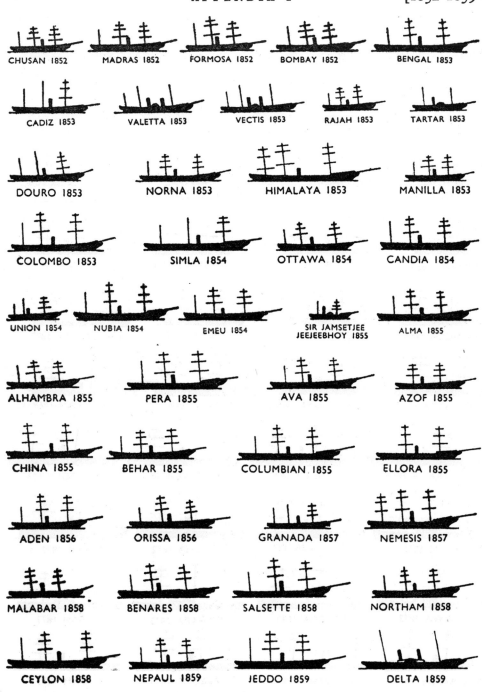

CHUSAN 1852   MADRAS 1852   FORMOSA 1852   BOMBAY 1852   BENGAL 1853

CADIZ 1853   VALETTA 1853   VECTIS 1853   RAJAH 1853   TARTAR 1853

DOURO 1853   NORNA 1853   HIMALAYA 1853   MANILLA 1853

COLOMBO 1853   SIMLA 1854   OTTAWA 1854   CANDIA 1854

UNION 1854   NUBIA 1854   EMEU 1854   SIR JAMSETJEE JEEJEEBHOY 1855   ALMA 1855

ALHAMBRA 1855   PERA 1855   AVA 1855   AZOF 1855

CHINA 1855   BEHAR 1855   COLUMBIAN 1855   ELLORA 1855

ADEN 1856   ORISSA 1856   GRANADA 1857   NEMESIS 1857

MALABAR 1858   BENARES 1858   SALSETTE 1858   NORTHAM 1858

CEYLON 1858   NEPAUL 1859   JEDDO 1859   DELTA 1859

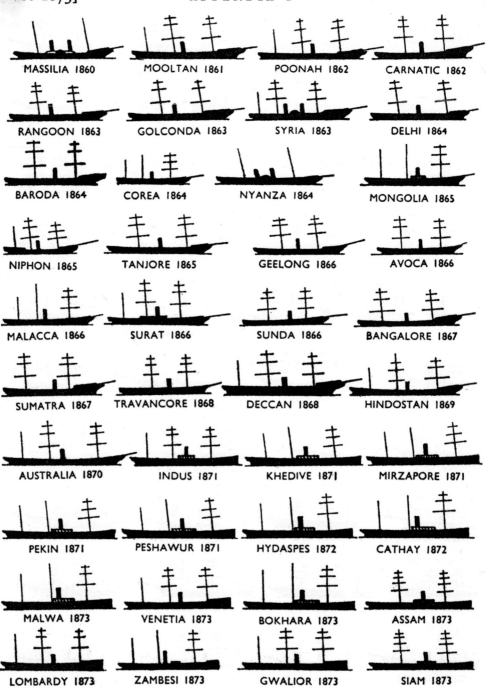

MASSILIA 1860   MOOLTAN 1861   POONAH 1862   CARNATIC 1862

RANGOON 1863   GOLCONDA 1863   SYRIA 1863   DELHI 1864

BARODA 1864   COREA 1864   NYANZA 1864   MONGOLIA 1865

NIPHON 1865   TANJORE 1865   GEELONG 1866   AVOCA 1866

MALACCA 1866   SURAT 1866   SUNDA 1866   BANGALORE 1867

SUMATRA 1867   TRAVANCORE 1868   DECCAN 1868   HINDOSTAN 1869

AUSTRALIA 1870   INDUS 1871   KHEDIVE 1871   MIRZAPORE 1871

PEKIN 1871   PESHAWUR 1871   HYDASPES 1872   CATHAY 1872

MALWA 1873   VENETIA 1873   BOKHARA 1873   ASSAM 1873

LOMBARDY 1873   ZAMBESI 1873   GWALIOR 1873   SIAM 1873

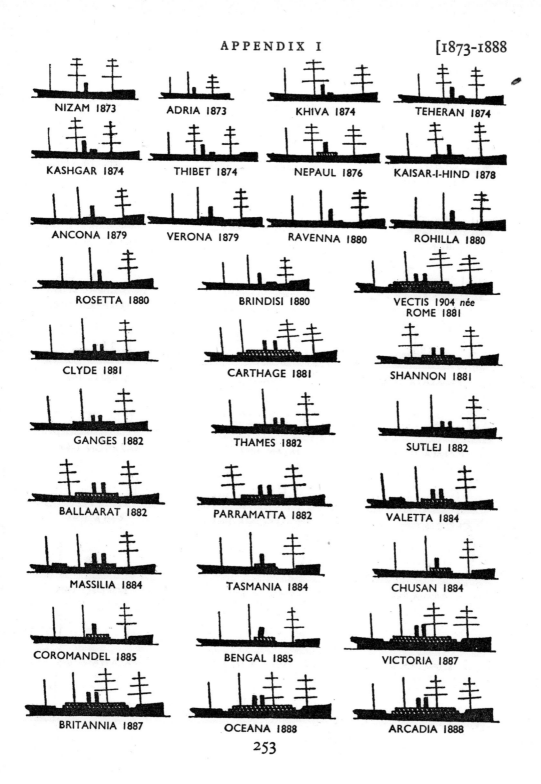

NIZAM 1873

ADRIA 1873

KHIVA 1874

TEHERAN 1874

KASHGAR 1874

THIBET 1874

NEPAUL 1876

KAISAR-I-HIND 1878

ANCONA 1879

VERONA 1879

RAVENNA 1880

ROHILLA 1880

ROSETTA 1880

BRINDISI 1880

VECTIS 1904 née
ROME 1881

CLYDE 1881

CARTHAGE 1881

SHANNON 1881

GANGES 1882

THAMES 1882

SUTLEJ 1882

BALLAARAT 1882

PARRAMATTA 1882

VALETTA 1884

MASSILIA 1884

TASMANIA 1884

CHUSAN 1884

COROMANDEL 1885

BENGAL 1885

VICTORIA 1887

BRITANNIA 1887

OCEANA 1888

ARCADIA 1888

PENINSULAR 1888

NANKIN 1888

TIENTSIN 1888

PEKIN 1888

ORIENTAL 1889

BOMBAY 1889

HONGKONG 1889

SHANGHAI 1889

CANTON 1889

ADEN 1892

MALACCA 1892

FORMOSA 1892

HIMALAYA 1892

JAVA 1892

AUSTRALIA 1892

MANILA 1892

JAPAN 1893

MAZAGON 1894

CEYLON 1894

CALEDONIA 1894

SIMLA 1894

NUBIA 1895

MALTA 1895

BORNEO 1895

SUMATRA 1895

SUNDA 1895

PALAWAN 1895

INDIA 1896

CHINA 1896

CANDIA 1896

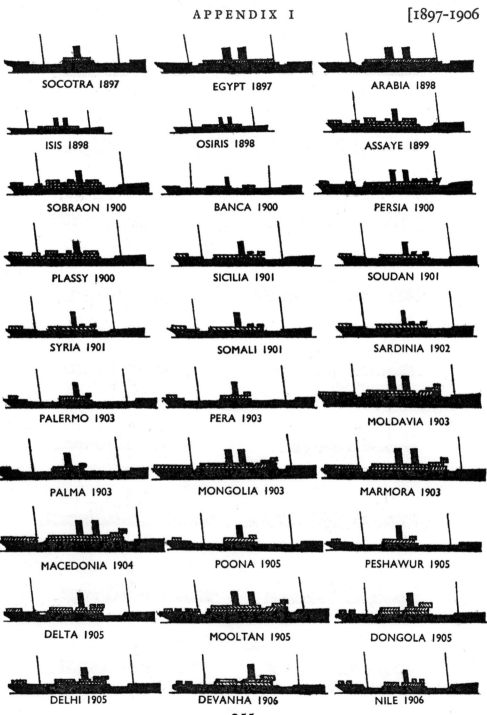

SOCOTRA 1897   EGYPT 1897   ARABIA 1898

ISIS 1898   OSIRIS 1898   ASSAYE 1899

SOBRAON 1900   BANCA 1900   PERSIA 1900

PLASSY 1900   SICILIA 1901   SOUDAN 1901

SYRIA 1901   SOMALI 1901   SARDINIA 1902

PALERMO 1903   PERA 1903   MOLDAVIA 1903

PALMA 1903   MONGOLIA 1903   MARMORA 1903

MACEDONIA 1904   POONA 1905   PESHAWUR 1905

DELTA 1905   MOOLTAN 1905   DONGOLA 1905

DELHI 1905   DEVANHA 1906   NILE 1906

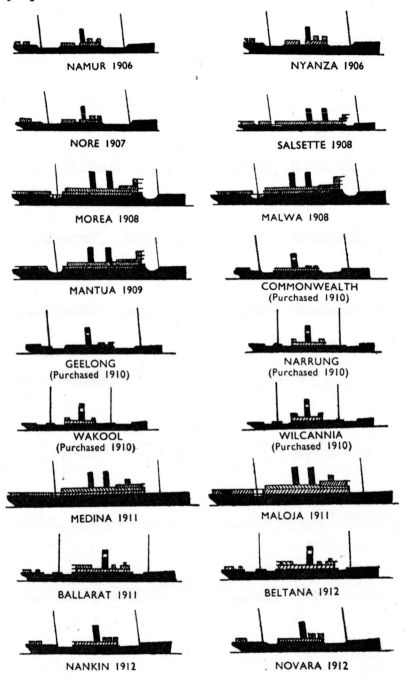

NAMUR 1906

NYANZA 1906

NORE 1907

SALSETTE 1908

MOREA 1908

MALWA 1908

MANTUA 1909

COMMONWEALTH
(Purchased 1910)

GEELONG
(Purchased 1910)

NARRUNG
(Purchased 1910)

WAKOOL
(Purchased 1910)

WILCANNIA
(Purchased 1910)

MEDINA 1911

MALOJA 1911

BALLARAT 1911

BELTANA 1912

NANKIN 1912

NOVARA 1912

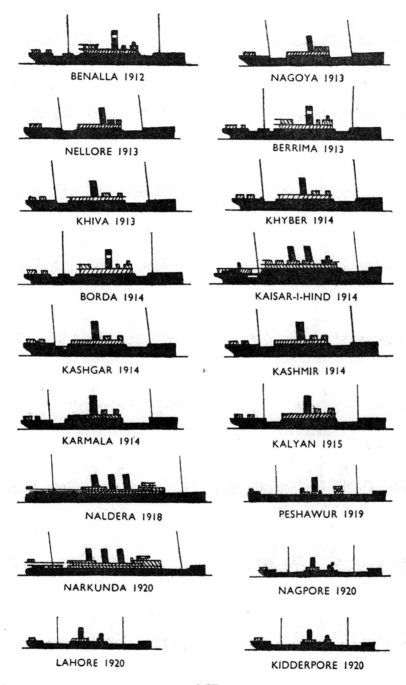

BENALLA 1912

NAGOYA 1913

NELLORE 1913

BERRIMA 1913

KHIVA 1913

KHYBER 1914

BORDA 1914

KAISAR-I-HIND 1914

KASHGAR 1914

KASHMIR 1914

KARMALA 1914

KALYAN 1915

NALDERA 1918

PESHAWUR 1919

NARKUNDA 1920

NAGPORE 1920

LAHORE 1920

KIDDERPORE 1920

S

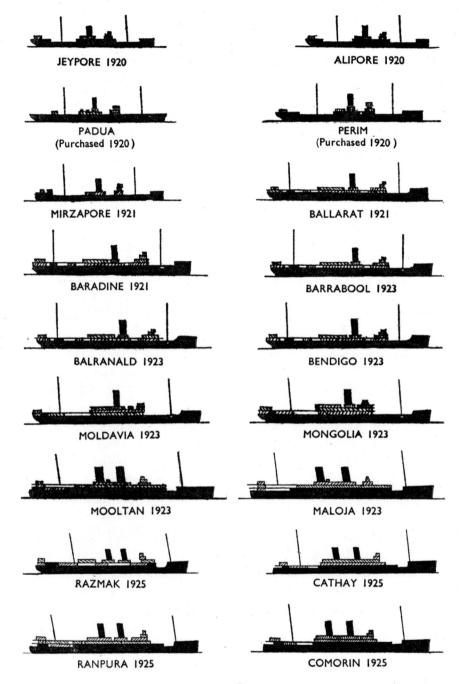

JEYPORE 1920

ALIPORE 1920

PADUA
(Purchased 1920)

PERIM
(Purchased 1920)

MIRZAPORE 1921

BALLARAT 1921

BARADINE 1921

BARRABOOL 1923

BALRANALD 1923

BENDIGO 1923

MOLDAVIA 1923

MONGOLIA 1923

MOOLTAN 1923

MALOJA 1923

RAZMAK 1925

CATHAY 1925

RANPURA 1925

COMORIN 1925

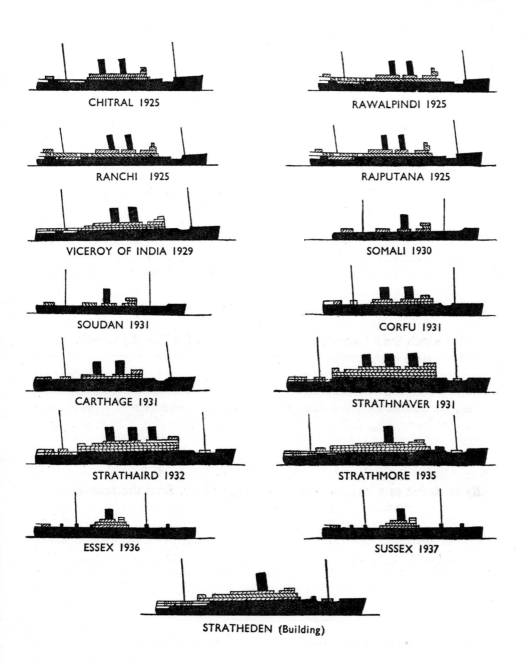

CHITRAL 1925

RAWALPINDI 1925

RANCHI 1925

RAJPUTANA 1925

VICEROY OF INDIA 1929

SOMALI 1930

SOUDAN 1931

CORFU 1931

CARTHAGE 1931

STRATHNAVER 1931

STRATHAIRD 1932

STRATHMORE 1935

ESSEX 1936

SUSSEX 1937

STRATHEDEN (Building)

The Development of the P. & O. Fleet

BY FRANK C. BOWEN

To the student of ship design as well as the student of trade there is, perhaps, no more interesting story than the progress of the P. & O. fleet during the century, for part of it was occupied by the construction of steamers to cover routes which all the experts considered to be quite beyond the steamer's reach, maintaining a steady and uninterrupted development to overcome the ever-present coaling difficulty, and the second part in improving the standards of comfort and efficiency on routes which are admittedly most difficult and on which the principal competition has been heavily subsidised by its various Governments. It is obviously impossible for any company covering a long route to produce ships which are comparable with those on the uniquely favoured North Atlantic trade; but to the student, the manner in which difficulties have been overcome makes the P. & O. ships more interesting than the New York flyers which attract so much public attention.

When Messrs. Willcox & Anderson started their steam service to the Peninsula, steamers had already crossed the Atlantic, and their venture does not seem to be nearly as daring as a voyage to New York. Actually, from the practical viewpoint, they were tackling a bigger problem, for none of the Atlantic pioneers which preceded them had for a moment considered a regular steam service, regardless of conditions, while that was what the business world wanted, and, in spite of colossal difficulties, they supplied it. Moreover, their tonnage was not promising, for most of it was either bought or chartered from other concerns and was not specially designed. The ships were all wooden paddle-steamers with the old-fashioned " splasher " wheels, but they were the best on the market and were handled with great care.

Of the earliest fleet, the " William Fawcett " of 1829 had a tonnage by the old measurement of 206, and had been designed as a ferry-boat on the Mersey but employed principally between Dublin and London. The chartered " London Merchant" had been built for the General Steam Navigation Company's Edinburgh service in 1831 and was of 306 tons burthen. The " Royal Tar " of 1832 was 165 feet long by 27 feet 10 inches, and the " Braganza " of 1836, whose design the P. & O. adapted to their requirements while she was under construction, was 158 feet by 24, but was later lengthened.

All these steamers were of the old " cod's-head and mackerel-tail " type with apple bows, but abaft the paddles they usually had as pretty a run as the scientific architect of to-day could devise. They were surveyed by the Admiralty, and all passed as being able to carry guns in wartime ; it is interesting to note how the conservative naval officers, while doing their utmost to ban steam from the Fleet itself as killing everything that was worth while in the Navy, fully appreciated the qualities of the P. & O. liners. To each was allotted the armament that she should carry in an emergency.

The " Braganza " is particularly interesting as being the first ship in which the Company was able to carry into effect its aim of securing greater economy in coal by the introduction of side-lever engines, which were infinitely superior to the simple engines of her consorts.

In the " Iberia," which was built at Limehouse in 1836, the Company was able to carry all its ideas into effect, for she was designed for them from the first and suited them to perfection. Her tonnage was 516, when she was later surveyed for the modern gross measurement ; she had side-lever engines of 190 horse-power, the pressure being 7 lb. to the square inch, and her sea speed was 9 knots. She was able to carry 290 tons of cargo with 150 tons of bunker coal, proportions that were regarded as being remarkable at that time. Her passenger accommodation was voted the finest afloat, and she logged a number of records, including 36 hours 45 minutes from London to Falmouth and 84 hours from Falmouth to Lisbon, including 4 hours stuck on Oporto Bar.

The " Iberia " was a most interesting ship, both by her design and her history of efficient service. She was handy and economical, and incidentally she started the century-old connection between the P. & O. and Messrs. Watkins, the London tug owners, for it was their " Monarch " which towed her from Limehouse to receive her engines from another firm. The Clyde-built " Montrose " of 1837 was very similar, but she demanded more bunkers and carried rather less cargo ; more modest were the " Peninsular," first chartered for the Branch service and then purchased, and the chartered " Glasgow " and " Manchester." The Company was by then doing so much business on the Peninsular trade that it was quite impossible to build ships to its own ideas fast enough, and it was constantly chartering ; by 1840 it had employed, in addition to those mentioned, the

"Ocean," "Soho," "Emerald Isle," "City of Londonderry," "Neptune," "Juno," "City of Hamburgh," "Royal Adelaide," "Vivid" and "Wilberforce"; they were the best steamers that were available, but they were not P. & O.

The next interesting ship built for the Company was the "Tagus" of 1837. In her the Directors looked ahead to an extension of their service, and her tonnage of 782 made her the biggest ship to be built on the Clyde. Her engines were an improvement on the previous side levers, and at nineteen revolutions per minute they drove her at 9½ knots. Of her three boilers, two were of the flue type and one of the newly patented tubular, which claimed great economy. They worked at what was regarded as the very high pressure of 12 lb. to the square inch and her 265 tons of bunker coal was enough for ten days' steaming at full speed, while she could carry 300 tons of cargo and 90 passengers. The contriving of so much in so small a ship won the admiration of shipping men, and the "Tagus" was extensively copied. The "Don Juan" was somewhat similar.

As the Company's position was strengthened, it reduced its chartering as much as possible and, when it could not build, it bought ships which could be adapted. The "Liverpool," which had originally been built as a sailing vessel, was added to the fleet in 1838 by arrangement, as described in the general history, although she was not completely taken over until 1842. She was called the "Little Liverpool" to distinguish her from the "Great Liverpool," which was built in 1837, and added to the fleet in similar fashion in the following year. She was the first P. & O. with two funnels, and made a very great impression, her tonnage of 1,311 being well ahead of any of her consorts. Her cabins and state-rooms were the finest afloat, the after saloon being 58 feet by 29 and the forward cabin 45 feet by 29. She was originally built for Sir John Tobin, and he was so proud of her that he commanded her himself, but the Company contrived to improve her greatly.

Another particularly interesting and successful ship was the "Oriental," built as the "United States," to be the crack transatlantic liner, with her tonnage of 1,787 and side-lever engines. She was acquired to extend the Peninsular service to Alexandria, and so to add the "Oriental" to the name. Her engines were regarded as being the finest set ever built, but such a service prevented the carriage of much cargo, and she could only stow 350 tons against 450 of bunkers. As a mail and passenger carrier she was exceedingly successful. When she was transferred and the necessary improvements carried out, a big party of guests were invited for a cruise in the Channel, the first occasion on which this was done.

When the Overland Route was firmly established, the Company sent out to Egypt some little ships, which not only vastly improved the comfort of the inland water section, but encouraged the tourist business. Three remarkable little vessels were built, the "Lotus" of 1838, which was sent out in 1840, the "Cairo" of 1840, and the "Delta" of 1842. Unfortunately, few details of these little ships have survived, for they must have been quite a triumph of naval architecture and many years ahead of their time. The draught of the "Lotus" was only 2 feet 2 inches; that of the "Cairo" was 2 inches less, yet she had a guaranteed speed of 15 miles an hour and could carry 100 passengers.

The Indian service was what really mattered, and pending their chance to enter the direct Bombay service, the Directors broke absolutely unknown ground to Madras and Calcutta, for the experience of the East India Company's packets, with naval methods and no check on the expenditure, was of no use to a commercial concern. Coal and stores were the greatest difficulty, for practically all had to be taken round the Cape by sailing ship, with the spare parts of machinery which were essential for a regular service. They were lucky in finding the "India" on the market, built by Scotts of Greenock in 1839 and purchased two years later. Although only 871 tons, she was a remarkable vessel in many ways; the fact that she had an iron bulkhead at either end of the engine-room, carefully secured to her wooden hull, was a great factor for safety and at that date a novelty in Europe. Greater economy was secured by Hall's surface condensers, the predecessors of the modern type, although as a precaution the old-type jet condensers were there as well. She was given ventilation suited to the station, and her head room of 8 feet 2 inches in the saloon was unprecedented and appreciated.

At the same time they came to an agreement with would-be rivals and took over from the slips of Wood's yard at Glasgow another steamer which became the "Precursor," 1,817 tons, and proved a very useful ship, although she could only stow 200 tons of cargo with 550 tons of bunkers. Her trial speed was nearly $11\frac{1}{2}$ land miles per hour.

These ships, however, were quite eclipsed by the first two which the Company built to its own designs for the Indian station, the famous "Hindostan" and "Bentinck" of 1842 and 1843 respectively. They were built after a most careful study of the conditions, and although their tonnage differed slightly, 2,017 against 1,974, the greatest possible care was taken to make them sister ships. This had great advantages. The regular passenger found himself in familiar surroundings as soon as he got on board and settled down to feel at home, and the training of native ratings and supply of spare parts were greatly simplified.

They were wooden paddlers, but had numerous iron bulkheads and special fire-extinguishing apparatus. Each had sixty cabins, accommodating 102 cabin passengers, twenty being single-berth rooms in the fashion that was not generally adopted for many years afterwards. After a good deal of discussion it was decided that for the Indian station absolute reliability was more valuable even than coal economy, so they were given flue boilers instead of tubular, working at a pressure of 5 lb. and burning 6½ lb. of coal per I.H.P. per hour. Fawcett's supplied side-lever engines, and the machinery was all that could be desired. Their two funnels, 40 feet apart, greatly impressed the natives, and the Navy regarded them as an invaluable reserve on a station where it was very short of cruisers, each being able to carry four of the heaviest guns and two lighter pivots.

On the Home Station, as the Peninsular and Alexandria services were called, the conditions were not so exacting, so that it did not demand such big ships as the Indian, but it was necessary to build for quality, as the Iberian service, at least, was coming within the reach of many competitors. The Company was therefore very careful over its new tonnage. The " Lady Mary Wood " of 1842, 533 tons, was noted for her speed. The " Pacha," 590 tons, was the first iron vessel in the P. & O. fleet, and when fitted with new boilers became a record breaker as well. The " Madrid " of 1845 was designed when the two services had been divided and had a gross tonnage of only 479, but she did nearly 13 land miles per hour. The " Tiber " of 1846 was considerably bigger, 762 tons gross, and was designed for either service according to demand.

The " Ariel " of 1846 was specially designed to run on the new Overland Mail service between Marseilles and Alexandria, and was remarkably speedy, an iron paddler of 709 tons gross and 300 h.p., while the " Erin " of the same year, 797 tons, was of somewhat similar design but with greatly improved engines.

After that the services were more sharply divided, and the Alexandria route, and the one to Constantinople, which had become very important, were covered by bigger ships. The " Ripon " of 1846 was an iron paddler of 1,508 tons, the " Sultan " for the Constantinople service was 1,090, and the " Euxine " of 1848 was 1,164. The ships primarily intended for the Constantinople run were given rather less power and more cargo capacity than the Alexandria mail steamers. As the Company could find steamers on the open market suitable for the Spanish service, they were content to buy or charter for a time, and devoted their resources to building special iron-hulled steamers for their Eastern business.

The " Pottinger " of 1846, an iron paddler of 1,401 tons—1,850 after she had been lengthened—attracted great attention as the biggest and most powerful iron steamer to be built on the Thames, and after certain alterations was very successful. The " Haddington " was 1,647 tons and was a fine-looking brig. For the " Pekin " of 1847 the Company turned to a Clydeside firm which had greatly decreased the space demanded by the engines, and she gave equal service on a tonnage of only 1,182. She was intended to work at certain seasons, when the expenses of the bigger ships were not justified, but her contemporary, the " Indus," was 1,782 tons, and was built at Wigram's famous yard at Blackwall.

Far smaller and less important to the public, but equally interesting to the naval architect, was the little " Canton," built in 1848 for the Chinese feeding service, an iron paddler of 348 tons. As a protection against pirates, she was given two 32-pounder shell guns, and some ex-naval seamen gunners were included in her crew. She was treated with great respect by the pirates, and did excellent work against them. The 1,218-ton " Malta " was intended for the main Far Eastern run.

It is interesting to note that many of these paddle-steamers long outlived the technical development of their machinery, and several were lengthened and converted into screw vessels. This generally meant very great improvement in their speed and economy, so that they ran for many years on the P. & O. service, and were at least equal to their newer rivals in other fleets. With modern steel vessels, of course, such a conversion would generally be most uneconomical, but the Company was giving its ships hulls of such immense strength that it was carried out repeatedly with complete success.

At the same time the Directors were still willing to consider wooden construction for their smaller units if it had particular claims. Messrs. White of Cowes had evolved a remarkably strong wooden hull, and the " Vectis " of 950 tons was accordingly laid down in their yard, but when she was practically ready for sea, she was bought by the Sicilian Government for conversion into a man-of-war. So successful did she prove in their service that the " Ganges " and " Bombay," which had been intended for the Indian run, were snapped up in similar fashion.

The " Ganges " was very soon replaced by another of the same name, an iron paddler of 1,189 tons, which, in accordance with the Company's custom of that day, was tried on the Mediterranean route before she went to the Indian station. On her maiden voyage she broke the record from Southampton to Malta with a run of 8 days 4 hours, and then went on from Malta to Constantinople in 84 hours. On her second voyage she logged a record from Alexandria to Malta with 72 hours, and when, after three Mediterranean trips, she went out to the Indian station, she was called upon to take troops out to South Africa, and did the run from Southampton to the Cape in 37 days 22 hours. This was regarded as a remarkable performance, and was of great service to the sorely-pressed Army at the Cape. The " Singapore " of 1850, 1,190 tons gross, was an up-to-date iron paddler for the Eastern service.

As the Chinese business was growing rapidly, it demanded bigger tonnage for the feeding service, and the " Chusan " and " Shanghai " were accordingly built in 1851, the first iron screw steamers in the fleet. The " Shanghai " was 546 tons gross, but the " Chusan " was 700, and although she was built for the local feeding service, she was to become better known, indeed world-famous, as the ship which

opened real steam connection with Australia, in which she was joined by the
" Formosa," 677 tons gross, built in 1852.

The striking success of screw propulsion in these little vessels suggested it in
bigger ones, but in this the Directors had to fight the Admiralty on every point,
for they were still in favour of the paddle for full-powered ships. The sisters
" Madras " and " Bombay," iron screw barques of about 1,185 tons gross, had the
most up-to-date engines which had proved their efficiency and economy in the
latest Atlantic liners. The difference that they made to the P. & O. service may be
judged from the fact that these ships, smaller than many of the paddlers, had far
better accommodation for 80 first-class passengers, and carried no less than 600
tons of cargo on 300 tons of coal.

On their success Napiers of Glasgow were called upon in 1853 to build the iron
screw barque " Colombo " of 1,865 tons, her beam engines being geared to the
shaft and giving both speed and economy. The " Bengal," 2,185 tons, had the
distinction of being the biggest steamer in the world for a short time, but people
shook their heads at the rashness of the Company in spending as much as £70,000
on one ship, while admitting that such features as a whistle and speaking-tube to
the engine-room were undeniably interesting. In the same year the " Douro,"
which had a gross tonnage of only 810, was completed, thoroughly tested, and then
sent out to the East. The " Tartar," on account of the shallow draught required
by the Canton-Shanghai feeding service, reverted to the paddle, but although her
wooden hull was regarded as one of the strongest to be built to that date, her
tonnage was little more than 300. The screw " Manilla " and " Rajah," 646 and
537 tons respectively, were bought to take coal and stores out to the ships on station.

The Company had to bow to the old prejudices of the Admiralty when it came
to the subsidised mail services, and the " Valetta " and " Vectis " of 1853 returned
to the paddle principle and wooden hulls. Extraordinary strength was obtained
by diagonal planking, the " Valetta " being built by Mare of Blackwall, with a
gross tonnage of 823, while the " Vectis " was built by White of Cowes, with a
gross tonnage of 751 on their very latest principle. They were both engined by
Penn's, with oscillating engines of rather more than 1,000 I.H.P. and Lamb's
boilers, but actually the machinery was far too powerful for their small hulls, and
although they were phenomenally fast ships, making between 13½ and 14 knots, it
was a strain on their hulls, and it was not until they were fitted with superheaters,
nowadays generally regarded as quite a modern innovation, that they became
profitable.

All these ships were unusually interesting, but the finest ship of all at that period,
and the wonder ship of her time, was the " Himalaya," which had been laid down
by Mare as a paddler, but which was permitted by the Admiralty to be converted

to screw while still on the stocks. She was an iron ship with dimensions 340 by 44 by 35 feet depth of hold, giving her a gross tonnage of 3,508, making her by far the biggest steamer in the world, and she was given horizontal direct-acting engines by Penn, the two cylinders being 84 inches in diameter with a stroke of 42 inches. She was the very last word in naval architecture, her saloon being nearly 100 feet long and seating 170 passengers out of the 200 that she carried, while she had bunkers for 1,200 tons of coal, which she consumed at the rate of nearly 18 tons a day, and stowage for 1,000 tons of cargo.

When she was tried she comfortably maintained 14 knots with her engines running at 56 revolutions per minute, and on her maiden voyage she broke record after record. With full sail spread in addition to her engines, she actually did 16½ knots, an astounding performance for the 'fifties, but it was not long before the Directors realised that the trade offered was not sufficient to keep such a very expensive ship running, and after she had proved herself the most efficient of the chartered transports in the Crimean War, they were glad enough to sell her to the Admiralty. She served as a naval transport for many years, and was finally converted into a coal hulk. After the war she was sold to private bunkering interests and, being surveyed, her stout old hull was pronounced to be fit to be towed anywhere in the world. It may be mentioned that she is still fulfilling the function of coal hulk at Portland.

Expensive as she was, the " Himalaya " performed one service which was invaluable to the Company in its desire for progress ; her qualities did much to persuade the Admiralty that the paddle was not really necessary, although it took time. For the subsidiary services, however, they permitted several paddlers to be converted to screw, and this was generally carried out with an improvement in the hull lines to reduce resistance, which must have been exceedingly difficult for the Company's architects before the introduction of tank experiments.

The national services of the fleet during the Crimean War were a serious disadvantage to the Company, and it became very difficult to carry on the normal services. Some had to be suspended, but the Directors looked well ahead, and in spite of the high shipbuilding prices which naturally followed a war boom, they built as rapidly as they could. In 1854 they obtained the iron screw steamers " Candia " (1,961 tons), " Nubia " (2,096 tons), and " Simla " (2,441 tons), each built to the design of a progressive yard in order that the Company might benefit by the best of private effort. They were followed in 1855 by the " Alhambra " (642 tons), " Ava " (1,373 tons), " Pera " (2,014 tons), and " Alma " (2,165 tons). The " Pera " was described as the most perfect steamer that ever left the Thames, although she had to be launched hurriedly, and before she was ready, in order to prevent her being seized by her builders' creditors.

The supply was still insufficient to satisfy their demand, and they had to purchase a number of ships. These ranged from the little wooden paddler " Sir Jamsetjee Jeejeebhoy," built at Bombay in 1849, to the " Ottawa " of 1,274 tons. Several ships were bought from foreign owners, the " China," " Ellora," and " Orissa."

In the meantime they did not relax their efforts to get more ships to their own standard. The " Aden " of 1856, although only 812 tons gross, was a very useful little ship whose engines served well for experiments to get greater economy. The " Granada " was 561 tons, with an excellent turn of speed, but the " Nemesis," given that name at the collapse of the Indian Mutiny, a very fine ship-rigged iron screw steamer of 2,018 tons gross with geared trunk engines, was noted for her immense strength, and could contrive her 13½ knots. In 1858 the Company built a number of iron screw steamers—" Malabar," " Northam," " Salsette," " Nepaul," and " Benares "—again following the policy of going to different yards and getting their designers to do their best.

Perhaps the best of the ships added in 1858 was the " Ceylon," an iron screw barque of 2,376 tons built by Samuda on the Thames with direct-acting engines by Humphrys & Tennant. She had a steam pressure of 20 lb. to the square inch, which was then high, and averaged 13·34 knots on trial, but her stout hull survived many alterations to her machinery, and she was always a great favourite. She had a very long career, both in the P. & O. service and later as a cruising yacht.

Within the next few years quite a number of ships were added to the fleet of the same general type, their size varying according to their service ; but in 1859 and 1860 the Company reverted to the paddle with the " Delta " and " Massilia." They were built under the last expiring effort of the Admiralty to bolster up the paddle system. The two hulls came from the Thames, with a tonnage of 1,618 and 1,640 respectively. In their case the Company was not altogether sorry at the Admiralty's attitude, for it permitted them to use the magnificent engines which had been put into the " Valetta " and " Vectis," whose only fault was that they were too powerful for the small hulls, but which gave wonderful service in the bigger ships. One or two other vessels were also given paddle engines, but they were of secondary importance.

After them the Company reverted to its policy of attempting to get the greatest possible economy, firstly, for obvious reasons, and secondly, to enable the ships to reduce prices as much as possible and to carry the greatest cargo. The " Mooltan " (1861 ; 2,257 tons) was the first to be fitted with compound engines, these being on the very complicated tandem system. Her magnificent decorations of carved mahogany and teak were criticised as being too expensive, but she was the most comfortable ship of her day, her fittings including an ingenious hydraulic machine for making ice for the passengers' use during the voyage, while the Company was very satisfied by her burning 630 tons of coal on her first voyage against 1,200 by a consort of older design. The " Baroda " was given compound engines, with which Humphrys & Tennant guaranteed the greatest possible economy, which was certainly realised, and the " Delhi " of 1864 did still better as regards coal consumption with Ravenhill's horizontal compound engines, superheaters, surface condensers, and 25 lb. pressure, averaging 13·4 knots on her maiden trip. In the same year the " Nyanza " (2,082 tons) was the last paddler for the fleet, but even her surface condensers could not prevent her being very extravagant.

During that period there were many ships of lesser importance built : " Carnatic," " Poonah," " Syria," " Rangoon," " Golconda," " Corea," and " Baroda," while such vessels as the " Geelong " and "Avoca" were bought before completion.

Among many, the " Tanjore," an iron brig of 1,971 tons, was noteworthy as doing no less than 17 knots on trial with improved compound horizontal engines, and these proved so successful that many ships which had simple engines were converted to them. Their rig varied, but the graceful clipper stem and bowsprit were retained until the " Australia " of 1870, a very well-remembered ship of 3,468 tons, which was so strongly built that she was always known as " the P. & O. Ironclad." The vessel which followed her, the " Indus," built by Denny in 1871 (3,478 tons), was the first to have a straight stem, while her compound engines, which gave her a speed of 13·3 knots on trial, had a pressure of no less than 60 lb. to the square inch. This was regarded as being a very risky pressure even for the Navy, with its long Service personnel, but the Company had for years taken very particular care over its engineers, and had attracted some of the best naval men who had become disgusted with Service conditions, and the higher pressure gave its economy with remarkable freedom from accident.

This strengthened the policy of conversion, often with the provision of greater earning capacity with greater length. The changed conditions, after the opening of the Suez Canal in 1869, required many new ships, as did the shipping boom of 1871, and British yards could not satisfy the demand.

The early 'seventies therefore saw a great increase in the Company's fleet, but the great majority were of normal design, good dividend-earners which carried a lot of cargo and afforded their passengers great comfort, but not particularly interesting to the layman. Most of these ships were later greatly improved.

The ship which stands out among all others in the 'seventies is the " Kaisar-i-Hind," built by Caird in 1878, an iron screw barque whose tonnage was just over 4,000, and whose compound engines of 4,000 I.H.P. worked at a pressure of 70 lb. She had accommodation for 176 passengers in the saloon and 64 in the second class, and her trial speed of 15 knots was remarkable in a ship for economical running.

She was intended primarily for the Indian service and nicknamed the " Bridge to India," justifying this name by many years' very successful service.

In 1880 came the famous " R " class, originally for the Bombay run, of between 3,370 and 3,500 tons, the " Rosetta," built by Harland & Wolff, the " Rohilla " by Caird, and the "Ravenna" by Denny. " Rosetta " was the first P. & O. to be built in Ireland, starting a long connection with the Belfast Yard, while the " Ravenna " was the first steel ship in the Company, and was such a success that iron was abandoned as soon as possible, although supplies of shipbuilding steel were so difficult in those days that it was not always possible, and her cost was great, several thousand pounds more than that of her bigger sisters. All had compound engines of 3,600 I.H.P., but those of the "Rohilla" had a pressure of 80 lb., while the others were 75. Together they formed an exceedingly useful class, which influenced P. & O. design for many years.

During 1881 and 1882 the Company was very active in its building, generally in classes. The " Rome " and " Carthage " of 1881 had to be built of iron on account of the shortage of steel, but otherwise they marked another big increase in the standard. Introducing the rig of four masts and two funnels, which became so popular for years, they were the first to exceed 5,000 tons gross, while their two tiers of deckhouses made them as impressive in appearance as they were comfortable. They each originally had a tonnage of 5,013, while their hulls were of tremendous strength.

They were given four-cylinder compound engines, those of the " Rome " being 5,000 I.H.P. and of her sister 5,250, steam being supplied by four double-ended and two single-ended boilers at a pressure of 90 lb. The Company broke away from the tradition inherited from the sailing ships, and put the best accommodation amidships instead of aft over the screw, and they were the first ships to have their saloons forward. Another innovation was the provision of a steam launch and large refrigerating machines and cooling chambers, so that they very soon became the most popular ships on the Australian service for which they were particularly designed, and on which the Company soon had to fight heavily subsidised Continental competition. Their designed speed was 15 knots, but that could always be exceeded.

Smaller than the " Rome " and " Carthage " were the sister ships " Clyde," " Thames," " Sutlej," and " Ganges," steel-built, of between 4,100 and 4,200 tons, with engines of 4,500 horse-power, similar to those of their predecessors. They were 15-knot ships, again comfortably exceeded whenever necessary, and they not only carried big bunkers, but had a large cargo capacity in addition to accommodation for about 170 first- and second-class passengers, and the ability to fit the 'tween decks for emigrants or troops when necessary. They were primarily intended for the Eastern services. The " Shannon," with two masts instead of three, was very similar in general design, but had a rather higher pressure and several minor differences.

As an improvement on the " Rome " class, the " Ballaarat " and " Parramatta " were built in 1882 by Cairds, their steel hulls permitting the gross tonnage to be reduced to about 4,750 without any sacrifice of qualities. Their compound engines were simpler, having two cylinders supplied by four double-ended boilers with a pressure of 90 lb., the I.H.P. being 5,000 and the speed 15 knots. They were regarded as the very last word in passenger luxury, particularly in the public rooms. The saloon extended the full width of the ship for 42 feet of the length, immediately abaft the engine, and that of the " Rome " was decorated with really remarkable carving. They were originally brig-rigged with two perfectly pro-portioned funnels, and their appearance was particularly pleasing to a people as essentially " ship-minded " as the Australians.

The subsidised German competition on the Australian service was countered by the steel-hulled " Massilia " and " Valetta," built in 1884, ships of nearly 5,000 tons, which loaded excellently as well as having first-class passenger accommo-dation. In the " Massilia " the experiment was tried of fitting hydraulic winches and windlasses instead of steam, and in spite of their being pioneers, these were so successful that they were fitted into all the passenger ships for many years, their comparative silence making them a boon to passengers when cargo had to be worked at ports of call. Among the other qualities which made these two ships favourites was their extraordinary steadiness at sea, while the installation for fire-fighting and fire-tracing, which had been a feature of the Company's ships for some years, was carried many steps farther. The fitting of electric light, although it was not on a very elaborate scale, was a boon to the passengers as well as an additional factor of safety.

Next came the " Tasmania " class—the others being the " Chusan," " Coro-mandel," and " Bengal "—of 1884 and 1885, rather smaller ships of about 4,500 tons, with a speed of 14½ knots only. They were essentially Indian ships, but ran on the Eastern and Australian services when necessary, and although they were less ornately decorated than the Australian ships, they were exceedingly comfortable and excellent dividend-earners. The " Coromandel " and " Bengal " were the first P. & O. ships to be given triple expansion engines, their three boilers working at a pressure of 145 lb. to the square inch, while the others had the more usual compound engines and worked at 90 lb.

These ships were specially designed in consultation with the Admiralty for easy conversion into transports or cruisers in war time, although that was an act of pure patriotism on the part of the Company, for there was no subsidy involved. One of the features introduced on this account, on the initiative of the P. & O., was that all watertight doors could be closed from the upper deck, which made them much safer than most of their contemporaries. The value of such ships for national purposes was very soon shown in the Russian War Scare of 1885, when the Navy was found to be appallingly short of cruisers for the protection of commerce.

The service of these ships as auxiliary cruisers led to the Admiralty forming a proper organisation with reasonable recompense to the owners, and this had a big influence on the design of the famous " Jubilee " class of 1887, four remarkable ships to the same general design, but built in two pairs of sisters, the " Britannia " and " Victoria " and the " Oceana " and " Arcadia." They were all steel four-masted barques with two funnels, the first pair being just under 6,100 tons gross and the second pair just under 6,200. Not only did they mark a big increase in the size of the P. & O. ships, but also in the accommodation, carrying about 250 first-class and 160 second-class passengers, in addition to nearly 4,000 tons of cargo. Each was given triple expansion engines of 7,500 horse-power for a contract speed of 15 knots, which was what was demanded by the Australian mail contract, but they were good for well over 16, although they had to burn 110 tons of coal per day to get it.

They were better subdivided by bulkheads than any ships built until then, their ventilation was the wonder of naval architects and fully appreciated by their passengers. Two of them received an annual subsidy from the Admiralty, while the Company voluntarily held the other two at the Navy's disposal without any payment. They cost about £200,000 apiece, but they were so popular that they were probably the best investment that the Company ever made.

They were followed in 1888 by two ships designed specially for the Bombay service, the " Peninsular " and " Oriental." They were much smaller, rather less than 5,000 tons gross, but while they were designed for 15 knots, they were always good for well over 16 with their triple expansion engines of 6,000 horse-power, and although their rig of three masts with a single funnel may not have been as impressive as that of the " Jubilee " class, they were perfect yachts in their lines, and their graceful appearance gladdened the eye of any sailor. Naturally, they were always great rivals, both on the Indian run and the secondary services to which they were later relegated. The " Oriental " broke the Bombay record when new, but the " Peninsular " held the Shanghai record for several years.

After the " Pretty Sisters " came a number of ships which were essentially cargo vessels for the Indian and Eastern services, each fitted with limited passenger accommodation. They included the " Bombay," " Shanghai," " Canton," " Hong Kong," " Aden," " Malacca," " Formosa," " Japan," and others, built between 1888 and 1894.

The construction of first-class mail steamers recommenced with the "Hima-laya" and "Australia" of 1892, similar in outward appearance to the "Jubilee" class, but a great improvement in design. Their gross tonnage was about 6,900, and the indicated horse-power of their engines 10,000, which gave them a speed of 18 knots. They were intended to run on the Bombay or Australian service according to demand, and they were really beautifully fitted for their time, their saloons being the finest that had been put on any long-distance service, and their very complete bathroom facilities being a great feature which made them par-ticularly popular with the Australians. Both of them were exceedingly fast: in 1893 the "Australia" landed the mails at Adelaide in a record time of 26 days 16 hours from London, but was beaten next month by the "Himalaya."

The design of these two very successful ships was improved in 1894 in the "Caledonia," another remarkably good-looking ship with two funnels and four masts, but her gross tonnage was increased to 7,558, her passenger accommodation was considerably enlarged, and her engines, five-cylinder, triple expansion, work-ing on the tandem principle on three cranks, developed 12,000 I.H.P. They were a peculiar design, but they ran remarkably well with the engineers who knew them thoroughly, and although she was only contracted for 18 knots, she made 19½ on trial, and this reserve was exceedingly useful to her when it came to beating her rivals under the French and other flags.

Her lines were beautiful, and she was exceedingly comfortable for her pas-sengers, but cargo capacity was sacrificed, and the bill for her construction ran into a quarter of a million. When she came out she was given a white hull and yellow funnels, which showed off her grace to perfection, and this colouring was kept for two years. Then she was given the Company's black hull and funnels, but she kept her boats white to maintain her individuality. When she was a new ship she broke the Bombay record with a run of 12½ days, and even when she was getting on in years, she held the Calcutta record with 24 days 21 hours and the London–Marseilles–Colombo record with 19 days.

The construction of the "Caledonia" completed the passenger fleet for the time being, but the enterprise of the Company in working up the cargo side, and the large number of passengers who liked to travel to India and the East in the intermediate steamers, with their solid comfort and lack of pretension, made the increase of the minor fleet a business proposition. Several ships of rather varied design were built or bought on the stocks.

After that the Directors felt themselves in a position to build classes of inter-mediate steamers again, designed to their own ideas entirely. The "Simla," "Nubia," and "Malta" were sister ships, a great improvement on the "Japan" class, with a gross tonnage of about 5,900, good stowage, and greatly improved

T

passenger accommodation. Their indicated horse-power was 4,500 for a sea speed of about 14½ knots, and they made excellent troopers. The " Borneo," " Sunda," " Sumatra," and " Palawan " of 1895 were smaller, round about 4,650 tons, with a sea speed of 13½ knots, but in many ways were a further development, carrying more passengers, but aiming primarily at running economy. At this time a new departure was made by the purchase of the " Harlington," of just over 1,000 tons, to maintain a coastal feeding service for the big ships.

For the passenger and mail services a great forward step was made by the construction of the " India " by Cairds in 1896, the biggest ship built at Greenock until then, and the prototype of the famous class whose other units were the " Persia," " China," " Egypt," and " Arabia." Their dimensions were approximately 500 by 54 feet 3 inches, varying slightly with the different ships, and their gross tonnage round about 7,900. With their two funnels and two pole masts, they had just the appearance and dignity that a P. & O. mail ship should have, while their triple expansion engines, developing 11,000 I.H.P. and supplied by three single-ended and three double-ended boilers, gave them a sea speed of well over 18 knots. As auxiliary cruisers they were to prove remarkably efficient, while as troopers they could carry no less than 2,500 soldiers, and their normal passenger accommodation was between 460 and 500. They ran on the Australian and Indian services with equal success.

The " Candia " of 1896, although she was only a cargo steamer, was a particularly interesting ship, as she was given twin screws for the purpose of making the experiment on the long routes. She was designed essentially for the Australian service, one which had not been given special cargo tonnage before, and with per gross tonnage of 6,482 she created quite a sensation as being the biggest ship to go up the river to Adelaide. The " Socotra " was a somewhat similar twin screw ship of 6,044 tons, with a trial speed of 13½ knots.

In 1898, the Company bought the Eastern service of the Hall Line, together with the steamers " Locksley Hall," renamed " Pekin," " Rufford Hall," which became the " Nankin," and " Branksome Hall," which was the " Tientsin " in the P. & O. fleet. They were useful cargo ships of rather less than 4,000 tons, and were always employed on the Eastern service.

In the same year appeared two steamers which, while they were comparatively insignificant in size, were a remarkable addition to the P. & O. fleet and made a great name for themselves. The " Isis " and " Osiris," built by Cairds in 1898, were designed for the new express service between Brindisi and Alexandria or Port Said, and were perhaps the most remarkable vessels of their day. They were twin screw ships of about 1,700 tons, and in appearance they were real miniature liners with their two well-placed funnels and two masts. Each had two sets of

274

four-cylinder triple expansion engines supplied by two double-ended and two single-ended boilers, and they contrived a speed which was undreamed of for such vessels before the advent of the turbine. When she was new the " Isis " lowered the Brindisi–Port Said record to 46 hours 14 minutes, but they were always great rivals, and the crew of the " Osiris " would not accept this. The healthy rivalry, which spread to the regular passengers of each ship, was all to the good, and these two wonderful little vessels performed invaluable service in connection with the Overland Route until it had to be abandoned in the early days of the War.

Ever since 1894 the Company had been covering the Indian trooping service with steamers which it could ill spare from its regular services, replacing the famous troopers of the " Serapis " class with so much more comfort for the troops, and economy to the Treasury, that there was no question of returning to the old system. At the turn of the century the Company decided to build a special class of three troopers which could be used for the normal Indian and Eastern services when required. These were the " Assaye," " Plassy," and " Sobraon," twin screw steamers of about 7,400 tons with triple expansion engines of 6,500 I.H.P., giving them a speed of 16 knots. They could carry both passengers and cargo, but they were essentially troopers, and, while there was no sacrifice of comfort, the decoration was very much simpler than usual, while the wide decks which were provided for parades were fully appreciated by passengers when they were on commercial service. This seldom occurred, for they were such a great advance on the ordinary transports that they were constantly employed.

The " Banca," built in 1900, was unique in the P. & O. fleet, in that she was a turret-deck cargo steamer of nearly 6,000 tons whose design was not repeated, but which was very successful for its particular purpose.

The " Sicilia," built by Barclay, Curles, in 1900, started the phenomenally successful " S " class, her sisters being the " Syria," " Somali," " Soudan," and " Sardinia." They were designed to be intermediate passenger ships with excellent accommodation, adapted for trooping when required, but normally intended for the Calcutta and Eastern services. Triple expansion engines of 4,500 I.H.P. gave them a speed of 14 knots.

After the " S " class, in 1903, the Company started the famous " M " class with the " Mongolia," which was built by Cairds, and which was followed by the " Moldavia " and " Mooltan " during the next two years to practically the same design. With dimensions rather more than 520 feet by 58, they had a gross tonnage of about 9,500, but they were a vast improvement on the popular " Egypt " type, principally because they had all their accommodation above the main deck, a great boon in tropical waters. Another great improvement was that they were driven

T*   275

by twin screws, and the basic design was so successful that it was maintained for years.

Their triple expansion engines developed 14,000 I.H.P. and gave them a comfortable 18 knots, well above the requirements of the mail contract. Although it varied in the different ships, the passenger accommodation was about 350 in the first class and 160 in the second, and it was on a standard which had never been approached on any distant service. Most of them were first tried on the Bombay service, and then ran regularly on the Australian.

Close on the heels of the Caird pioneers came the " Marmora " and " Macedonia," built by Harland & Wolff, introducing the quadruple expansion engine into the P. & O. service and having a gross tonnage of about 10,500. The " Morea " was a single ship differing slightly from the others. She was built in 1908 by Barclay, Curles, and with quadruple expansion engines was always a good and economical steamer whose big funnels gave her a particularly handsome appearance. The " Malwa " (1908) and " Mantua " (1909) were Caird products, and were a steady development of the same general design.

The final development was the " Maloja " (Harland & Wolff) and " Medina " (Caird), both built in 1911 with a tonnage of nearly 12,500, quadruple expansion engines of 16,000 I.H.P., giving a speed of over 19 knots when it was required, and very much greater passenger accommodation, while for the Australian service they were given a big stowage for refrigerated cargo. The entry of the " Medina " into the P. & O. service was delayed, as she was taken up as a Royal Yacht for the Delhi Durbar celebrations, a function which she fulfilled very much better than any warship could have done.

While the " M " class was steadily developing to the limits of size which the Suez Canal permitted, the Company was building up its fleet of secondary vessels, which were nearly as important from the business viewpoint. In 1903 the " P " class was built by various yards, 14-knot, 7,600-ton cargo ships named " Pera," " Palermo," " Palma," " Poona," and " Peshawur."

For the intermediate business the popular and successful " D " class was built as an improvement on the " S " class, " Delhi," " Delta," " Devanha," and " Dongola," 16-knot ships of rather more than 8,000 tons with comfortable passenger accommodation for the first and second class and good cargo stowage. Like the " S " class, they were used on both the Indian and Eastern services.

Although less pretentious, the " N " class was even more profitable, and included the " Namur," " Nile," " Nyanza," " Nore," " Novara," " Nankin," " Nagora," and " Nellore," whose construction was spread over a considerable period. They were reduced editions of the " D " and " S " classes, with a gross tonnage of about 6,700, economical quadruple expansion engines, and a speed of 14 knots, with comparatively small passenger accommodation, but an excellent capacity for cargo.

In 1908, the Company had built a particularly interesting steamer, as striking in her way as the " Isis " and " Osiris." She was the " Salsette," designed to maintain the " shuttle service " between Aden and Bombay, connecting with the weekly mail steamers when the sailing was to Australia and taking their mails and passengers to Bombay. She was a steel twin screw steamer of 5,842 tons, with quadruple expansion engines of 10,000 I.H.P. for a speed of 20 knots. Her hull was that of a yacht, and there was not a parallel section in it, while her white paint and yellow funnels showed her beauty off to perfection. She was the first ship to break the " Macedonia's " great record between Marseilles and Bombay, and she logged a Bombay–Aden record which was not beaten until the P. & O. commissioned an even more remarkable ship, the " Razmak."

For many years the Company had been aspiring to a service to Australia by way of the Cape, but one or two experiments that had been made had used tonnage which was far too good for the purpose and had not been successful financially. In 1910, they got their opportunity by the purchase of Lund's Blue Anchor Line, together with the steamers " Commonwealth," " Narrung," " Wakool," " Wilcannia," and " Geelong." These were ships of between 5,000 and 7,000 tons, designed for the service, which was largely concerned with emigrants, and they had been regarded as excellent for it, but as soon as the P. & O. took it over, they decided that something very much better was required, and laid down the first " B " class of 1911 and 1912. These were the " Ballarat," " Beltana," " Benalla," " Berrima," and " Borda," and they were twice the average size of the Lund steamers. Twin screw steamers of well over 11,000 tons, with twin screw quadruple expansion engines giving 14 knots, they carried roughly 1,100 third-class passengers, on a standard never before attained on the route, with a very large cargo capacity, including a big insulated stowage for meat. They were very fully appreciated on the trade, especially by the type of settler accustomed to his standard of comfort and possessing a certain amount of capital to establish himself, which was most desired by the Commonwealth.

Meanwhile, the improved tonnage which the Company had put on to the secondary services had so increased the demand that something bigger and better was required, and the " K " class was built in 1914 to satisfy it. This consisted of the " Khiva," " Khyber," " Kalyan," " Kashgar," " Karmala," and " Kashmir." They were roughly 9,000 tons apiece, with quadruple expansion engines of 7,000 I.H.P. for a speed of 14 knots, and although the number of passengers was strictly limited for the greatest possible comfort, they carried a large cargo and, but for the War, which amply proved their national value, they would have been extraordinarily profitable ships to Calcutta and the Orient.

Just as the War prevented the " K " class showing their full value, so it stopped the development of what might easily have been as interesting a type as the famous " M " class. Only the " Kaisar-i-Hind " was built by Cairds in 1914, a twin screw steamer of 11,430 tons with quadruple expansion engines of 16,000 I.H.P., which were designed to give her a speed of 18½ knots, but which have always been available, both in war and peace, for a far higher speed when it was demanded, so that the pretty " Kaisar," unfortunately without any sisters, contrived to break a number of records in addition to making herself a great favourite with regular travellers.

She was designed specially for the Bombay service, and her cabin comfort and ventilation were well ahead of any ship running to the East. Compared with the ships which the P. & O. has built since, when the size could be increased through the improvements in the Suez Canal, she is comparatively small, but her extraordinary popularity, lasting until she was well past her first youth, is a tribute to the qualities of her design. She is a ship which will always stand out by her individuality, and in spite of the fact that it could not be repeated, her design was very successful.

During the War the Company had no chance of building new ships, principally because it was too busy serving the nation—incidentally at a heavy cost to itself. The ships which it had under construction were subject to the demands of the authorities, and their owners got no benefit from them. Immediately after the Armistice, however, the Directors naturally took steps to catch up, and as the ship-building industry was more than fully occupied, they had to take their turn. Standard ships of the " B " type were bought on the slips, altered, and entered the fleet as the " Kidderpore," " Alipore," " Jeypore," " Lahore," and " Nagpore." The " Peshawur " was a bigger ship, and the " Perim " and " Padua " were purchased German prizes.

In addition, the Company had for a short time the use of the surrendered German liners " Berlin " (17,324 tons) and " Prinz Hubertus " (7,523 tons), but they were neither of them P. & O. ships, as the phrase had come to be understood.

The Company really wanted the ships which they had designed themselves, of which the most important were the " Naldera " (15,825 tons) and " Narkunda " (16,227 tons), launched in 1917 and 1918 respectively, but held up by the Government. They were the first three-funnelled ships in the P. & O. service, with quadruple expansion engines, and although it was said that they had been altered so many times by order of the Government that they had been everything except submarines, when they were ready for service in 1920 they were just what the Company wanted and were both great favourites.

After some interesting, but unimportant, coasting steamers, the Company next turned its attention to the Australian emigrant trade, which then gave every promise of booming with so many ex-soldiers looking for a new opportunity, and built a new " B " class, which was almost as great an improvement on the old as those vessels were on the Lund fleet. " Ballarat," " Baradine," " Barrabool," " Bendigo," and " Balranald " had been ordered during the War, but had to wait. They were designed for third-class passengers only, and were ships of over 13,000 tons, with twin screw quadruple expansion engines of 8,000 I.H.P. for 13½ knots, carrying nearly 500 passengers in conditions of greater comfort than had ever before been considered on the run. When the Australian emigrant trade collapsed, these ships were given Bauer-Wach exhaust turbines and oil fuel, and their trial speed was increased to 17 knots, over 15 knots on service, so that they could carry mails on the Suez route.

Next came the mail steamers " Moldavia " and " Mongolia " of 1922. They had a gross tonnage of round about 16,300, with a speed of 16 knots, and, apart from a purchased cargo steamer, were the first geared-turbine vessels in the P. & O. fleet. There was some prejudice against them on account of their only having one funnel, although their graceful lines satisfied every seaman, and the " Moldavia " was later fitted with a second dummy stack.

To build up to the limits of the economical possibilities of the trade and the capabilities of the Suez Canal, the " Mooltan " and " Maloja," built by Harland & Wolff in 1923, had a gross tonnage of nearly 21,000, but for absolute reliability they had quadruple expansion engines instead of turbines. Bauer-Wach exhaust turbines were later added, and their speed thereby improved, their magnificent steadiness, broad decks, and solid comfort making them popular favourites.

The commissioning of these two ships permitted the P. & O. to carry out its scheduled service, and the Directors wisely determined not to build more than was necessary when building prices were at their peak, and when it was an obvious impossibility for any new ship to earn her depreciation. With great caution they waited until 1925 to start another programme. This consisted of the " C " and " R " classes, exceedingly popular ships which were designed so that they could be interchanged between the services. The former consisted of the " Cathay," " Chitral," and " Comorin," of rather more than 15,000 tons, having an I.H.P. of 13,000, with quadruple expansion engines for a speed of 16 knots and excellent passenger and cargo accommodation. The " R " class consisted of the " Ranchi," " Ranpura," " Rawalpindi," and " Rajputana," of about 16,650 tons, with a speed of 17 knots, but otherwise very similar to the " C " class.

At the same time a particularly interesting single ship was built for the Aden–Bombay shuttle service, replacing the " Salsette," which had been sunk by enemy action. That was the " Razmak," of 10,600 tons, with a speed of well over 18 knots, which was a great favourite until the reconstruction of the services rendered the shuttle unnecessary, when she was sold to one of the subsidiary companies and immediately broke the transpacific record. In conjunction with the Hain Line, a subsidiary, the P. & O. then built four remarkable purely cargo ships in pairs, the " Bangalore " and " Burdwan," and the " Behar " and " Bhutan." With a gross tonnage of rather more than 6,000, these ships were among the fastest cargo carriers afloat, and were fully appreciated on the Indian service. They were followed by the similar P. & O. steamers " Soudan " and " Somali."

The next mail and passenger ship built for the Line was of revolutionary design for the Indian trade. The " Viceroy of India " of 1929 has a gross tonnage of 19,684, and outwardly somewhat resembles the " C " and " R " classes, and was the first big British ship to be propelled by electricity, her two steam turbines generating the current for motors of 17,000 S.H.P. for a nominal speed of 19 knots, easily exceeded on service. She lowered the London–Bombay record with a time of 16 days 1 hour 42 minutes. Another innovation was that only single-berth cabins were fitted, and both on the mail service and yachting cruises she has proved herself extraordinarily popular and successful, her absolute freedom from vibration being specially appreciated.

So successful was the electric drive in the " Viceroy of India " for the Indian service, that it was adopted in the " Strathnaver " and " Strathaird " of 1931, built for the Australian run. These ships were given the white hulls and yellow funnels which had periodically been favoured for the crack ships of the Company, but in their case the colour scheme was so successful, and showed up their appearance to such good effect, that it was retained permanently. Twin screw ships of over 22,500 tons, turbine engines drive their generators and electric motors of 28,000 S.H.P. give them a speed of 22 knots, which was far in excess of any contract requirements. They were given three funnels, although their four side-firing water-tube boilers are so compact that only the midship one is genuine, the others being put in to give the ships a good appearance.

In spite of the advantages of turbo-electric drive, it was decided, after careful consideration, to return to the geared turbine for the " Carthage " and " Corfu," which were intended primarily for the Far Eastern service. They have a gross tonnage of about 14,300, and 15,000 S.H.P. gives them a nominal speed of 19½ knots, but they have sufficient reserve to permit them to beat any competitor. The same system was adopted in the " Strathmore," 23,428 tons, built in 1935. In general design she followed the " Strathnaver " type, but was an improvement on minor points, while the Company determined to disregard public prejudice, which was still inclined to think that a single-funnelled ship was not as safe or powerful as one with two or more, and fitted her with a single stack only, which greatly improved the comfort of her passenger accommodation below decks. It was a daring experiment, but she was such a fine vessel in all respects that the public forgot its quaint prejudice and took her into full favour at once.

At the present time the " Strathallan " and " Stratheden " are building as an improvement on the " Strathmore," and the " Canton," building for the Far Eastern service, is something which is even better than the " Carthage " and the " Corfu."   After a hundred years the P. & O. pursues the policy which paid so well in its early days, making each design an improvement on the last, but remaining faithful to the same general principles so that the regular passenger may feel himself at home the moment he steps on board.

P. & O. Capital

THE original capital of the P. & O. Company, as authorised by the Charter of 31st December, 1840, was £1 million, and power was also given to borrow up to £100,000. The former amount could be increased to £1,500,000, and the latter by " any further sum or sums " with the consent of the Treasury. By 1849 the power to increase the capital to £1,500,000 had been exercised, and the Directors' report issued in December of that year contemplates the issue of shares in respect of this additional £500,000, provided the Company proved successful in obtaining the Australian mail contract. These shares were issued at the close of 1850.

In the report of 1852, the Directors state :

" . . . The Directors have deemed it expedient to avail themselves of the present favourable state of the money market, and of the powers vested in them by the Royal Charter of Incorporation and Deed of Settlement, to take up, on Debenture, for terms of three and five years, such sums as they may find necessary."

A Warrant of the Treasury was accordingly obtained, whereby moneys might be borrowed up to £400,000 in addition to the £100,000 authorised by the original Charter.

The Third Charter, 1854, empowered the Company to increase its capital to £2,500,000, and also authorised an increase in the amount of debentures from £500,000 to £800,000, and the Fourth Charter, of 1867, authorised a further increase of capital from £2,500,000 to £3,500,000.

The Fifth Charter, of 1876, authorised the issue of not more than £800,000 Debenture Stock for the sole purpose of repaying the existing debentures. The debentures then existing were actually paid off out of the assets of the Company, and the power given by the Fifth Charter to raise £800,000 was not, in fact, exercised.

The Sixth Charter, of 1887, gave power to issue fresh debenture stock to the extent of £800,000.

APPENDIX III

At the date of the Seventh Charter, 1889, the issued Capital was as follows :

	£
50,000 Shares of £50 fully paid	2,500,000
20,000 Shares of £50, £20 paid	400,000
	£2,900,000

the Authorised Capital then being £3,500,000.

This Charter authorised the reduction of capital to £2,320,000 divided into :

	£
50,000 Shares of £40 fully paid	2,000,000
20,000 Shares of £16 fully paid	320,000
	£2,320,000

This reduction was accomplished by returning £10 to the holder of each fully-paid share of £50, and £4 to the holder of each share on which £20 only was paid up, and by extinguishing the liability of £30 in respect of these latter shares. The nominal amount of shares was reduced respectively to £40 and £16. The same Charter authorised the conversion of capital, each share, whether of £40 or £16, being divided into equal moieties of preferred and deferred stock. After this operation the capital was £2,320,000, divided into £1,160,000 Preferred and £1,160,000 Deferred Stock. The Seventh Charter also empowered the Company to increase the capital by £1,180,000 by the creation of not more than £590,000 each of preferred and deferred stock. This power was not, however, exercised, and the Ninth Charter subsequently revived the right to issue a further £1,180,000, with authority for this amount to be issued as " either preferred or deferred stock or partly preferred and partly deferred stock."

Exercising powers granted under the Sixth Charter, £800,000 3½% Debenture Stock was issued in 1894 and 1896.

The Eighth Charter, of 1899, gave power to issue debenture stock up to £1 million subject to the debenture stock issued under the Sixth Charter, and in 1902 this power was exercised to the extent of £600,000 3½% Second Debenture Stock, the balance of £400,000 being issued on the market in 1904/5.

In addition to the increase of capital mentioned above, the Ninth Charter, 1903, authorised the raising of moneys, in particular by the issue of debenture stock, provided that " the total nominal amount for the time being secured by any debentures or debenture stock issued by the Company and for the time being outstanding shall not at any one time exceed £1,800,000 and a further sum equal to three-fourths of the nominal amount of any stock for the time being issued and paid up in addition to its existing preferred and deferred stock." The powers of borrowing given by the Sixth Charter were, by the Ninth Charter, cancelled, excepting in respect of the issue of new debenture stock in substitution for any debenture stock purchased and cancelled under the provisions of the Trust Deed securing stock issued under the Sixth Charter; similarly, the Ninth Charter cancelled rights of borrowing given by the Eighth Charter, except in respect of the issue of new debenture stock in substitution of any debenture stock purchased and cancelled under the provisions of the Trust Deed securing stock issued under that Charter.

Under the provisions of the Ninth Charter, the capital was increased by £1,180,000, by the creation and issue of preferred stock of that amount, the capital then being :

£2,340,000 Preferred
1,160,000 Deferred
———————
£3,500,000 (authorised and issued)

Subsequent to 1912, the acquisition, by the exchange of capital, of the British India Steam Navigation and other Companies and the issue of a further £1 million Deferred Stock in 1927 increased the capital of the P. & O. as follows :

—	PREFERRED STOCK. Entitled to a Cumulative Dividend of 5 per cent. per annum.		DEFERRED STOCK.	
	Authorised.	Issued.	Authorised.	Issued.
	£	£	£	£
Existing 1912	2,340,000	2,340,000	1,160,000	1,160,000
1914	700,000	700,000	638,133	637,874
1916	—	—	906,720	905,820
1917	—	—	500,000	496,774
P. & O. Bonus Issue, 1919 . .	—	—	200,000	190,705
P. & O. Bonus Issue, 1920 . .	—	—	205,000	201,345
New Issue, 1927	—	—	1,000,000	1,000,000
—	£3,040,000	£3,040,000	£4,609,853	£4,592,518

Total Issued Capital as at 30th September, 1936 :

	£
5% Cumulative Preferred Stock	3,040,000
Deferred Stock	4,592,518
	£7,632,518

It should be noted that holders of Preferred Stock and holders of Deferred Stock rank equally as regards subscription for new stock and distribution of surplus assets in the event of a winding up.

The liability of members is limited.

In pursuance of Trust Deeds of 1922 and 1923, £3,500,000 $5\frac{1}{2}$% and £3,500,000 5% Debenture Stocks were respectively issued, and by a conversion scheme of 1933 these were repaid, as to £1 million in cash and as to £6 millions by the issue of $4\frac{1}{2}$% Debenture Stock, 1943/72. This latter stock is redeemable by purchase in the market and/or drawings.

The amount of Loan Capital outstanding at 1st April, 1937, was :

	£
$3\frac{1}{2}$% Debenture Stock	657,300
$3\frac{1}{2}$% Second Debenture Stock	830,260
$4\frac{1}{4}$% Debenture Stock, 1943/72	5,743,000
	£7,230,560

INDEX